THE IMMORTAL BL...
NORTH: STONE MEMORIES OF
ARTHUR

Fiona Mulgrew

Published: June 2016 by

Iudeu Publishing

ISBN 978-0-9935850-0-5

This work is registered with the UK Copyright Service: Registration No. 284683383.

The cover photograph is the Emperor's Map taken by Fiona Mulgrew

Dedication

To Bernie and Maeve

Table of Contents

Acknowledgements vi

Abbreviations viii

The Archivist's Preface ix

Chapter 1: Historical context and the emergence of a Stone Archivist 1

Chapter 2: The Red Castle and the White Palace 18

Chapter 3: Strategic Position and never heed Bede 40

Chapter 4: The Bear's Battles begin. 56

Chapter 5: Bloodlines and the Sea Baby 91

Chapter 6: Over the Gannet's Bath, Arthur and the Gwyr Y Gogledd in the lands north of the Forth. 116

Chapter 7: The Bears of the North 155

Chapter 8: The Painted Hill 172

Last Words 212

Appendix 1: The Emperor's Map 215

Appendix 2: The Glass Map 218

Appendix 3: Sketch Maps 220

References and Bibliography 228

Index 246

Acknowledgements

To write a book has never ever been something that I planned to do, 'some day'. So it still seems a little bewildering to me that I have come to the end of doing just that. Without the ancient makars and those who left their beautiful work in the landscape of Scotland this book would not exist. The skilful complexity and content of the pictorial narratives had me seeking out sources from the lettered world.

With regards to these I wish to thank Derek Bryce for giving me permission to include extracts from *Arthur and the Britons in Wales and Scotland* by F.W. Skene and edited by Derek Bryce (1988). Thanks are due also to Llarnerch Press Ltd for their supportive response in the process.

Many thanks to Peter Burns of Birlinn Ltd who gave permission for me to include extracts from W. J. Watson's (1926) *The Celtic Place-Names of Scotland* the 2004 edition with the introduction by Simon Taylor. I have made reference to Watson's etymological analysis throughout my book as his work came to contribute much to an essential strand in my research and exposition. Any errors of interpretation are mine.

I much appreciate being able to reproduce a chapter extract from *Kings, Clerics and Chronicles in Scotland 500-1297* edited by Simon Taylor (2000) namely T.O. Clancy (2000) 'Scotland the 'Nennian' recension of the Histora Brittonum and the Lebor Bretnach' pp87-107 thanks to Four Courts Press for providing permission to do this.

I am very grateful to Edinburgh University Press for their permission to quote both an extract from James Fraser's (2009) book *From Caledonia to Pictland Scotland to 795* and a translation by Simon Taylor from Royan and Broun's (2007) chapter entitled 'Versions of Scottish Nationhood c850-1707' pp 168-183 in *The Edinburgh History of Scottish Literature vol1. From Columba to the Union (1707)*

I would like to thank the National Archives of Scotland for the access to archival material and in particular to those who gifted or deposited the documentation I refer to within the book.

In my research I made much use of the historical maps which are available to all within the online archive of the Map Library of the National Library of Scotland, Edinburgh. I would like to thank all who made this wonderful resource possible. Also I am very grateful to Ian C.

Cunningham for permission to quote from his translation of the Latin text of *Blaeu's Atlas of Scotland (1654)* reproduced from the Blaeu Atlas website.

Finally without the steadfast support of Bernie over the years of researching and writing I may never have completed this book. Mar seo a Bernie, moran moran taing!

Abbreviations

AFB - Am Faclair Beag

CCD- Chambers Concise 20th Century Dictionary

CSD –The Concise Scottish Dictionary 1987 3rd edition.

NAS –National Archives of Scotland.

NLS –National Library of Scotland.

The Archivist's Preface

Written close to the Wanton Wall, Mill Sea, East Lothian, Scotland.

From almost the beginning I knew that I had made an important discovery. I did share my initial findings with archaeologists but failed to interest them. I am on my own reluctant to press my finds upon the established knowledge builders. I think that the sea and the land will continue to weather unabated the stories of this people and their world for many more generations. Pressed budgets and other projects and priorities will serve to keep them hidden. What to do? Who will believe this? A culture, a history, the expressions of a people long gone lies unnoticed. I will record all that I have found until there is something approaching a coherent body of work to present.

Perhaps I should contact the archaeologists again and tell them of my findings. Perhaps not, if I broached the subject of Arthur they would dismiss me as a wishful thinking crank. I think sometimes that I can't write this book. This will not be a conventional piece of work in which the research of others provides something of a secure pathway towards new knowledge. I am by no means sure that I will find the 'background literature'. However, I know that I am not raving and my eyesight is good. There is a big history here and it is forgotten. The ancestors' world that is now Scotland should not remain unseen. Like the rest of Scotland there was a thriving and vibrant society living out its time in this southern part of the country. Why should their story be left untold when vestiges of it lie close to us?

The Uotadini or the Votadini, which is what the Romans called them, left us stories or narratives which should be studied for the cultural and historical light they may shed upon a period of history that has been often termed the Dark Ages. Not only that, the more I find the more convinced I am that if Arthur was factored into Scottish history, much would be revealed about past events and places in my country. More enlightenment may come too if the actual absence of Arthur from historical documentation and literature was explored. This will no doubt seem presumptuous of me, being neither historian nor archaeologist, but I have to remind myself that my views have developed and matured from grounded observation time. What I have found was never hidden from view and the only mystery is why it has not been seen for the wonderful ancient archive that it could become. So yes, I am going to make some effort to let the heirs to the memories and art of these ancient people know how much has been bequeathed to them.

Such were the internal conversations and mulling as I started upon this work. A counter weight to all this circular debate was a strong emotional motivator to press on with the project. It seemed to me that the pride, bravery, love and sadness of the people who lived here were expressed in the art and craft that they left behind. Many hours of looking at their work has meshed these feelings into my perception of my home. Their way of interpreting their land has caused me to see this small corner of Scotland in a new way. The avian ancestors of the little birds that flit around the garden and their larger cousins of the big sea and endless sky of East Lothian were major subjects of the native people who lived here. They were the Gwyr Y Gogledd, the Men of the North, whose existence was immortalised in the old poetry of Cymru (Wales). Listening to birdsong now has a time altering effect upon me, setting me thinking of horsemen racing across the land to fight off enemies from the south and the north and of victories and celebrations in a great fort.

The greatest of all the emotions that the worked stone, wood, iron and clay and other materials evoked was that of adoration for their great defender, Arthur. The vast numbers of images that I have found speak of the love many had for him. He successfully fought off those who would take their way of life from them and they were very grateful. Steeped as I have been in the iconic imagery that has been left by the people here, I too became an admirer.

Chapter 1: Historical context and the emergence of a Stone Archivist

In around AD43 the Romans invaded Britain, landing in Kent. In AD80 they crossed the River Tweed into what became Scotland. Their leader Agricola orchestrated a pincer movement up the south- eastern and western parts of this future land arriving at Inveresk close to the Forth. From there they marched north to the Tay. The construction of a garrison town was begun at Inchtuthil a few miles north. A chain of forts were built between the Forth and Clyde estuaries to ensure the security of the territories gained. At the battle of Mons Graupius the Romans inflicted a resounding defeat upon a large Caledonian force. This victory was to be the peak of their success in North Britain. Demands for forces elsewhere in the Empire meant that they were not able to continue with Inchtuthil. Various campaigns followed aimed at gaining control on the north-east to little effect. Within twenty years the Romans had retreated, destroying their forts as they went with an alliance of northern tribes harrying them as they moved southwards.

In 122AD the Emperor Hadrian ordered the building of a line of fortifications, including a continuous wall 1.8 metres thick across Northern Britain from the Solway coast in the west to the River Tyne in what is now North East England. This emperor was of the view that the peoples to the north were not amenable to Roman rule. For some reason that is not clear to historians, Hadrian's Wall was abandoned between 138AD and 161AD in favour of a new wall and Imperial frontier further north across the Clyde-Forth isthmus commissioned by Hadrian's successor Antoninus Pius (Fraser 2009 p22). At thirty seven miles, it was half the length of the southerly wall and would have needed less manpower to defend. However the geography meant that it could easily be outflanked by the peoples on the northern banks of the two estuaries. It was abandoned after only a few years and Hadrian's Wall was settled as the northern Imperial frontier until the late 4th century (see Map 1) ......

On an early evening in January (Winter 2009-2010), very cold with a huge full moon hanging low over the headland, I had the beach to myself excepting the very occasional jogger. There was half an hour before I had to be at the station. It was enough time to walk to the Fairy Burn and back. The sand was made a rosy hue by the early moon light. This, no wind and waves seen but unheard on the low tide, transformed the winter shore into the unearthly edge of a distant sea. As I neared the burn I looked for the little forest of wild roses that grows close by. In the summer this patch of dune is a perfumed heaven of white blooms. Always when I see them now I imagine the low-lying memory house sheltering from the fierce winds that can bombard this coast whatever the season. Reaching the little river I stood for a few minutes taking in the changes to the character of its flow. One day it is slow-moving, attaining estuary dimensions as it joins the sea, another, a mad noisy pump. That evening it was a sedate trickle. A few minutes after turning back I noticed something that was half covered in the sand.

The summer before this I had found a dark heavy stone. It was cold, flat and smooth. It seemed shaped by man, easy to hold in one hand. I thought perhaps it was a tool from the time of the very oldest peoples who had had summer hunting camps along this coast of Scotland. Later, in the shadowed light of my home, the stone took on an additional identity. Covering its surface entirely were minute complex carvings, tiny vestiges of colour and the outline of a very different place to the outskirts of the small seaside town that exists here now.

The more exposed I am to the visually incredible materials I keep finding, the more I start to panic. My literate being wants to take notes. Who were these people and what was the story and why was it being told? Coming from a data organised 21st century, I want to categorise. Six months of squinting at tiny sculptures, carvings, 'mixed media' pieces and I know I have some knowledge to put toward answering these questions. For a while I will be an archivist for this long gone society. I will start a library of documents hewn from the local rock or made from the lime that may have been sourced from here. Perhaps as a collection, the worked stones will reveal to the modern world, the patterns of ideas and values held by the community who lived here. As I start writing this though, I know that I am on a journey which should be cherished as a first contact experience with the cultural artifacts of an unknown people when all that is observed needs to be recorded. The later understanding and interpretation will be an unpredictable process.

The aim of this conversation that I am about to embark upon with you, fellow Traveller, is to contribute new understandings of the history of the people who lived their lives out in a portion of time within what is sometimes called the Dark Ages or Early Historic period. This was the period after the Romans withdrew permanently from southern Britain to fight battles closer to home. It was a 'dark' time because there has been a lack of materials, written or otherwise from this era, which could bring some greater knowledge. 'Traveller' is to be my name for you as surely it is a journey into a hardly known era when myths and legends were the history of a people. Till now it has been thought that such a distant time could not be reached and the vestiges of it that slipped through into ancient poetry or chronicles are just that, unsubstantiated traces. In the case of Northern Britain, the darkness seems to have been deepest and longest lasting through till the end of the seventh century. I am aware that much work goes on in the study and interpretation of ancient texts and archaeological discoveries that shed light upon the lives of our ancestors of that period, but I wish to suggest that there is another line of investigation that could contribute to such research. That a contribution is possible will be revealed I hope as this archive progresses. One ancient legend in particular, rarely referred to in contemporary historical texts may sometime in the future be part of that contribution. The legend I refer to is of Arthur, stone revealed as the Bear of the North.

It is very likely that such an assertion from someone who is not a specialist, will be received with much scepticism even derision. However that is only to be expected when a new form of study emerges. I hope, through this conversation to convince you fellow Traveller, that it should be considered as a valuable source for the illumination of these 'post Romano' years. Indeed it is possible that this line of enquiry will open a series of windows which look out onto vistas of human experience long before this time. Research of the 'Early Historic' seems to rely a good deal upon what is uncovered by the archaeologists. Most of whatever paper documentation is known or conjectured to have existed about the people of that time in what is now Scotland is considered to be lost or destroyed. Sometimes the only way to discovery, in this case a new locus of knowledge is to put to one side, to some extent at least, the established ways of seeing (De Bono 1967). Not such a difficult feat for someone unversed in such ways.

Although I will refer to a variety of written materials, historical and others, the main source of my ideas about a people who lived over fifteen hundred years ago is pictorial. This people lived in the the Central Lowlands of present day Scotland, including the lands close to the estuaries of the Rivers Forth and Tay. That my database is firmly embedded in the visual arts of the ancient world should not be surprising as despite contact with the literate Romans, the native British communities of these areas apparently chose not to adopt the written word. Why would they? Their cultures were developed and maintained through a strong oral tradition supported and elaborated upon, I would suggest, by an equally robust penchant for illustrative arts and crafts. Such *mores* were integral to belief systems which revered gods and respected the mysteries of the natural world. Much then was invested in being other than literate. Regarding their dealings with the Romans, it could be conjectured that the leaders of these northern British tribes or communities may have considered a degree of cultural opacity as politic. Being mysterious in the eyes of a powerful invader is a defence of sorts.

A large proportion of the pre-literate documentation that I have found and subsequently sought to interpret is in miniature form. The materials upon which these tiny works of art have been wrought are mostly of stone and vary in size between a few millimetres and what can be comfortably held in one hand. Given the dearth of miniature work on display at the National Museum in Edinburgh, I am certain that I am in the midst of an altogether different layer of historical evidence. I often had to use a magnifying glass to glean the full details of the story that has been crafted. A digital camera has also been employed. There will be those who would scoff at the very notion that such art and skill could have been possible but perhaps not the art historians. From my observations this distinctive mode of expression has a much longer pedigree within the British Isles than previously thought (Ackroyd 2002) and was manifested in a vast array of mediums and techniques (Note 1).

Although some of the worked pieces that I have found have been crudely made and easy to observe unaided, most as I have said, are small to miniature in dimension. Tiny figures are distinguishable due to skilled sculptural detailing. For a long while I thought that this meant that the crafts people here had access to some sort of magnification technology. Where ever the source of this, through trade with the Roman world or native innovation, the use of some form of lens with around 2 to 5 times magnification had to have been in frequent use in this part of Scotland in the sixth century. Recently however, I have come across an object that provides another explanation. Minutely decorated and made of what looks to be some sort of dark flint-like material, I have found what looks to be a pin-hole viewer. Using it the small comes closer to the eye and I have no need of my reading glasses. The technology consists of a light proof box with a hole in one side. Light travels through the hole and an

4

inverted image is projected onto the other side of the box. Referred to in ancient texts, it is still in use today, for example in the safe observation of solar eclipses and in space exploration. I would guess that the use of such a methodology would have been controlled and commissioned by the powerful in the society. It is not difficult to imagine the magic and mystery that would have been associated with miniature work. The digital eye has been invaluable in revealing the faintest engraving. Even more remarkably I suggest, this technology has on occasion, had the almost magical effect of consolidating colour and form making pictorial sense of what had been fashioned so long ago.

People have always sought different ways to express their ideas and values and their stories or history and they have used whatever materials that have been to hand. This part of Scotland is considered a geologist's dream because its landscape betrays the vast amount of volcanic activity and ice age machinations that took place here millions of years in the past. For the people who lived on the coastal lands of East Lothian more than fifteen hundred years ago, the results of such cataclysms provided them with a truly magnificent range of minerals and stones to work with. It is clear to me that the artists and craftsmen of this time were very knowledgeable as to the characteristics of the medium they were using. I would like to hypothesise that here, near the Wanton Wall there was a knowledge and practice centre for arts such as sculpture and ceramic work with access (apart from the local stone) to dyes, iron ore, tar, clay and lime. The large quantity of worked material I have found suggests to me that many of the people who lived here sought to express themselves through art and craft. Out of a large craft base there would have been a greater chance that masters would emerge and with them particular styles of representation. I have found objects that suggest this, for example, the use of a particular selection of dyes or sculptures that are recognisable as being copies but with varying levels of skill execution. With the accumulation of the theoretical and the 'how' and the 'doing' forms of knowledge (Carr 1981) associated with particular skills, there develops an increasingly sophisticated network of ideas and ways of working a medium. In the case of the people who lived here, this was expressed in what I would like to call *artfulness*.

From my experience this artfulness was principally about entertainment. Exploring a piece of work has often been an adventure where there was the anticipation of a surprise waiting to be admired and exclaimed over. Stories were being told or events recounted and dramatic flourishes were an important part of the pictorial telling. For example, travelling across a stone taking in the small scenes of action one's eye would catch a glimpse of shadow and taking a closer look, the outline of a figure dressed unlike the others, in long robes, would emerge from a shaped indentation in the rock. With just the slightest movement the figure would begin to disappear and with it some of the surrounding pictorial detail. There are I would suggest, whole categories of artfulness such as this.

As this archive proceeds there will be instances noted of where in my view, the pictorial presentation of the stone hewers has left traces in the language and literature of Scotland. An extract from Walter Bower's (1418) *Scotichronicon* chosen by Royan and Broun (2007) to illustrate the chronicler's ability with words provides I would argue, an example of the transfer of the artfulness in stone into drama and thence committed to manuscript. In his description of King Alexander III's wedding Bower, Abbot of Inchcolm Abbey, wrote this about an entertainment put on for the occasion:

"At the head of this procession were skilled musicians with many sorts of pipe music including the wailing music of bagpipes, and behind them others splendidly performing a war dance with intricate weaving in and out. Bringing up the rear was a figure regarding whom it was difficult to decide whether it was a man or an apparition. It seemed to glide like a ghost rather than walk on feet. When it looked as if he was disappearing from everyone's sight the whole frenzied procession halted, the song died away, the music faded and the dancing contingent froze suddenly and unexpectedly." (Translated by Simon Taylor)(Royan with Broun 2007, p173)

My reading of this is that Bower witnessed the dramatic equivalent of what could be termed a *stone journey* reminiscent of the mysterious recessed figure that comes into view as a stone is manipulated and then as it begins to fade, so too does the associated narrative. Other stories or the next part of the same one may appear as the stone is manipulated further. I have no doubt that the stone shadow represented a member of the Druid caste whose influence had a bearing on the surrounding storyline. Unlike the dearth of written documentation concerning the Druids in Scotland I would argue that their presence was made clear in the sculpted stones of East Lothian. In his book *A Brief History of the Druids* (2002), Ellis makes a cogent case for the Druids as the intelligentsia of pre-Christian Celtic societies and for their presence in

6

Scotland. The meaning of *'druid'* is thought to be *'immersed in knowledge'* (Ellis 2002, p38). Up to twenty years of learning and apprenticeship was a requirement to attain competence. The Druids were the professional class, the advisers and teachers of the secular leaders sometimes taking precedence over them, the judges, the healers, the philosophers, the scientist and the artists. The beauty and cleverness of the story stones seems to provide good evidence as to the depth of knowledge held in the last two specialities in particular.

From my observations the artfulness revealed from the stones and other artefacts were a display of artistic brilliance. A craftsman's knowledge of the medium used and the availability of a huge amount of time that would have been required to produce the miniature detailing are also evident. I have been able to distinguish many artistic forms. There is the technique in which multiple figures are fashioned into the one, usually zoomorphic representation. That is the image of an animal that personifies a god or perhaps a tribe or community. Sea birds were frequently portrayed in fortress scenes. The wren thought to have been associated with the Druids (Ellis 2000 p223) is occasionally to be spotted in stone too. The underlying image(s) of these representations often replace each other as the angle of observation is altered. There are tiny mosaic scenes upon sandstone and the use of a smear of mortar close to shade, to create a hide-and-reveal tiny picture. There is the use of a red dye to depict a scene of carnage. There seems to be the deliberate manipulation of stone which already bears the actions of the sea and sea creatures or of fossils upon its surface to fashion an image. Then there are the shell and mortar portraits within stone cups and hidden pictures within the light porous interiors of shells and the use of metal to depict the strength of a fortress. Histories have been sheltered in the camouflage of patterned stones and picture messages inscribed upon bark.

Why is a good proportion of the work so small? As I have already hinted earlier, miniature work must have had great value in the creation of mystery and magic. That there is so much of it here might suggest that it was at the centre of such creative industries. Consider the power that magic must have bestowed upon the controllers and possessors of such tiny work. Given the ever present insecurities of the time, miniature work may also have been important to a people who wished their story to elude the wrecker's eye. If this was the case miniaturising was a successful strategy. These pictorial records have been lying unrecognised as generations moved into a future where ways of seeing have been increasingly directed by wordsmiths (Berger, 1972).

The tiny art could have been about pride in presenting detailed workmanship as in the case of the English miniaturists who, it might be suggested, were the inheritors of this native British tradition (Ackroyd 2002). There may have been several other explanations for the original miniaturist tradition. The most likely I would guess would have been an established penchant for small tool-making. Also such work may have held some value and been in demand as something 'magical'. Presumably the stones; wood; shells and small pieces of pottery found are only a remnant of the miniature work produced. The sheer quantity of these however and the similarity of theme and portrayal of character as well as where they were found, may shed light upon the role of this place with its 'wanton wall'.

Aside from the relative invisibility of the miniature work, most of my stone finds appear to be just what they are, stones, with no obvious human interference upon their surfaces. Many of them may have been brightly decorated when first fashioned and the effects of weather and time have erased the paint, dyes and ceramic. Often though on closer inspection, faint traces of these materials and distinctive shaping can be discerned. I can only speculate as to the treasures that would have once been sited here.

As well as there being objects to be admired and entertained with, I would hazard a guess that some of the worked pieces I have found were aide memoires for whoever was the chosen story teller. Others were ornaments with a flat base to allow their display. Some were so small they could perhaps have been talismans for adults or children. These things were from a world when the knowledge and history of a people was apparently not written down using an alphabet but I would contend that it was documented nonetheless. In today's world there are vast libraries and museums whose raison d'etre is to preserve the work of generations of writers. Papyrus, parchment, leather and paper and any other medium which holds words is protected to varying degrees. Over fifteen hundred years ago people were not so different. Our ancestors also wanted their lives, loves, stories and history to be remembered for those who came after them. They just did it differently and very creatively (Note 2). In this small corner of Scotland, the ancient heritage of this country exists and lies waiting to be recognised.

There are Roman written sources about the Empire's campaigns in Britain and although like all 'evidence', they have to be placed in the context of the period in which they were penned, they are thought to shed some light on who were the northern peoples of Britain. How much the Roman presence affected the socio-political relations between the various communities of the native population is not definitely known. Suffice to note that there is much room to conjecture a complexity of history that would have arisen out of the survival strategies adopted in the face of the well-oiled fighting machine of Rome (Fraser 2009).

The Brigantes are thought to have been an alliance of people who lived in lands now called Yorkshire extending into today's Anglo-Scottish border country. Hadrian's Wall was to be built through their territories effectively cutting off communities from each other. The Dumnonii whose lands early in the occupation seemed to have ranged between the Clyde in the west to Strathearn in the east, were later referred to by one Roman source as the Maiatai (Dio 216AD in Fraser, 2009). Their territory seems to have been reduced somewhat by the second century AD and was littered with the fortification efforts of the Imperial Army. The Maiatai were perhaps one group of people who were part of a larger Dumnonii confederation, and are thought to have lived on the surrounding lands of the Forth-Clyde isthmus reaching north almost to Stirling and encompassing the plain of Manau that lay between the rivers Carron and Avon near the head of the Forth estuary. The Uotadini occupied the eastern lowlands of this firth. Fraser (2009) posited that the Uotadini were a Miathi people. Like most of the Dumnonii they would have found themselves between the two Roman walls. The northern neighbours of the Maiatai were the Calidones. Their territory was delineated variously in terms associated with Roman military achievements and installations. In the main it is thought to have encompassed the lands north of the Clyde across to the Moray Firth.

The fallout from the Roman depredations and separations of communities behind and between walls upon the peoples of northern Britain can only be, in the main, conjectured. Fraser's analysis suggests a complex picture of what may have resulted from these experiences. North of the Forth-Clyde line there may have been a coming together of peoples at least into some sort of federated structure with regard to matters of further military threat. Fraser (2009) suggested that there came a time during the Roman rule when Northern Britain became divided between those who had become Romanised and those who had resisted Roman rule. In other words the Uotadini and other Romanised peoples between the Walls distinguished themselves from those 'barbarians' further north who had resisted the Empire, the non-Romanised. The latter came to be known by the the Latin word 'picti', a term previously used by the Romans for all the people of North Briton but thought to have had its origins in native forms of the word Watson(1926). The word means *painted* and is thought to be an allusion to the painting of the skin or clothes. Acknowledging that what I have observed were the cultural efforts of one group of people, who in a state of defeat, siege and fight back that seemed to exist when Arthur entered their story, would tend to portray a 'them and us' scenario in line with Fraser's view. However, it would appear possible that when telling a story/history the stone sculpturors using colour and the occasional tribal totem, may have differentiated between different communities within this generic term. Details of these methods and their significance will be explored in later chapters.

For the people living between the two walls, the experience of living to all intents and purposes, in a military buffer zone that shielded Roman southern Britain from the 'barbarian' north must have been similar to what happens in the contemporary world. That would be: world power providing military support such as training and hardware to 'friendly' or least threatening peoples to fight its battles. Perhaps a good dose of espionage and regular distribution of 'sweetners' such as the often referred to stash of Roman silver found at Trapain Law would also have been in the mix (Note 3). However, it is not known what the exact relationship between the Uotadini and the Roman occupiers was. Were they 'protected or contained' by the fortified road from Eboracum (York) to Inveresk that lay west of their lands (Fraser 2009, p24)?

Around 79AD the Romans are thought to have wrested the territories close to the Rivers Forth and Tay from the native population and viewed this achievement as very significant (Fraser 2009, p17 source Tacitus). Stone observations detailed later in this book point to lands north of the Forth, (East Fife and coastal Angus) being anciently (long before the Roman invasion) held or roamed over by the same people in control or residing in parts of the Clyde Estuary and Argyll. By the time of Arthur the descendants of these people were still settled on the Forth and the Tay fighting to defend their lands from incursions from the north and the south. If anything can be drawn together from contemporary academic research and fifteen hundred year old stone narratives, it seems possible that the relationship was one of service to the Roman military in which the monitoring and defence of the Forth and Tay estuarys may have been a significant part. Stone pictures suggest that the Uotadini may have had many generations of expertise in monitoring these eastern waterways and responding rapidly to sea-borne raiders. Some of the islands of the Forth, those close to the southern shore perhaps, may have been used as naval havens enabling ships to be rapidly scrambled without the hindrance of tides.

Of these islands the great bastion, the Bass Rock should be given separate consideration. It is precipitous on all sides except to the south where it faces the Lothian shore. From its summit those who possessed this natural phenomenon had a full view of the estuary, its islands and its rivers. That it was to prove impregnable against a variety of foes over the better documented future of Scotland, emphasises further the importance of Uotadini territory to Rome. Control of the coastal lands and waters of the Tay and Forth would have been important in keeping a curb on any raids from hostile peoples further north.

Holding the Forth estuary would also have meant power over the trade and military movements of the central hinterland of Scotland via the rivers Carron, the Lothian Esk as well as the river Forth itself (Note 4). Perhap given their role as possible gate-keepers of the estuary, the Uotadini had held quite an influential position in their own relationships with their neighbours. It is possible perhaps that the Romans recognised this and saw the advantage in using them to maintain some sort of stability within the buffer zone and defend the seaboard extension of the Antonine fortification. The Uotadini though subjugated may have been well rewarded to carry on as they had from time immemorial. It may be of no significance but according to Pausanius a 2nd century Greek geographer and traveller, the Romans punished the Brigantians for incursions into the territory of a people called the *Genuini* who were vassals of Rome. Dunbavin (1998, pp54-55) posited that this tribe must have lived on the northern side of Hadrian's Wall.   Could it be that Pausanius was referring to the Uotadini who lived on the lands of south-eastern Lothian?

In the century after the fall of Rome in 410AD and the consequent absence of support from the Empire in protecting southern Britain from the incursions of the Picts and the Irish, the decision was made to invite Saxon barbarians into the country. The use of Germanic mercenary forces had long been the practice within the old Empire and the Saxons were skilled seamen well able to take on the seaborne attacks from the north and west. However the Saxons revolted against their Brittonnic paymasters in 442AD and then began years of battle and devastation of Roman Britain. Before 461AD the southern Brittonnic forces had accepted defeat and a portion of their people emigrated to what is present day Brittany. However for the last third of the 5th century the Britons successfully fought back (Morris, 1973/2004, p43). Arthur was to become the leading figure in this campaign as the focus shifted to freeing the lands between the two Walls.

Prior to my discovery I possessed only a little knowledge of Scotland's history as it was only fleetingly covered in school. I certainly knew nothing of my country's story of more than a millennium ago, nor of the legends and myths associated with that time or earlier. As I have progressed through this exposure to a long forgotten world, it has always been the crafted narrative that prompted a direction in which to search for a literate corroboration and not the reverse. Mostly there were no written materials to help explain the pictorial rather it has been the accumulation and observation of carved stories that has enabled understanding as well as provoking a search for further illumination.

How do I help myself and you, Intrepid Traveller, navigate this almost hidden world of visual expression? By as many routes as possible I think, given the levels of incredulity you will experience within yourself and from those with whom you share the contents of this book. Some of my finds have made me take a closer look at the land around me today. At the same time the sculpting of topographic features on stone is leading me towards an obsession with studying the old maps of Lowland Scotland. The online access to the map catalogues at the National Library in Edinburgh is making this exploration very rewarding. Five hundred year old maps are not cluttered with the infrastructure of a post-industrial society. The physical features of the land are given the sort of attention that the people a thousand years before would have appreciated. A rocky mount with defence potential, a river leading into the heart of a territory and the legions of place-names, many gone now or much changed serve to smooth the observer's passage into the reality of what was important for survival to our distant ancestors.

The more stone observations that I have done, the more research pathways have developed and I have become immersed in what the written word might reveal of this long distant time. The pickings were lean at first, because few North British records of the 5th or 6th century seem to have survived, until I came upon etymology, the study of place-names. This was to be a fruitful area of enquiry specifically with the localities and events stone-portrayed. On an experiential level etymology impressed upon me the complexity of language, ethnicity and history that eventually resulted in the formation of my homeland.

I had another resource which in retrospect, I should have looked for earlier given that I had read of the strong oral traditions of ancient cultures and how knowledge was passed on through apprenticeships in the methods of memorising. However, for a long time I thought that most verse of or about those times was inaccessible to me due to it being in Old British (or Welsh), Gaelic, Latin, old English or Norse, the languages that were in use at different times and places in ancient North Britain (Note 5). I have been fortunate to be writing this in a period when there has been a growing academic interest in early Scottish literature leading to the translation and publication of poetry previously unknown to most people in Scotland (Clancy 1998). Some of these works may be a direct inheritance from rhymes retelling of 'Dark Age' events. Some I think, were written in direct response to an Arthurian narrative held within the strong oral tradition of Northern Britain, but given today's ignorance of the hero, this remains 'hidden' with the agenda which may have motivated its composition. Others still may contain a brief allusion to places and people of those times as it helps to inform or entertain an audience with a taken for granted knowledge of times not yet forgotten. My use of such materials has always originated in the pictorial stone narratives. In many instances paper corroborated stone and in some cases stone solved a mystery identified by the wordsmiths.

As I have already mentioned photographs of some of the finds have been useful. In many instances the camera's pixcel eye discerns the colouring and form of carved and sculpted work that is almost opaque otherwise. Initially on my quest for knowledge I began by trying to document all my finds in sketch form and I littered paper with descriptive labels and exclamations denoting my amazement at the degree of artfulness concealed and then revealed by sleight of hand. I soon had to give this up as there was so much material. I decided to observe as much sculpted work as possible. This turned out to be the way forward as by observing large numbers more quickly over a continuous period I began to recognise patterns and styles of presentation.

The more materials I look at, the more convinced I am that some of the worked figures should be represented in my exposition. Warriors, old and young, women and children, tradesmen and farmers and philosophers/Wise ones, shepherds, carters, many birds and some animals and fish are all featured. Sometimes I find a very decorative stone which on closer inspection is covered in dozens of faces looking right back at me! So I am giving some of these characters a little talking space. Their accounts will be mercifully short as I am no story teller. They will be placed within this book where it seems appropriate to the theme under exploration. My notes that follow will represent a distillation of my interpretations and understandings. In these different ways I hope to persuade you, the literate reader, that the non-literate world has something to say to the inheritors of their lands.

From my early observations as archivist the protagonists in the North seem to have been stone depicted as the Picts and the Saxons. The latter, represented by a young warrior with a very unfriendly visage, may have been based somewhere close to present day Lothian's southern border. I wonder if it is possible that the war-like portrayal represented the ancestors of the Bernician people (*Berneich*, British word for *gap people*), who had either been part of the invited mercenaries or were later settlers who had taken over the coastal area of the Tweed Basin coming across the North Sea during the English (Anglo-Saxon)-Britonnic wars in the last half of the 5th century (Fraser, 2009). Suffice to say now that stone documentation suggests that although the Saxons operated as a separate unit, their campaign may have been given an edge by the actions of the Picts who seemed to have held strategic locations and may have got involved in some guerrilla tactics against the Britons. Arthur and his forces faced a formidable task.

Chapter notes

Note 1
Besides the miniature artifacts themselves, the only evidence for the use of pinhole or magnification technology by Uotadini artists may lie in a re-interpretation of one or perhaps two of the forty Pictish symbols that have been identified on Pictish stones found in Scotland (Historic Scotland 2010). I would like to posit that the 'triple disc' and possibly the 'mirror case' may have been representations of the possession of this technology. The former consists of a central 'disc' or circle which has three inner concentric circles which could be signifiers for changes in layers of increasing detail. Attached at opposite edges of the central circle are two rings. It is not difficult to envisage these being the mode of holding the pinhole/magnifier steady for use when both hands are needed such as in sculpture. Such a design is similar to that used today. The 'mirror case', which has a single concentric circle within looks more like a magnifier with less magnification strength. Could it have been designed for use by the owner of miniatures? The attached shape looks like a stand and would make examining one's tiny pictorial treasure much easier than a handle when seeking out its 'secrets'. Did the presentation of these particular symbols identify a people who possessed the 'magical'knowledge of miniaturisation? Could it be that such signs indicated Druidism? I will not say there will never be answers to these questions given the immense pictorial data base waiting to be attended to.

Note 2
In the summer of 2010 I visited the ' Neolithic Tomb of the Eagles' on Orkney Mainland and during the preliminary group talk was handed for a brief moment, a very smooth and regularly faceted stone that had been found in the tomb by the farmer on whose land it stands. We were told that the function of this stone was a mystery. In the short time I had to view it I could discern small faint figures etched onto the surfaces. Perhaps this was a narrative stone, each facet holding a part of the history of a family and the stone was passed from person to person, each taking a turn to learn/tell the tale. This hypothesis seems all the more credible when similar sized and faceted stones have been found in the graves of people who lived in Kilmartin Glen, Mid Argyll, one to two thousand years after they were made (Kilmartin Museum) (see chapter 7). I would suggest that such objects were cherished, as 'working

heirlooms' that were a record and a prompt for an oral tradition reaching very far back in time. Perhaps there came a time in a particular family or community when it was thought appropriate to bury the stories with one individual. It seems to me that the present day interest in genealogy and social history continues an ancient concern to contextualise and structure the past.

Note 3
The silver consists of Roman plate broken into pieces. The hoard is on view at the National Museum of Scotland, Edinburgh.

Note 4
It seems very likely given the milder and wetter climate of that time, that there would have been a significantly larger body of water flowing across the Forth-Clyde isthmus. The Carron River is about 14 miles long and arises from the Campsie Hills about half-way along this 'waist' of Scotland. A 17th century observer William Nimmo (1770) described the Carron Bog as a 'vast plain and meadow' (p1) which was about four miles in length situated mostly in the area of *Fintry* parish not far from its origin. He thought that this part of the Carron may have been a loch in earlier times. In the Bartholomew (1912) map of Scotland the *Endrick* Water, a small navigable river formed from burns from the Gargunnock Hills, turns at Todholes and heads west and after 18 miles enters the southern end of Loch Lomond . The two rivers are for a mile or two almost parallel flowing in opposite directions and a portion of the Endrick does continue easterly and joins the Carron near Kirk o'Muir. A couple of miles downstream at Temple Denny boats would need to be carried for a while due to waterfalls.   Such a waterway may have enabled, not only sudden raids on the peoples living along the Clyde-Forth isthmus but perhaps also trade and cultural exchange across this region and beyond.

Note 5
Old British originates in the 'P Group' of prehistoric dialects associated by their treatment of the 'qu' sound within the primitive Indo-European language. It was turned into the *p* sound. The other group of dialects held onto the *qu* which produced the Irish, Scottish and Manx forms of Gaelic. 'P Celtic' and 'Q Celtic' are a relatively recent way of referring to the peoples of ancient Britain around two thousand years ago. It is not known when the Celts arrived in Britain, perhaps several centuries BC, but of course there would have been an indigenous population already

there, and no doubt conversing in their own particular dialect. Towards the end of the sixth century AD, the Old British or Brythonnic language was mutating into early Welsh, Breton and Cornish (Watson, 1926, p2).

Chapter 2: The Red Castle and the White Palace

I called them 'the story stones of Rodes' at first before I discovered others along the miles of coast land that border this part of East Lothian. 'Rodes' was the name given by the early map maker Adair (1682) for this area at the edge of the town of North Berwick. The name is the Scots spelling for *roads* and I like to think that when the cartographer came to this place, the local people gave him what was a description of its terrain that had been passed down through the generations of local families. Empty of all signs of habitation, this name seemed initially at least, to be the only memory trace of the old ruins of the ancient, vibrant civilisation that lived here. The land adjoining this area has a *wanton wall* hidden for the most part under turf (Forrest 1802). When I first came to live here I was told that this eastern edge of town was church land which perhaps suggests another spelling, that of *Roods*. If this was the case then other meanings may have been attached to this place. The Scots words *'rood'* or *'rude'* signify the cross of Christ. Alternatively the name is also a Scots measure of land and the burgh *'rudis'* was ground owned by a burgh that is feued or rented out (CSD 1987). I would suggest that a multiplicity of place-name meanings and unexplained roads and walls are significant hints of much earlier forgotten times.

On a reddish coloured stone there is a girl in short skirts and her long hair loose watching a leave-taking. Two small boats moored alongside each other are filled with people embarking from a guarded sea cave....

Mae

We waved to my cousin Aiken as he and his fellow rowers manoeuvred their canoes out from under the cliff and headed out to sea, away from the tall rocks which surrounded the entrance to the cave. My aunt had allowed me to come down with her because this was the day my oldest brother was getting shore leave. The boat that had taken my cousin away was returning with Hugh. He was a sailor with the navy and spent many weeks away at a time. While we waited for him, my aunt sat down in the little recessed area and I walked out onto the wooden jetty. Staring down at the water, I thought about all that had happened since my big brother had been home last.

It was a spring morning and Hugh with Buckie and Lachlan, my other older brothers, had been helping my father with the lambing. I was forbidden from joining in on this heavy work but I had the task of climbing up the steep slopes above the village with a parcel of food for the workers. It was a crisp, clear day and looking out to the east I gazed beyond the little scatter of cottages on the ridge below that is Tranent, towards the wide fertile plain golden edged by coastal dunes. Gwanannon it is called, the land of gods and kings. The sea beyond this was a shimmering azure that day. My family had lived in the hills of this beautiful kingdom for a long, long time. The stories of my father's hearth are filled with how its history had shaped the lives of generations of the sons and daughters of Naiton. I filled a jug from a burn close to the path. As I looked up from my task I thought I saw my favourite bird, the thrush, peeking at me through the blossoms of a hawthorn bush. I felt glad that she was making an appearance as it meant I would have a lucky day.

I had strict instructions not to loiter as my Aunt Lillith was expected. In a week's time she was to take me to live with her in the citadel. My mother and Lilith were sisters and came from a long line of Reciters. I had passed the memory tests set by the Druid College and had been awarded an apprenticeship with the Company of Bards to the Guinnion Court. To have the chance to become a Reciter was a great honour for my family. It would take till my fifteenth summer to learn all the history and the stories of my people. When I returned from the hills she had arrived and was sitting with my mother beside the hearth, my baby twin brothers playing on the rug between them. My sisters Morna and Etnach were serving honey cakes and milk, and listening avidly to Lilith's news from the royal palace. My aunt was a tall woman with dark auburn hair which was very like my mother's, tightly curled and difficult to subdue under her veil. Lying at her feet was Murn, her faithful hound. The King called my aunt the 'Linnet' as she could sing out the poems and the lineages of his ancestors so beautifully. Even now, as a middle aged matron she was called upon to perform at festivals and entertainments for visiting dignitaries. It had been arranged that I would stay with my aunt and Uncle Cerres, her husband, and attend my classes every morning. I was to help her with her household duties in the afternoons.

My mother and my older sisters had made me two new dresses and a woollen overcoat and my father presented me with a pair of warm moccasins to wear indoors. My brothers had carved and painted two little green stones for me. One was of an eider duck resting its head in its feathers and when I turned it over on the other side it had morphed into a baby seal. The other carving was of Dougal, the little spaniel, from the family of dogs much loved by the King. I put both of these stones into the amulet I wore around my neck. They would, I hoped, help protect me from misfortune.

Early one morning the following week, my father walked us down to the piers at Pans. Murn of course, as dogs do, ran on ahead, wheeling back and then high tailing it off again. It was only a mile or so to the river, so it was not long before I had said goodbye to my father and had stepped into the skiff which was to take us to the great white citadel. While the boatmen rowed, my aunt, once she had calmed Murn began to talk about some of the places we passed on our journey. Far to the east across the firth was the land of our kindred. The twin blue beacon hills that were its main landmarks were all we could see from the boat. My aunt had been there and described a beautiful place with many settlements around the loch that lay at the foot of these hills. She said it was a blessed land that everywhere sparkled with little lochs. Lilith was truly, I think, a poet herself as well as a Reciter. Close to this nirvana many battles had been fought in years gone by. There has been peace now for the last eight summers.

The distant land was shades of blue above the glittering sea. It's outline of hills falling down to the last headland of the Firth before the Great Northern Sea. The coast that I knew on this southern shore was a swathe of sand bordered by dark woods and interspersed with jagged stone outcrops. In the sea, but close to the beaches, lie a row of little islands. They all have names and are beloved by my people because of their calming influence on the rough sea that rolls in to mingle with the more gentle rivers that flow into the firth.

Soon we were passing Federary Island. I could see ships anchored and some little buildings close to its first headland. This place was fortified against attack, and men were stationed there as lookouts all year round. During the wars a small garrison of soldiers was stationed on this island, on call for any attack upon the coastal lands. Before long, other islands came into view and further east and north of these is the huge Rock named after of our bird god Gana, a glimmering, shimmering white jewel during the summer and forbidding sentinel through the dark and stormy winter.

Now my aunt began to talk about the upcoming harrying (Note 1) of the young gannets from the Rock but I was hardly listening. My gaze was firmly fixed upon the coast now as we neared the sheltered waters of Guinnion. The royal city stood above a golden crescent of sand protected on one edge by a range of ragged rocks and by a steep headland on the other. Tucked close in to the headland, the crenellated walls of the stronghold could be seen climbing high up onto the cliffs that rose from the beach. Enclosed by the walls and clutching on precariously to steep indents in the heights was an imposing red sandstone fortress with a collection of windowed turrets that faced out to sea. At the summit of this vertiginous manmade edifice I could see the white painted wall of the adjoining palace. Built into this great bastion and forming part of a combined entrance with the old red fortress is the great white tower, the Light of Guinnion, so called because, it has, at its summit, a life-saving beacon. Lit at night, it is a warning of and a guide through, the wrecking rocks below. Dominating all of this of course was the great Hound Stone that shelters the most sacred grove of our Wise Ones. Lying a half mile inland, it is a little mountain seen big against the flat, southern plain in its trailing wake and the coastal citadel sited close to its northerly slopes. Both land and people benefit from the fresh water it gives up. I wondered when I would see the Mother Hound, Agnes, the enchanted dog who chases the wind as she scales the Mount. She is said to lie at its summit with her pups, guarding the Sea Kingdom from the dangers that surround it.

As the boat drew closer I could see the much acclaimed King's Causeway, the elevated approach to the stronghold. The road builders had extended the edge of the cliffs to accommodate this, the main way in. Partially hidden by trees, it was about a mile long beginning at the road from the rocks called the Sisters at the western end of the bay and snaking high up and around the cliff edge. Halfway along the road disappears and I knew that it had arrived at the dark glen where it continues along its way over the King's Brig, a stone pillared bridge, spanning the deep chasm through which the Fairy Burn flows below. Not far after the brig the road ends, and the huge drawbridge of the red fort and the adjoining snowy white palace begins. All along this great highway there is much activity. Carts loaded with hay, fisherwives carrying the morning catch on their backs, soldiers on foot and on horseback. My aunt drew my attention away from this busy scene as she was telling the boatmen about my apprenticeship to the Bardic masters and as she did so nodding towards a green bell-tower rising above the woods that bordered the precipitous roadway. I realised that this was the Bard House where I would learn how to be a Reciter.

****

I have given names to various places in Mae's narrative based on my study of the story stones and my subsequent trawl through relevant paper documentation. In particular I have called the clifftop citadel 'Guinnion'. If you will bear with me, dear Traveller, I will explain my choices as it seems most pertinent in the exploration that I have undertaken. My detailed description of the citadel is down to stone documentation alone there being no apparent paper record of a native British citadel on the edge of town. It has been generated from an amalgam of many carvings showing all or part of the picture of the fort and its environs. As someone familiar with the shapes of the landscape in this coastal corner, I recognised the setting of the fort. Common to almost all the carvings is the shape of the Law hill of North Berwick (in Mae's narrative the Hound Stone) (see Map 2 and Map 4).

Another distinctive feature seen frequently in what I will term the 'citadel carvings' is the curved shape of what is now called Milsey (Mill Sea) Bay. There are a large number of these stone representations which are very consistent in their detailing. According to these the citadel was of two parts (see Map 4). The eastern section was a castle-like building with its levels built into the niches and plateaux of that part of the cliff face which is closest to the headland. On the west side where the line of the cliff is relatively even there was a long wall on the seaward and landward sides which was portrayed as enclosing a distinctly separate set of buildings situated around a central open area. There was a door in the landward wall that gave access to this space. I have named this part, the 'palace'. The pictorial suggests the need to distinguish between the two structures. Sometimes the castle, but never the palace, has been represented in iron. More often than the palace, the castle has been represented in red. The palace most frequently has been portrayed as painted white or built with light coloured stone. The impression made is that the castle was, or had been strongly defended and that perhaps it was the older of the two. Within both representations of the structures there are carvings that are sometimes discernible. In the red or iron castle a chieftain or king figure and several others, a queen, a servant and sometimes a clutch of warriors were distributed within its different levels. There is more decoration of the palace. This consists of carvings of a variety of dogs, of seabirds including a gannet and a gull and lastly a

22

single hare. Two sea birds have been fashioned beaks meeting that suggested an imposing doorway. The tiny sculpturings are always arranged in the same way, situated around the borders of a space often populated with humans and dogs, battles and other events. In my journey of discovery in 'reading' these scenes, I came to the conclusion that the animal and bird sculptures may represent the location of the accommodation of the various family members and supporters of a royal household within the palace grounds. Perhaps even the name of the head of each dwelling has been communicated!

Slightly west of the central space or courtyard I have very occasionally observed what looks to be a large sculpture. In the north-west corner of the palace, depicted on only several stones so far, there is a deepened circle with human figures arranged in rows into its depths, suggesting some sort of amphitheatre. From my observations, round meeting places may have been a common feature of Uotadini culture. I have identified several locations in or near to Guinnion apart from the one already described. A couple of early (Note 2) crafted stones 'tell' of a table positioned close to the landward wall of the citadel on the little plain at the foot of the Heugh (see Map 2). Another is in the palace area but at its eastern end. A few others have been wrought in a very sophisticated fashion in which scenes were depicted within the depth and circumference of an open circle. There are usually figures seated in a round and sometimes with others standing further back. Often there is a 'crowned' figure to be seen in this circular scene. Another, spotted on a map of stone was positioned a little to the south west of the North Berwick Law. In that vicinity today there is the hamlet of Kingston. Early maps (Blaeu 1654; Moll 1745) have it called 'Kingseat'. Of further interest is Forrest's 1802 'Map of Haddingtonshire' in which he inserted the term/name 'hole' beside Kingston. Could this be written corroboration of the same indented circular space (Note 3) ?

On the seaward side of the citadel an arched entrance to the castle was portrayed as joining it to the palace wall. A drawbridge linked the entrance to the elevated road described in Mae's narrative. The road must have been of some width as I have seen carts as well as horsemen approaching the drawbridge. There was also a lower route into the castle that ran parallel to the highway and ended in a little door in a crennalated wall that enclosed the lower reaches of the cliff. This scenario is very distinctive don't you think, a citadel with precipitous access that included two bridges? The higher of the two which straddled across the Fairy or Glen Burn must have been a famous construction in those times consisting of two stone built towers of some considerable height to maintain the cliff-top route, and strength to house the drawbridge apparatus. It is my impression that the 'King's Brig' was a split bridge with the facility to draw up the two sides separately in times of threat.

Apart from these dramatic northern approaches, it is a possibility that the other access points on the landward side of the citadel may also have involved bridge-building. A bridge is known to have spanned the loch above the *Glen Burn* or Fairy Burn that was created through the damming of the waters from the Law to power the grain mills situated in the Glen and owned in medieval times by the Priory of North Berwick. There is today a *Lochbridge Road* nearby that commemorates that long gone feature. The Blaeu Atlas (1654) does document the loch and there is no reason to suppose that the burns from the Law hill were not exploited in much earlier times. Although with regard to there being a bridge over the loch, at the head of the burn, in the time of the stone sculpturers, I have found no pictorial evidence. However, what I have observed is the suggestion of a moat directly in front of the landward edge of the citadel. Given the much wetter weather conditions and undrained land in the East Lothian of those times the development of a natural or man-made stretch of water there at the foot of the Heugh seems very possible. If this was the case the fortress on the cliff may have had at least three and perhaps four bridge approaches. Perhaps vestiges of such edifices were visible or remembered or even in use into medieval times.

Returning to the magnificent towered 'King's Brig', such a feature can live long in the memories and stories of a place and I found documentation that might be a written trace of its existence. A memory of the great bridge access to the citadel may exist in the 'Lebor Bretnach', the Gaelic translation from the 11th century of the 'Historia Brittonum' (more about this later (chap4)). Cogent to this part of the archive is the listing of specifically Scottish 'mirabilia'. There are several of these 'wonders' which relate to the stone narratives but the following, I suggest was about the 'King's Brig':

"A do deg : cloch for eas i mBrebic.

12 : a stone upon a waterfall in Brebic."

(From 'Scotland, the 'Nennian' recension of the Historia Brittonum and the Lebor Bretnach' Clancy 2000, in Kings, Clerics and Chronicles in Scotland, 500-1297 p93)

In Clancy's (2000) analysis it is possible that this name (*Brebic*) was meant for North Berwick. It is a small place now and no one knows it for its waterfall but even today after a bout of rain, the town's Glen Burn flows fast and furious down the ravine that divides the cliffs of Milsey Bay. In a time when the rainfall was greater and the waters of the Law and the Heugh were pouring down the narrow gorge, the appellation 'waterfall' would have been most appropriate. The stone that is the *wonder* I would suggest refers to the stone towers that supported the span of causeway through the ravine (Note 4).

Perhaps there is also a reference to the cliff-top citadel within the king-lists of the Picts. If this is the case it would be quite remarkable in itself as apart from the lists which may have a Pictish source, no other written Pictish documentation has been discovered. The stories/history and poetry concerning the Picts has been in the main, from medieval Irish texts. In these compositions they were called 'Cruithni' which has caused some confusion as there was an unrelated Irish community of that name (Calise 2002). Their place in the story of the land now called Scotland is traceable in the named places within it and most tangibly from their sculpted symbol stones. As a stone archivist of Uotadinian craft, the latter seem to be the products of a distinctly different artistic tradition as regards the art engraved upon them. However I will tentatively suggest that the Brittonic penchant for the miniature and less visible sculpturing seems to be present on some Pictish stones.

The lists are thought to be sequential records of kings that ruled the Pictish peoples over a period of about a thousand years. Interspersed within them are the reigns of thirty *Brudes*. There is inconsistency in recording these in that not all versions of the lists include the thirty. It has been thought that 'brude' was a title with Pictish or Irish names attached (M O Anderson referred to in Calise 2002). There is an alternative interpretation which I favour. No need to try and squeeze extra kings and years into a poorly known history. According to Calise (2002,p190) 'brude' can be sourced to the early Welsh word 'brud' or 'brut' meaning 'prophecy' or 'chronicle' and he suggested that there may have been a tradition at special events to recite the king-list and at certain points elaborate with some detail or narrative.

The greater the exposure to the artistry of the stone sculpturers the more aware I have become of the distinctive styles and patterns of presentation that had been wrought. One sort of presentation arrangement in particular came early because it was easy to spot and that was king or chieftain lists. These quite frequently were chiselled at the edges of a stone. No doubt it was a good way to create profiles. A column of heads one on top of the other created a sense of lineage. To the side of this column were tiny scenes. Even to an inexperienced eye like mine it was clear that these were placed there to provide some significant narrative about this or that head/ruler personally or his/her reign. This early differentiation of the sculptured work would not be the last which suggested to me that the written documentation of ancient 'dark' times seemed to be closely linked to stone versions of the same era. It hints at a point on the time continuum when the traditional telling, known by heart, or perhaps failing that, a miniature stone crib in the pocket was finally written down. However, in the case of the written regnal lists there was either a lost 'Brude Appendix' which elaborated upon each chronicle or it was never written as it may have seemed inconceivable that anyone would forget them. Discovering written translations of pictorial presentations may be another way of reaching back to the ways that our ancestors sought to organise their world in living and remembering it. I have already intimated that as this archive progresses, some examples will be given of how pictorial narrative may have been the source and/or inspiration for later wordsmiths.

Wonder no longer, dear Traveller, what all this has to do with the cliff-top citadel of Guinnion. One of the several versions of the Pictish king-list (Regnal List SL3 (Lec.2) K. Muchrone Book of Lecan (Calise (2002, p7) states that there were 30 'Bruides' but names only one, 'Bruda Pont' (Calise 2002, p190). 'Pont' is the Welsh for 'bridge' from the Latin 'pontis' or 'pons'. However this name has more likely meanings with regard to Guinnion for example also from the Latin, 'pont' may translate as 'sea' ('pontus') which would not be incongruous with the location of the citadel. I would like to argue though that there may be a much better connection with this remnant of Pictish record that locks in to a variety of other sources linked over time to the story of North Berwick

References to the presence of the great fortress at the foot of North Berwick's little hill the 'Law', in memory and place-names were I would argue, interwoven into the wording in the old documents preserved in the National Archives of Scotland. These are to do with the ownership of the land on the eastern edge of the town where the citadel once stood. In the feuing (feudal tenure) of a William Matheson's croft in 1539 there was a reference to a *'ponti [fc] raig'* or *'ponti [fe] raig* (line 33, GD1/453/5, no 15 NAS) (*'craig'* being a rock or hill). In another document from the same collection of papers, there seems to be corroboration of this as there was written, '*[tou]* or *[ton]ttspont arrondafiont'* (line 24 GD1/453/5, no 17 NAS). If *'pont'* in this context was the source of the Latin *'pontifex'* meaning *'a college of high priests'* (Chambers 1985) then the Law and the surrounding lands east of it seem to have had a history that involved an elite priesthood.

Further medieval documentation recording the lands and a family called 'Puntoun' may provide some credence to this proposition. In 1487 a Thomas Puntoun 'dwelling with the Prioress of North Berwick' was buying the 'lands of Ruchlawfald' from the Archar sisters one of whom was the widow of a William Halyburton. This property lies south of the *Ferrygate* area between North Berwick and neighbouring Dirleton and was otherwise known as 'Duns Falde' (GD6/4NAS) (see Map2). In 1500 when this Thomas Puntoun, was making his will and leaving some of the old Archar/Halyburton property to his youngest son Thomas, it was revealed that he also had a croft

"between Welly's Land on the east and Kayis Wynd on the west which he had in tack from the prioress's convent of North Berwick"

(GD110/218, NAS) (Note 5)

Kayis or *Kay's Wynd* was within the royal burgh boundary and so west of the Glen/Fairy/Mill Burn whilst Welly's Land was about 3 miles east of North Berwick. *'Toun'* it should be noted was frequently used within Scottish place-names to denote *'a cluster of houses belonging to tenants'* (CSD 1987). Early names were often acquired from where the person/family had lived and so it is possible that Thomas was *of Puntoun* which lay to the east of the town. More documentation locates his croft close to the burgh boundary. In January 1587/1588 the last Prioress of North Berwick gave over the convent lands to her kinsman Alexander Home (GD110/20, NAS). In 1560 the Estates of Scotland had abolished the authority of the Pope in Scotland and forbidden the celebration of Mass. The new reformed faith was to be adopted. In the years before this and after valuable lands and properties of the Priory were passed to the Home family who were related to the last two Prioresses (Ferrier

1980). Pinning down more tightly the location of Thomas' croft was done in a document dated 15th June, 1596 in which a Robert Hume 'of the Heugh' signed a charter that apportioned his grandson Alexander Home (Hume) the lands of 'Horsecruik' which were described as:

" between lands of Tamptalloune (Tantallon) on east, lands of **Croceflatt** and Laichfaldis on south, lie lonyng from town of Northberuik to manor of Heuche on west, lands occupied by Andrew Home of **Roddis on north**, lands called **Puntoun Rig and Puntoun Myre adjacent....**"

(GD110/177, NAS).

It seems that alongside 'Roddis' were the cultivated and bog lands of the settlement of 'Punt'. The year 1607 finds a John Puntoun and his sister Isobel Puntoun giving up 'ad perpetuam remanentiam' their three properties in the barony of North Berwick, held by the Home family, two of which appear to approximate the lands on which the old citadel stood. Again in 1642 *Puntoun* and *Puntounrig* are recorded (GD110/211, NAS).

'Horscruik' is *Horsecrook* today and is situated across the Tantallon Road from the ancient citadel site and the Glen. Until the building of a supermarket adjacent to this in recent years there was signs that there may have been a burn flowing off the Heugh and into the Glen opposite Horsecrook while there would have been waters and bog on the west from the Law. 'Cruik' can mean 'lameness' particularly of horses and so could relate to there being a danger in that locale for horses due perhaps to the amount of surrounding bog land (CSD 1987). Certainly no horsemen long ago would have chosen to approach the fort from a westerly direction. Note too 'Croceflatt' with regard to the citadel site having some religious association.

From these various references including the 'milne' which may have been one of the mills by the Glen Burn there seems to be sufficient evidence that the word 'punt' was linked to the site of the old citadel on 'Roddis' land. It seems even more likely that this was the case as 'pontifex' is thought to derive from the pre-Latin Oscan and Umbrian word 'puntis' meaning 'propitiatory offering'. From this it looks as if the citadel and the Law were associated with a priesthood/high priests and pilgrimage. More traces of the ancient history of this place beside the Wanton Wall will come to light as the archive progresses. Apart from the sheer antiquity of the site there may be other reasons why there is apparently nothing that directly refers to the existence of any kind of fortress on the edge of town. An English visitor to North Berwick who
28

made reference to a castle there alerted me to one explanation. This was Bishop Pococke who undertook a tour of Scotland in 1760. The bishop wrote regularly to his sister during his travels. The following is an extract from one of his letters in which he refers to his visit to North Berwick:

"It is said that King Edward First after the Battle of Banock Burne gave up this Castle (at North Berwick) and retired to the Castle of Dunbar.

I proceeded two miles to Tantallon Castle at the mouth of the great bay, called the Firth of Forth......"

(From letter LXVII Pococke Tour of Scotland 1760, Publications of the Scottish History Society 1887 Vol 1 and quoted in Ferrier 1980,p62)

Interestingly aside from pointing out that the bishop had got the king wrong (was Edward II) Ferrier (1980) dismissed Pococke's words concerning the castles at North Berwick and Tantallon as mistaken. He clearly thought that the latter was the castle 'given up' by the English king. However, stone observation suggests that he was referring to the old cliff-top stronghold almost two miles west of Tantallon (see Map3). That Ferrier did not take the Bishop's observation as valid was due in part it would seem, to the assumed presence of the remains of another 'castle' in North Berwick. Its location is said to be on the grassy mound, called *Castle Hill* that lies to the east of the modern day harbour. This construction is thought to have been a motte built there in the 13th century by the Earls of Fife to protect a pilgrimage route to St Andrews that enabled people coming from the Borders and the north of England to reach the saint's shrine across the firth. Crossing from North Berwick was the shortest distance to travel for the pilgrims. At that time (until time of Robert II) apart from owning large tracts of Fife the Earls held the barony of North Berwick 'with the castle' (Ferrier, 1980 p13). Many thousands of pilgrims throughout the Middle Ages took the ferry established for them, from North Berwick over to Earlsferry in Fife. The presence of a motte, if it really existed, may have been an effective deterrent to anyone who would seek to harm the pilgrims. The castle and palace depicted by many stone workers, unlike the Castlehill site, had the dimensions large enough to house many men and host King Edward II of England in 1314. For a time perhaps a force which could have staffed a motte was billeted in the cliff top citadel. The 'motte' may have been a small onsite military station, tasked with ensuring law and order at a busy ferry point and all that that must have entailed in goods and services.

In a search to find out what happened to the Uotadinian citadel it might be fruitful to mull over why the English king would give up one castle after a major defeat and take up residence in another just ten miles away. Was this place particularly significant in the history between the Scots and the English that absenting himself from it was fore'gone after such a major defeat? In other words, were his actions to do with the narrative attached to this ancient stronghold? Rivers were physical boundaries for different territories and I would hazard that the Lothian Tyne may have marked an ancient and not forgotten border. Dunbar lies to the south of this river. I will return later in this archive to explore how the citadel's story may have continued to feature in the history of Scotland.

Further castle confusion seems to have been added with the building of Tantallon Castle by William first Earl of Douglas. The Douglases acquired the Fife earl's lands on the southern banks of the Firth of Forth in 1371 including the barony of North Berwick. As a result the town seems to have been identified with Tantallon. The original burgh charter was destroyed by fire but in 1568 James VI granted a replacement charter that renewed the rights and privileges of royal burgh status that the town had had since the 14th century. As stone archivist for the cliff top citadel I have noted that the burgh boundaries identified within this document, very clearly did not include the land on which it is sited (Ferrier1980,pp26-27). The eastern burgh boundary was the length of the 'Millburn' (called Glen Burn today, Fairy Burn in Mae's narrative) from the sea and up through the glen. Perhaps this separation of the site of the old fortress from the town could be a trace of the very distant history. 'Castlehill' (motte) on the other hand is very clearly situated on the burgh side of the 'Millburn'.

Interestingly the burgh charter makes particular mention of the mill on the burn in the lowest reaches of the glen as having an 'acqueduct' that boundary lines must not affect. One old paper map of North Berwick (Ainslie, 1775) identifies a 'Wall Tower Mill'. It is clearly labelled as in the lower glen area. It is a name which seems to corroborate my stone observations that there was a tower within the grounds of the citadel close to the 'King's Causeway' entrance. The name seems to suggest that there was still evidence or memories of this tower presumably centuries after the citadel had fallen into ruin. The reference to a 'wall'
30

also hints of the presence of a substantial building east of the burgh. A further possibility is that the 'tower' referred to may have been an allusion to the remains of one of the stone supports for the 'King's Causeway' where a bridge spanned the burn. To conclude, the small amount of paper documentation available consistently seems to record a separation of the eastern lands of the barony and the western burgh. Suffice to say it is perhaps time to question what 'castle' was being referred to in any paperwork concerned with the history of North Berwick. Castlehill, the site where the motte was supposed to be has never been excavated. The power of the written word is very great indeed.

Perhaps a clue as to when Mae's 'White Tower of Guinnion' was no longer in situ may be in the adding of a tower of 'some considerable height' (Ferrier 1980, p19) onto the west side of the parish church sometime after it was built in the 12th century. This church was on the tidal island gifted to the North Berwick Nunnery by the Earl of Fife which is now the promontory at the present day harbour. Although the rest of the church was destroyed in a storm in the 17th century, the tower still stood until early in the 19th century acting as an aide to shipping. A tradition of ensuring there was always a sea mark in the dangerous coastal waters in this area of the estuary, may have existed long before the parish church was built. If this was the case the citadel's tower may have been fulfilling such a role for at least six hundred years after the stone crafters left their memorials of the citadel's structures.

Returning to the pictorial narrative, there looking over the sea-facing palace wall, the heads of four youths have sometimes been worked. From my observations they are of high status, sometimes being portrayed as children with a king figure close by. The latter is usually represented as extremely fat presumably because he was in life or perhaps the obesity is a signifier for great wealth and power. I would contend that the pictorial impact of the children or sometimes a row of babies close to this figure conveys that there was a significant historical destiny for them as a group or individually. Whatever the future held for these princelings it involved some sort of evil. In several pieces this is glimpsed through the distance placed between the group and a young man with a threatening visage (black hair, facial lines black, countenance nasty).

With regards to Mae's 'Guinnion', the citadel sculptures I have observed have been painted white frequently on one flat side. In addition to these portrayals I have found a very large number of stones, of varying proportions, from extremely tiny, to small boulders, upon which there is a white painted delineated area. The consistency with which this fortress was depicted as white had made me wonder whether this was the Guinnion stronghold referred to in the 'Historia Brittonum' as the location of one of the battles of the mythical Arthur. The P-Celtic meaning of 'guinnion' is the *white* or *holy place*. In Mae's narrative I describe how I think this great fortress of the ancient Britons must have looked like around the time of Arthur in the fifth to sixth centuries AD. A good proportion of the stone fragments I have found seem to corroborate the portrayal of the actual site as white or whitened. On dark shades of stone the sculptured fortress is painted white or white stones are modelled into its outline.

This whitened representation perhaps can reveal something of the religious and practical world of the people who lived here sixteen hundred years ago. At this period in time the Romano- British peoples of what is now southern Scotland were becoming Christianised or at least their elites were. The Uotadini people came to call themselves the *Gododdin*, meaning the '*Baptised*'. Old beliefs and ways of representing the world would have existed, perhaps for a long time, alongside those of the new religion and some would have endured, being rebranded or adopted by it. Whether the whitening signified the citadel was at that time a Christian site cannot be assumed. With regard to the pictorial art, out of the many worked pieces I have found so far, only a handful of them have some distinctive trace of a Christian narrative. One of these is a portrayal of an important event within the whitened stronghold. In the centre of the scene there a king faces the figure of a warrior who has a cross on his arm and upon his shield. Accompanying these Christian accessories, the warrior has been portrayed as wearing what appears to be a pagan garland or crown of feathers upon his head. Adherence to pagan and Christian beliefs may well have co-existed in a very harmonious way in many areas of the lives of the ordinary people. I will talk again about this scene in a later chapter.

The Bass Rock, 'Gana' in Mae's narrative, is a steep sided volcanic plug, situated about five kilometres north east of North Berwick. It stands 107 metres at its highest point about two kilometres out into the Firth of Forth. Inaccessible to humans on all sides except for its southern aspect where there is a steep falling away from the summit which has in the past allowed the building of a 15th century chapel and various forms of a castle or fortress, the latest dating from the 16th century, the earliest version of which is not documented. In the time of Charles II the castle was converted to a state prison and early into the 20th century the governor's house and part of the castle was refashioned again and the Stevenson lighthouse was built in 1902. At its base above the water line there is a tunnel 105 metres long that reaches into the depths of the Rock. Today no one lives on the Rock and it is known for being the world's largest single rock gannetry with around 150,000 North Atlantic gannets returning from southern climes every January to re-establish their nesting territories on the Rock.

Throughout its known history the Bass has been involved in various dramatic and usually violent events in Scottish history including the imprisonment of a royal hostage and many religious zealots as well as sieges and attacks on enemy ships entering the Firth. That for many centuries the Bass was perceived as a potential threat to the security of the state seems to be hinted at in the institution of joint ownership of the Rock. In 1425 King James confirmed that a Robert of Edrington, a member of the Lauder family held 'one half of the Bass in the barony of North Berwick and constabulary of Haddington' and this connection has been traced back to 1316 when the Lauders had received one half of it from Robert the Bruce and the other from the Bishop of St Andrews (Reid 1885 pp59-60). Interestingly the 1425 charter makes clear that the county of Haddington had no independent sherriffdom and was still under the jurisdiction of Edinburgh.

There is a also a trace that it's impregnability may also have meant that it was used as a place of safety for very early state documentation as in 1650 the Church of Scotland sought to have its public records placed there when it was known Cromwell was planning to invade Scotland the following year. From a requisition sent to the keeper of the Rock there were these words,

"that the bass might be made secure for the registers as it had been in a former day of calamity" (From 'The Bass Rock. Civil and Ecclesiastical History' McCrie 1848).

Unfortunately Cromwell was to send all these national documents to London when the Bass was surrendered to the Lord Protector in April 1652.

In the spring and summer the North Berwick area is in thrall to the huge and glorious white pearl that the Bass Rock becomes when its gannet population is in residence. A goodly number of stones seem to delineate the stronghold as a snowy mirror image of the area of avian luminescence on the Rock. I would suggest that for a people who, from their art, paid homage to the seabirds of their sky and estuary, whitening their home may have been part of that respect for the phenomenon of nature that dominated their part of the River Forth. This respect and celebration of the natural environment is communicated again and again in the worked stone and the presence of islands close to shore and in particular the Bass, would have made the seabirds the predominant representatives of nature to man. It can only be conjectured how large the bird presence was for these 5th-6th century coastal people but given that rats had not reached these shores at that time, it is likely that the numbers were considerably greater than today. One stone seems to portray some sort of competition held on the almost sheer side of the Law in which men are disturbing nesting birds. The old practice of 'harrying' or harvesting of young gannets from the Bass Rock is a matter of record but not with regard to the little mountain half a mile inland.

The whitened citadel sculptures may relate to a particular practical reason. Whitened buildings on a sea cliff may have had obvious maritime uses in an area with many rocky hazards to shipping and no lighthouses to warn or guide. In addition given the copious amount of coal to be found around the coast, it is not too fanciful, I think, to suggest as I have in Mae's story, that the white castle tower had a beacon at its top. Indeed one stone appears to portray an old woman handling coals near the top of a tower within the fortress.

McDiarmid (1983) in his examination of 'Y Gododdin', an early Welsh language poem attributed to a 6th century poet called Aneirin, about a disastrous Gododdin campaign to 'Catraeth' posited that the referral to 'mountain called Gana' may have been within the 'land of Gwanannon'. This was a place-name that was probably sourced to the Welsh 'gwen' meaning 'white' (McDiarmid 1983, p17). I will include the details of his analysis later but crucially he argues that this land must have been quite close to Eidyn (Edinburgh), from where the force had been sent on the orders of a Gododdin king/chief. From my observations of the pictorial, I would argue that 'Gana' was a reference to the Bass Rock. Long ago, as now, it must have been the 'mountain' most closely associated with seabirds, in particular the gannet and it is probably through this bird's name that there is a source of these long ago forgotten names. Watson (1926 p445) demonstrating the evolution of Scottish place name endings gave an example that may have relevance in the meaning of 'gana'. *Glean Geunaid* (now anglicised as *Glen Derby*) in Perthshire, which had been documented as Glengaisnot in 1510; -*ganot* in 1511; 1521; 1538; -ganacht in 1516; -*gynit* in 1629 and –*gennet* in 1630. This glen he explained was known locally as a feeding stop on the flight route of wild geese heading east to west. The origin of the word 'gannet' comes from a prehistoric Germanic *'ganitaz'* or *'ganaton'* a word from the same source that resulted in the English *'gander'*. That the similarity in appearance between the gannet and the goose is acknowledged in word construction can be traced further through the gannet being known traditionally as the solan goose, *'solan'* being a compound formed in the 15th century from Old Norse 'sula' 'gannet' and *'ond'* 'duck' (Ayto 1990, 2005). 'Ganot' is also the Old English word for 'sea fowl'. Establishing I think that there is a very good possibility that 'Gana' was the Bass, Aneirin's poem places this sea mountain and therefore the North Berwick area in the land of Gwannanon. From all this it may be that the 'Gwanannon' of poetry is traceable through the mists of time by virtue of the highly specific characteristics of the natural world in this small part of Scotland.

Mapping the white area to the geography of North Berwick suggests Guinnion was of significant proportions. I have calculated that it amounted to about 51 acres. It's boundary to the west being the Glen ('Mill' or 'Fairy') Burn and in the east it's walls I am not so sure of, but would at least have encompassed the land on which the Rhodes Farmhouse stands and probably more including the grounds of the adjacent council camp and private caravan sites. Given this and the carved evidence of human habitation and activity closer to the modern day town centre, I think there may have been at least several hundred people living there. According to descriptions of Lothian a thousand years after this time (Blaeu Atlas, 1654, NLS), the land, rivers and the sea were rich in grain, game and fish. The agricultural revolution had still to take place so the hills and plains of Lothian were likely to be little changed from the time of the Uotadini. This sort of landscape a given, it might not be too great a leap to envision a community large enough to support the differentiation of trades and crafts. The stones seem to make clear that Guinnion was the prestigious residence of a chieftain or king. In such a scenario there would be the need for people who could maintain and preserve the knowledge of such a dynasty and its people. Several stones have scenes which portray the playing of a wind instrument. On one particularly complex flat and dyed stone a musician has been fashioned playing a sort of lute (in the shape of a bird) sitting on top of what appears to be a graphic king list.

I have inserted the Druid tower into Mae's story as I noted on one stone a single tower some   distance away from the palace closer to the westerly end of the 'King's Causeway'. North-west of this location is a large sloping public park. Interestingly, at the foot of this and facing into Quality Street once the site of a medieval market place, stands the 'Lodge'. Before 1783, this house once the residence of the Dalrymples formerly barons of the town lands, was called the 'Wall Tower' (Ferrier 1980). This makes two locations less than a mile apart where there are paper and stone references to there being stone wall towers in North Berwick. A shared name but with no known history attached.

With regards to the Law or 'Stone' or 'Maen' (Welsh for stone), it is never difficult to isolate even in the most complex of carvings. It is perhaps the most frequently carved topographical feature of the area. It seems likely that the Law was an integral part of the Uotadini culture. The Law was never left unadorned. Sometimes the whole shape of it outlined the head of a dog. One stone has a female hound at the summit feeding three or four puppies and another, a hound racing up its steep slopes. Occasionally the head of what looks to be a baboon, an animal not native to Scotland, has been chiselled into its outline. In addition there was another sculptured being linked to the Law. This was of a bear, its distinctive profile worked into its shape.   The whole of this great creature was also very frequently presented as in or around the citadel site. Apart from this representation in the stronghold pieces, it is almost a constant feature of all the other sorts of portrayals I have found in my study of the stones in the locality.   That this bear was the representation of a very important person became clear from the sheer quantity of worked pieces in which it was featured in human settings and activities amongst an assortment of birds mainly, and humans. Occasionally indeed this central figure was presented as a man with a human face but with a bear's profile facing backwards. Later I will refer to specific examples of the not infrequent use of a brown colouring which through experience I came to understand was a signifier of the bear's presence.   As an observer, the frequency of this animal's appearance in the pictorial narrative communicated its pre-eminent position in a particular history of the people of the citadel.

It was after a few months of observations and I had begun to look at some of the paper work that referred to the Early Historic period in
36

Scotland that I came to realise that the bear portrayals signified a particular historical figure. What I had found were picture stories of Prince Arthur of legend 'told' by the people who lived in or very close to a time when he and a confederation of *Gwyr Y Gogledd*, the Men of the North, fought to recover and defend the lands between the old Roman walls. Gwry Y Gogledd was the name the people of medieval Wales had for the warriors and kings whose exploits and history largely took place in what is now southern Scotland. Stories and poetry are thought to have been preserved within the oral tradition of verse and rhyme till a time when they were written down. Over the generations the origin of the Gwyr Y Gogledd came to be associated with northern Wales itself and the real Old North was forgotten (Moffat 1999).

The English word *'bear'* was *'bera'* in Old English and has its origins in a Germanic family of names for the bear originating from the adjective for *'brown'* and the noun, apart from denoting the animal also meant *'warrior'*. It is thought that Arthur's name originated from the old British or Brythonnic word *'arth'* meaning *'bear'* and was used also to denote a warrior. In some languages there seems to have been a taboo in the use of the word and other terms developed such as *'the brown one'* (English *'bruin'*) or *'the honey-eater* (Slavic *'medved'*). It is thought that this taboo was to do with its Proto-Indo-European meaning of *'harm, injury'* (Wikipedia 'Bear'). No such prohibition seems to have troubled the artists of Early Historic East Lothian. And what about the owners of 'bear work'? It seems likely that he was 'The Bear' to them. His exploits and achievements, his story meshed with theirs, told and retold for many generations (Note 6).

Stone observations that were the inspiration for the starting of this archive have been the main resource for the descriptions and discussion about what lay on the edge of the small seaside town of North Berwick. There have been few traces within existing paper documentation. So few indeed that without the miniature stone narratives they may never have raised much curiosity. Emerging from the sculpted lines and faded paints are scenes of great drama and grandeur. The overall impression to the observer was that the great citadel perched on cliffs above the Forth Estuary was a very important centre of power in Dark Age North Britain. How important will become evident as we move on Fellow Traveller, in pursuit of Scotland's ancient history.

Chapter notes.

Note 1
The method of 'harrying' or hunting the gannets on the Bass Rock – Men tied by ropes would club and knock the young gannets out of their nests and into the sea where they would be gathered up by the waiting hunters in the boats below.

Note 2
The stones referred to were large and crudely carved and so I have assumed that they were earlier than the miniature work.

Note 3
Interestingly the old maps show that there were similarly described places in other parts of Scotland. For example, in Fife, *Hole Kettle* (Ainslie 1775) and Hol *Ketttill* (Bleau 1654) near Kettle of course, which is a little south of Falkland (Nicolaisen posits that 'Kettle' is derived from a personal name,p151) and Gladshole (Ainslie 1775), a little north of present day Markinch. These Fife sites are relatively close to each other but sixteen hundred years ago a large area of bog would have stood between them. 'Holl Baldrick', north of Dunfermline (Bleau 1654),' may be another instance. In West Lothian the Blaeu Atlas (1654 and in Pont's original mapping used for the Atlas) locates another '*Kingseate*' east of present day Denny in the bend in the River Carron. From my observations this area, now labelled '*Kirkland*' was a settlement of high status in the time of the Uotadini/Gododdin.

Note 4
I would posit that there are three other of the 'wonders' located in East Lothian two of which are linked to the place-name given by the 'Lebor Bretnach' as '*Megongan*' (my emphasis) as having an unceasing flow of grain from a 'well'. Clancy (2000, p94) suggested that the '*meg*' may be derived from '*mig*' the Pictish for '*bog*'. The fertile plain of East Lothian comes to mind for this name, particularly that closest to the gannet isle of the Bass Rock upon which after the summer of rain (2012) there were clear signs of an ancient area of bog. The other 'mirabilia' the 'Lebor Bretnach' associated with Megongan: a well spouting bird bones and

" innumerable birds there on a certain rock, and they fly under the sea as if in the air"

(Clancy 2000,p93)

seem very likely to be an allusion to the gannets of the Bass Rock.

A further 'wonder' recorded was of tuneful 'limpets' found far from the sea ('30,000 paces' which is about 16 miles).   Perhaps this may have been a reference to Gella Bridge in Glen Clova, Angus where fresh water mussels are to be found in the Gella burn that flows through the glen (Montrose Basin History Society, 2008).

Note 5
' *Welly's land'* may be in 1607 Thomas Scowgal's land called '*Woolies croft'* to the east of North Berwick, now spelt Scoughall (GD110/218 NAS) but pronounced or rather referred to by local people as '*scaldie'*.

Note 6
This habit of placing the definite article before the name of important or well known people is still a distinctively Scottish cultural trait.

Chapter 3: Strategic Position and never heed Bede

On a flattish stone depicting a battle the youth Thomas is seen riding in the vanguard of The Bear's cavalry. He tells his story...

I can't believe that I am riding so close to my hero, the Bear, Guledig of all the Kindred forces (Note 1). The sound of over two hundred horses at hard gallop behind me, fill my ears. The fear that had been with me before has gone. I am concentrating hard on staying on the mount. Every rider is intent on covering the miles to the fort.

All morning in the fort the atmosphere had been tense. The guard was doubled and the women had been told to make ready for an evacuation inland. The Saxon ships had been seen at anchor by one of our patrols returning to Gana the evening before. It was most likely that a raid was coming and the fort was not at full muster. Men and horses had been assigned to the Bear some weeks ago. Battles were being hard fought in the north of the kingdom. The palace guard set about checking the fort defences and the fastest horses in the stables were prepared to carry messengers out of Guinnion if need be. Meanwhile beacons were already sending word along the coast to alert other forts and settlements. Guinnion must fend for itself should an attack occur before reinforcements arrive.

My father who was Master Smith had me helping him with the extra work generated so I was exhausted by night fall. I heard the night guards calling to each other. After a cold meal, the fires were all out, fighting tiredness, I saw to the horses. I fell asleep on top of a pile of hay and dreamt of saving my people from the fierce, uncombed ravagers of my people.

I was shaken awake by my father. Signals had come from the lookouts on Gana. The Saxons were heading our way with the dawn hurrying behind them. Father told me to run and report to the guardhouse. All the youths were to escort the women and children to the Wamphray, a little hamlet where, in winter the cattle are kept close to barns in the south east lee of the Hound Stone. Dawn had not reached our coastland when I found myself squelching through the bog at the foot of that little mountain, carrying one bairn on my back and holding the hand of another. *Everyone was quiet, even the little ones.   Once through the marsh we all climbed a little to reach the grass lands of Wamphray.*

Our orders had been to return to the fort once the shelters had been reached. I and my two best friends, Marr and Jamie raced back together with the calls of our mothers and sisters in our ears.   Coming in sight of the sentries on the south wall of the palace, we could hear them shout for the great, carved oak door to be opened. As soon as we had passed through, there must have been about fifty of us, we were sent off in many directions to provide support to the fighting men on the seaward side of the citadel. Jamie and I were assigned to the soldiers on the cliff wall that winds its way steeply up from the sands a hundred feet below. A fearful scene of mayhem and carnage met our eyes as we neared the wall and were able to see what was happening. At least a dozen enemy vessels were just offshore. Some of our naval ships that had pursued the enemy craft were engaged in trying to block the advance of another six. The soldiers from the Gana garrison were already ashore, killing and being killed. Against the superior numbers of Saxon warriors they would not last long.

The main thrust of the enemy was concentrated on the very fortification that we were standing on. There is a stepped pathway from the shore which ends in a small door in the fort wall. All the way up this route were our enemy, holding shields high to protect themselves from the volleys of arrows and stones. Some of these missiles were finding their target and casualties were falling back and over the cliff but their places were quickly filled. Just as I had finished my pile of stones, somewhere far up on the tower, there was a shout. The enemy had been spotted coming from the east towards Guinnion's southern walls. Another landing must have taken place in one of the many coves around the coast. That or the Canty Landing had been overcome. Everyone knew what that meant, a siege. Our seaward defence would be weakened when men had to be taken away to strengthen the long boundary ramparts at the back of the fort. It was only a matter of time before the sea door would be breached and then it would be hand to hand combat in the maze of stairways within the old red castle.

Large heavy hands thudded down on my shoulders. It was my uncle, Rab the Thrasher. He shouted in my ear that he was taking me and Jamie to Angus, Captain of the Palace Guard. He steered Jamie and I through many passageways that twisted and turned on an upward trajectory. Finally we passed the great drawbridge firmly lashed closed against

41

assault and entered Guinnion's centre, the White Palace's square. Normally the royal houses that border it have their doors open, decanting royal personages and the many servants and slaves of these households into the gleaming paved space. No sign of domestic or royal activities now. Instead men were being carried from all directions to the field hospital set up in the middle of the square. Druid Allister and some of his monks were there ministering to the wounded and the dying. Close by Captain Angus stood with Farlan and Wynn, sons of Rhobert the Dyer. Four ponies had been made ready for us. It had been decided by the King and his advisors that the Guledig, who had to be on his way, must be apprised of the imminent siege. Angus told us to split up, two of us must head inland and the others follow the coast.

Jamie and I struck out directly ahead up the Heugh which began as rolling green meadow but quickly rises steeply into the precipitous ledge of the Hound Stone. Our route was to circumvent the sacred hill and ride the quite flat land that lies between it and the wooded coast. Looking back we could see the other boys splashing through the first of the many burns west of the city. They would have a watery descent and then with the help of the gods, make a good pace along the firth's edge. We pressed on passing within a mile of the women's camp. It was a possibility that the Bear would have rested his men and horses close to Goose Fort, an ancient place still used by our people. Only three or four miles away, this fort was built high up on the hills above the Peffer Valley with a clear view of the land and sea approaches to Guinnion. This was where we headed for.

We did not have to wonder long as to the whereabouts of our warrior kinsmen. My pony's pace accelerated with no signal from me, giving out a few excited whinnies as he did so. A few minutes later, surrounded by the Guledig's men, we were stuttering out our message. Some terse questioning followed and then orders were given. After this I am back to the start of my story. Close to the cattle shelters the cavalry split with some fifty men leaving the Bear's entourage. These men were to approach the fort from the coast and take on the enemy on the shore whilst the rest of the force would ride for the Heugh and attack those laying siege at the southern wall. Jamie and I were hoisted on behind two riders for the coast, our ponies being exhausted. Such an important task had been laid upon our shoulders by Prince Arthur. We were to alert the fort to his plan. When the defenders could make out the dog dragon on the shields of our men the gates of the citadel were to be opened. I *did not completely understand his instructions, but knowing that I was playing a part in The Bear's strategy was enough for me.*

When we reached the bog we had been through that morning, our riders slowed to allow us to slide off the horses. Skirting the muddy edges we made for the Fairy Glen. This is a small wood that borders the west side of the fort. It is divided by the entrance and confluence of two burns from the little mountain. After rain particularly, this combination of flows results in a small river that hurtles down the glen's deep ravine towards the shore. The King's Brig spans this ravine but we knew it would be pulled up against the attackers. Every boy in Guinnion knew of another way in. We scrambled down through the woods following the river to the point very close to the bridge. Here tucked into the boughs of a huge elm was the swinging rope. If pushed with enough force it was possible to get within inches of the windows of the household of the Hare Prince. In our games we had never tried to land on the fort side, just hold on tightly and swing back without falling to our deaths. We agreed that Jamie would go first as he had the longest legs. He would get help to catch me as I swung over. Our scheme worked after several tries, when Jamie let go of the rope and threw himself into a little courtyard between the Hare and the Gull Households. He disappeared and I had some anxious moments worrying that a stray Saxon barbarian would spot our manoeuvres.

Once in, we went about finding the Captain which was very difficult because there was all out fighting in the palace itself now with the Home Guard trying in vain to hold the enemy at the entrance to the white square. We found Angus in a very bad way but his lieutenant was with him and so the Bear's order was carried out. Crouching down on the floor of the southern ramparts we watched him and his men crest the Heugh and gallop down towards the siege camp. Taken by surprise and on foot, the enemy retreated, their backs to the fort walls. When the Gannet doors opened many of them were swept in by Arthur's host to be cut down or pushed over the sea wall along with those who had fought their way up the old cliff-clinging red castle. The Saxons who had scattered south met a similar fate. Their lives ended on the rocks of below. The black birds of death were quick to find them whilst in the other direction their comrades found themselves easy targets in the boglands of the Maen. It was a terrible sight that day in Guinnion, so many of our friends and family lay dead or maimed and many more of our enemy. The flagstones of Guinnion were no longer white.

****

In Thomas' story I have used the carved stone images of battles that were represented as taking place in the fort and its environs. From my observations there was more than one battle because several different conflict settings were portrayed just within the small area of the present day town of North Berwick. One small flat green stone shows a siege taking place, I could discern some sort of stairs, presumably representing a siege machine, assembled within the enemy force. There were horsemen coming down towards this from the Heugh as I have described through Thomas. Other stones show fighting on the shore and on the land at the base of the cliff and on the steep hill below the seaward portion of the fort. The last two sites are today part of a golf course. Another carving shows what looks very like a straight charge between two cavalries outside the southern walls of the citadel. Several stones I have looked at show men falling headlong over the cliffs and rocks on its northern boundaries. There are sculpted stories of a battle actually taking place on the slopes of the Law and finally, some carvings are of carnage within the fort itself. It seems clear from all these presentations of the defence of the fortress and its surroundings that this stronghold was of great strategic importance sixteen hundred years ago. This impression was to be reinforced when I became aware that there were also other stone narratives that told of battles taking place within a few miles east and west of the citadel. These will be elaborated upon in the next chapter.

I have through Thomas's narrative attempted to enlarge upon Mae's description of the citadel and its surroundings. On one side it was bounded by the sea, on another by the deep watery ravine which was probably wooded as it is today. One or two stones suggest that at some point the stronghold had a moat dug at its more physically vulnerable southern wall. As well as making strategic sense, it would have been easy to maintain a stretch of water given that the fort lay at the foot of the Heugh, the raised spine of land that makes up the easterly base of the Law. I have portrayed the north side of the Law as fairly watery. Today the land closest to it is a bog and as already detailed, in the medieval period, water running off it was dammed at the eastern entrance to the town. There are still two streams running into the Glen although one of these only when it rains heavily. In the time of the Uotadini therefore, this land approach to Guinnion could have been difficult if the infantry were caught there by horsemen.

Concerning the cliff defences referred to in Thomas' narrative, again this is based on stone documentation. The zig-zag steps crowded with warriors and the invasion of the king's part of the citadel is lifted from several of these story stones. Along the present road at the base of the incline to the car park on the headland of Milsey Bay, there is such a set of steps. The lower stonework of this may be very old! More old stonework can be discerned at the top of the cliff steps. There are the remains of an old wall on one side of the little path to the beach. Dog walkers and the holiday makers from the nearby camp sites make their way down to the steps and thence to the beach at Milsey Bay by this route. The path bisects the place where the drawbridge to the fortress would have been raised and lowered. Much of the old walls of the 'Red Castle' are hidden under grass and weeds but in the winter and coming from the direction of the beach, it is possible to see on your left, something of the old stonework peeping through the debris of centuries. The grass mounds rise to over ten feet in places. To your right, covering the whole site of the 'White Palace' are two housing complexes that extend to the eastern edge of the Fairy Glen. Perhaps it is the remains of the original wall that bounded the landward side of Guinnion that can be seen near the road that leads to Tantallon (see Map 2).

The Goose Fort in Thomas' narrative is any of the forts and castles built on the southern ridges and slopes of the *Garleton Hills* (see Map 3). There are today the remains of two forts and two castles in this vicinity not including the Iron Age *Chesters Fort* which lies around one mile northwards on lower ground (Note 2). The four fortified structures are situated linearly close to the B1343 road which skirts the Garletons on the way to the village of *Athelstaneford*. The arrangement of the hills begins in the east with the *Kae Heughs* and continues westwards becoming the Garletons. At around four miles from the coast at *Aberlady* and 175 metres above sea level (at Kae Heughs) there is a bird's eye view of what was once the vulnerable shoreline of the Uotadini (Note 3). Significantly as we shall see later, at least three of these forts have also clear sight of the low ground to the west of the Hound Stone which is the valley of the *Peffer Burns*. The preponderance of forts built through the ages along this stretch of high ground no more that about two miles long, provoked the thought that it may have featured on a stone that I found near the cliff-top citadel. It is a particularly large rough-hewn stone on which the stronghold of Guinnion is possibly represented by a bird in flight fashioned from iron impressed upon the rock. Not far away and easy to locate if led by the topographic hand of the sculptor, ie westwards, is another smaller iron sculpture melded to the stone in the approximate position, I would argue, of the fortified Garleton Ridge (Note 4).

As I have mentioned already, I have found what I would like to term 'battle stones'. These seem to be ancient stone narratives about strategic defence. Most of them are worn and it takes much effort to discern the story but it is possible. The ancient makar (artisan) provided a study of a land bounded by sandy bays and volcanic massifs to aid interpretation. A great proportion of the battle stones are about fighting off invaders from the sea around the long sandy coast between the mouth of the River Tyne near Dunbar to the beach lands of Dirleton, Gullane and Aberlady. The wide bay at Aberlady must have been very difficult to defend. Perhaps some of the stones date further back into time than the period I am concerned with. Here at this bay emerges the northerly (West) Peffer Burn. Close to the origins of this water stood the *Cole Mill* (Adair 1736).

It seems very possible that the stronghold's importance was linked with its geographical position in relation to the three 'mountains' of the coastal plain and sea: the Bass Rock and the North Berwick and Trapain Laws. From the stone pictorials of this place the holders of the citadel of Guinnion also held the Bass or Gana Rock and I have alluded in the previous chapter to that bastion's place in the documented vagaries of Scottish history. It's 'dark age' role in the strategic defence of the Forth estuary and the surrounding lands can only be conjectured. However, its position, close to the mainland yet far enough out into the waterway to be a watchtower, beacon, garrision with a fresh water supply and centre for piracy and policing, points to an ancient importance for the this sea mountain. Then there is the North Berwick Law which seemed to symbolise the watchfulness of the people here. Its shape is sometimes zoomorphed into a crouching hound facing out into the Forth estuary and the North Sea. According to Drummond (1991) *'law'* originates in the Anglo-Saxon word *'hlaw'* which in its earliest usage meant *'burial mound'*. It came to be a word for 'hill'. The significance of this etymology may become relevant to another aspect of the story of this 'little mountain' later in the archive.

Six hundred feet above the Forth, the Law would have given the people here a huge strategic advantage. This little mountain and the offshore islands of Fidra (Mae's narrative 'Federary') and Craigleith as well as the Bass would have provided close-by anchorage and look-out

46

opportunities for a sea-city situated at the mouth of the Forth estuary. Documented history has the Law being used as a beacon or signalling station. In 1544 the Prioress and Nuns of North Berwick, as owners of the Law were charged to light a beacon on the summit to warn of the advance of the army of King Henry VIII intent on the destruction of Edinburgh and the port of Leith. During the Napoleonic Wars watch towers were built along the coasts of the Forth as well as on the little mountain. The vulnerability to attack or invasion from the sea has continued into recent times. The remains of anti-tank defences on the beaches of East Lothian are proof of this.

Beacons may have not only been set with a view to warning the communites upriver. Look just a few miles south of North Berwick Law slopes to Dunpender (or Trapain) Law, the great fortified plateau upon which once stood a Bronze Age citadel and you will perhaps concur with my view that it was the third part of a strategic defence at the time of the Uotadini. With a summit 710 feet above sea level and 360 feet above its base Dunpender has a commanding view of the sea approaches to the area and in the south of any activity in the Lammermuir Hills (see Map 3). Occupied for at least a thousand years it is likely that it would have been reoccupied periodically in times of threat. Evidently there is documentation of a beacon being kept on 'Dunprendar Law' in 1547 (Johnston, F.I. 5/11/62). This great plateau, the sea mountain of the Gana (Bass) and the Hound (North Berwick Law) arguably constituted an important topographic trio of strategic significance, positioned as they were on a prominent coastal edge

The Blaeu Atlas of Scotland (1654) presented the Law at North Berwick as the 'North Law'. It is the only map that I have seen that shows this and though it may be of no consequence, I wonder if it is a trace of an ancient knowledge of the strategic significance of the position of the two Laws in relation to each other. Between them they would have guarded the Tyne Valley and Guinnion from an enemy raid. From the Tyne mouth Trapain, stone-represented as boar shaped, is in clear view. Military movements within the coastal plain could not fail to be spotted. The feat then would be dealing with such incursions into the Uotadini territory. For a certain period, given the strategic advantage of these three great watchtowers, defence of the surrounding lands may have been possible. This could have consisted of the deployment on land of an elite force of horsemen who knew how to use the distinctive features of their homeland to their advantage and in the estuary skilled seamen or even a navy. Perhaps in some circumstances, like the one described by Thomas, these forces would fight together as much of the action seems to have been located on the beaches. It might not be too fanciful to suggest that the sandy terrain of the Lothian coast may have been used at times as a highway. Apart from several rocky outcrops this coast has miles of 'bents' or links that horses would have found easier going than a land of few roads and many bogs and lochs (Note 5).

There are several stones which appear to document the presence of many ships. Each vessel has a long narrow necked prow with a variety of animal or bird figureheads. They were represented as broad and capacious with crew and passengers chiselled into, onto and overhead. The former usually clinging to the middle section of the single mast. Ships were also portrayed as if round the headland from the site of the stronghold. A walk at low tide reveals several possible locations that may have been natural harbours for flat bottomed ships to berth. The sharp-eyed may spot what looks like a hare's head moulded and painted onto the base of the sheer rock of that area of the headland with the ears fashioned separately and now partially destroyed.

With regards to there having been a naval force as narrated by Thomas, the stone sculptors have documented ships with hound and bird emblems which are also to be seen on many landward vignettes. Nature had presented the people here with an opportunity to defend their territory on a border that mattered particularly at that time, the sea. From what I have observed the Uotadini made the most of that advantage. Why wait for the invaders to come further into their coastal lands where there are many sites where raiders could be landed? Six hundred feet above the River Forth, the Law would have given the people here some strategic advantage. Control of the Bass as well as the offshore island of Fidra or as it may have been called in earlier times *Federary* with its natural harbour on the north side may have made the citadel the centre of an important sea kingdom (Note 6). I would suggest that it is possible that the Uotadini ships patrolled out from here, monitoring a goodly proportion of the waters at the entrance to the Forth.

Reading Fraser's (2008) analysis of how historians in the past have sought to solve the mystery of the North British citadel called *Iudeu* has made it clear to me that the fortress at North Berwick has a central place in this enigma. Iudeu, which may mean *'place of the king'* (Breeze 2004 cited by Fraser 2004) was referred to as *'urbs Giudi'* by the Northumbrian monk and scholar, Bede, in his 'Historia Ecclesiastica Anglorum' (731). It is thought that Iudeu may have been the original name and Bede's version was an attempt to translate the P-Celtic into phonetic English (Note 7). From the small number of allusions to Iudeu or Guidi it appears that it was the name for the Forth suggesting the place was of great importance and/or of significance with regards to the estuary. Historians have sought to locate urbs Guidi using Bede's reference. According to Fraser, Bede was very vague as to the location of Iudeu except for describing it as an 'urbs', meaning a native British citadel, and that it was located somewhere in the region of the Firth of Forth. From my interpretation of the carved work, I would contend that Guinnion and the elusive Iudeu/urbs Guidi were one and the same place with the former, a white or holy place that was a descriptive and perhaps poetic term for the latter. There are several threads of thought concerning this part of East Lothian which I think tie into a close knotted case for this view. One of these is Bede's (in Fraser 2008) linking the *Clyde Rock* or urbs Alcluith (Alt Clut), the fortress on the River Clyde at *Dumbarton*, with the eastern Iudeu. Along the Forth coastline it is the Law that most closely resembles the western rock. Looking east from the Braid Hills of Edinburgh, or south from Fife, it dominates the horizon, a giant pyramid on the coastal plain. From a little west, close to Fairmilehead at the foot of the Pentlands, the Law and the Bass appear to merge into a two peaked mountain on the edge of the land with a slight resemblance to the western rock.

Fraser's (2008) analysis of how others have interpreted Bede's description of the 'urbs' as 'in medio sui' (in the midst) of the Forth has thrown up some further descriptive criteria that appear to fit with the idea that Iudeu was situated at North Berwick. The coastline around North Berwick does constitute a broad peninsula. From the sea this feature may be accentuated by the indented nature of the coastal sands of the area. To the east are the deeply sculpted sands of the Tynemouth and to the west, the even greater concavity of Aberlady Bay. The effect may give the appearance of the land being 'in the midst' of the Firth of Forth. Together these geographical features create what could be called the *Iudean Peninsula*. I would suggest that the Gaelic-speaking peoples gave Iudeu an appropriate topographical moniker in *'Rinn fiadnach Fotudàin'* the *'conspicuous point of Fothudán'* which Watson (1926, p28) considered to be North Berwick Law. The etymologist also translated the term as meaning *'the conspicuous cape'* which describes well the appearance of the bulky East Lothian peninsula from the opposite side of the Forth. *Fothudán* is the Gaelic form of *Votadinoi* (old British) (Watson pp26 and p216). In other words the community of people called the Uotadini.

There are those (see Fraser, 2008) that posit the theory that Iudeu had to be an island or nearly an island (to be 'in the midst') of the Forth. The changes that took place through time to the physical environment of the *Conspicuous Cape* make it a clear candidate with regard to this requirement. Between ten and fifteen thousand years ago at the end of the Ice Age the sea levels rose producing a shoreline west of North Berwick, between Longniddry and Drem (or *Druim*, Gaelic meaning *'ridge'*), that was up to 35 metres higher than it is today. The same movement of water flooded the valley of the Peffer Burn from east of Aberlady reaching to the coast at Tyninghame cutting off the area around North Berwick from the rest of East Lothian (Whyte and Whyte, 1988). In 1885 Groome, noted that at *Balgone* about a mile south of the Law there was the

"Remains of a crannog or lake village"

(From 'The Gazzetteer of Scotland', (Groome 1885) vol1 p152)

That in 6th century the Conspicuous Cape was encircled to some degree at least, by a ring of water seems likely as the surrounding watery landscape appears to have still existed into relatively recent times. One contributor to the Blaeu Atlas (1654) revealed a topography that still could have given North Berwick and environs island status. Having described the Biel Water at Belhaven just west of Dunbar he continues

"Next is the Peffer or Phefer, better Pever or Bever; a stagnant lake with deep water rather than a river, it nevertheless discharges into the Scottish Sea, with one mouth on the east; on the west however, a small stream flows from it in the opposite direction."

(Contributer probably David Buchanan, Blaeu Atlas, (1654). Latin translation by Ian C. Cunningham reproduced from the Blaeu Atlas website http://maps.nls.uk/atlas/blaeu)

Watson (1926, p452) translated *'peffer'* as from the welsh *'pefr'* which means *'radiant'*, *'beautiful'*. Over a thousand years after the Uotadini held the sea plain, an island status for the Conspicuous Cape was still applicable although the topography was changing as revealed in the description *'stagnant lake'* . Adair's (1736) map of East Lothian not only shows the East and West Peffers as a continuous burn encircling the
50

lands around North Berwick but also documents the existence of a '*West Fortoun*' as well as the '*East Fortoun*' close by, situated just south of the burn(s). The latter is still mapped today as *East Fortune*. I wonder how these '*fortuns*' should be interpreted. Perhaps these settlement names referred to a tidal situation with the Forth intruding from west and east (as in Forthtown). However, referral to Watson (1926) and caution has to be the position taken. It may be that what is alluded to in these names is that some sort of fort or watch position existed on each side of a fordable site on the Peffer. If this was the case then it would imply that the Peffers were large enough (and/or the surrounding area bogland) at one time to deter raiders. I will return to this crossing place in a later chapter. Even today despite intensive farming, the two Peffer Burns are close to meeting south of the Law, almost separating the landmass that is between Aberlady Bay in the west and *Auldhame* in the east. The contemporary Ordance Survey map of the area (OSE 351, 2001) shows there to be two burns as described.

Further evidence I would argue, as to the location of urbs Guidi /ludeu as being here beside the Wanton Wall seems to lie in the Pictish Regnal Lists. Although I do reiterate my lack of specialist knowledge, there are recognisable words in the lists which appear to connect with other sources besides those of stone. In particular Regnal List SL3 (1289) and Regnal List SL3(D.iii.2) <u>Note 8</u>) are almost identical in the following phrase

"...UrCal **Pont** triot'c'ad, uir**gnit**, **Guidid**" (my emphasis)

(From '*Pictish Sourcebook : Documents of Medieval Legend and Dark Age History*' Calise 2002,pp158-159)

As you will remember fellow Traveller I have argued that it is possible that 'Pont' refers to the sea citadel including the Law and here it is in the same phrase with what appears to be the mysterious Guidi/ludeu. Other lists do not have the Pont Chronicle linked to a name so similar to Bede's Guidi but there are several which refer to *uirgnit* together with *Guidid* ('*B uirgnith Guidid*' from SL3(Bal.1), in Calise 2002,pp158-159, <u>Note 9</u>). '*Gnit*', '*gnith*' I would hazard were renderings of 'gannet' as already detailed. It would seem as if whoever wrote down this list was making clear the gannet isle referred to was in the Forth and associated with 'Pont'/ludeu.

That 'ludeu' may mean 'place of the king' is intrigueing in itself in that it raises the question 'What king?' I have already mentioned the presence of kings and queen figures or people of very high status within or close to the precincts of the clifftop citadel. Other signs of royalty seem, according to the story stones, to lie in what could be termed 'grave-mapping'. This took the form of sculpted open graves in the landscape in which clothed figures with circlets or bands on their heads were laid out. Most frequently the location of these resting-places has been situated at the base and on the slopes of the Law. Above this royal grave-yard and fashioned on what must amount to many thousands of stones was fashioned the representation of one individual. Most frequently he has been portrayed in bear form.

From stone observations I would agree with James Fraser's (2008) opinion that Bede, although writing almost two hundred years after the death of Arthur in 537/ 539, did know where Iudeu was and I would suggest he deliberately kept silent. Bede's book, which is thought to have had an important role in the development of the English identity was intent in telling the story of the religious and military achievements of the Anglo-Saxon Kingdom of Northumbria which at its peak (middle third of the 7th century) encompassed most of the Britain that lay between the River Humber and the Forth. From my observations of stones that narrate the end of the Bear, which I will explore in a later chapter, the Venerable Bede would have known very precisely where Iudeu was. As you will discover, Iudeu was at the centre of a long and important North British history. That Bede chose not to acknowledge this in any way, I would suggest, speaks volumes about how important Iudeu was. A wordsmith unable to pen what would have been common knowledge far and wide in his day and for centuries afterwards? The stone miniaturists of the Old North were less reticent.

****

Mae again

On that first morning of my apprenticeship I awoke to the sound of the hounds racing out of the Gannet Gate ahead of the hunters. From my little window I could see men and animals head off east towards the woods. The men leaning forward on their mounts, intent, holding their spears low whilst the hounds, were making a huge noise, a cacophony of excitement. I almost broke into wild shouting myself as I hurried to dress. However, anxiety dampened down this urge. I was nervous, wanting to do well. As my aunt walked me over to the Druid College we were joined by three other girls about my age. So I was not to be the only pupil beginning her apprenticeship. I was very relieved. We all made our way through the top end of the Fairy Glen. It was a very small wood and soon we were in a large cultivated clearing. The Bard's hall was situated in the middle of this. The green tower I had seen from the boat stood at one angle of a triangle of single level buildings. The walls of the triangle glittered rainbow colours in the early morning light. I found out later that between the dressed stones of red, black and green and a little yellow and white, a mortar mixed with mica had been used to magical effect. The roof consisted of light pink mortar tiles, very like those of the citadel. The whole effect was so bright and cheerful that my fellow students and I must have relaxed a little as we began to chatter amongst ourselves. As we all approached a large door my aunt, who had been been stepping out in front, turned and put a hand to her mouth to silence us. The door upon which was carved the huge bird dog Ino the Guardian was a little ajar and, after knocking, my aunt motioned us to enter.

****

Chapter Notes

Note 1
The title of *Guledig* which can be sourced to *Gulad* or *country* was used by the P- Celtic Welsh speaking Britons with reference to the *Imperatore*, the overall commander of the Roman army in ancient Britain (Skene ed Bryce, D. 1988, pp33-34). Skene argued that the referral to Arthur in the 'Historia Britonum' as the *dux bellorum* was the equivalent of this. Arthur's role was Guledig or Duke of Battles.

Note 2
According to Watson(1926,p366) many of the native British forts/castles between the Forth and the Tweed are identifiable in the name 'Chester' and sometimes by 'Rings' or 'Faulds' a reference to the circular earthworks associated with such constructions. There is another 'Chester' in East Lothian, south of the village of Spott.

Note 3
For those familiar with the Arthurian stories the name Kae may be remembered. Not a mile away and eastwards from the old fort on Kae Heughs there are two places called Pendrachan (Ordanance Survey, 2001)

Note 4
On the coast below, almost in a straight line from Chesters and north-east of Dirleton there was a settlement called Eldbotle. Recorded on a paper map as 'Old Battell', (Hondius, 1630), the name 'Eldbotle' is Northumbrian in origin and means 'old dwelling place' suggesting that it was old when the Anglo-Saxons came upon it. Recent excavations of the site confirm a thousand years of occupation, beginning around 400AD when East Lothian was still Uotadinian (Morrison, Oram and Oliver, 2008)

Note 5
That a beach route may have provided the speediest land access to the North Berwick area for a thousand years after this time seems to be confirmed in Herman Moll's map (1745) which indicates such a way along the coast from Cockenzie/Port Seton to close to Dirleton or rather Eldbotle. This route amounts to about 15 kilometres/10miles. (Moll died in 1732 so his map would have been a record of an earlier part of the 18th century.) Moll's map also indicates that the only overland route

in East Lothian was an east-west path/road which crossed the River Tyne near present day East Linton and continued on towards Edinburgh completely bypassing the ancient lands of Iudeu and/or Gwanannon. Even in the nineteenth century grass had to be cut on the western side of North Berwick to enable a stagecoach service between the town and Edinburgh! A further beach 'road' is recorded by Moll across the wide sands of the Tyne Mouth towards the Biel Water at the eastern end of Belhaven Bay at West Barns village close to Dunbar.

Note 6

From Watson's (1926) analysis of names such as *fedderis, fetters, fether* and *fother* mean the presence of a slope perhaps terraced in appearance (see pp 509-512) The island was referred to as such by Martine (1890). An earlier name for the island may have resembled the Welsh word *godir* which can mean hollow which fits well with the very distinctive appearance of Fidra which has a large hollowed out section of cliff on its eastern end.

Note 7

It may be of relevance given my theory that Iudeu/North Berwick was a place of high priests and pilgrimage that in Scottish Gaelic *guidhe* can mean 'an imprecation' or 'entreaty' (http://www.faclair.com).

Note 8

Calise (2002) sources elaborated (p152).

SL3 (1289):T.C.D., MS#1289,93 II.3-22(c1745, scribe Tadhg O Neachtain. Copy of *Book of Ballymote* Part of Rescension c of *Lebor Gabála*

SL3 (D.iii.2): R.I.A. MS Stowe D.iii.2, 95 1.33-96 1.21. (Scribe: Aodh O Dálaigh, copy of *Book of Ballymote*). Part of Rescension c of *Lebor Gabála*

Note 9

Calise (2002) sources elaborated (p152).

SL3 (Bal.1) Miller's SL3 Bii): *Book of Ballymote*, 43all-33. (1384-1406, scribe: Magnus O Duibgennáin). Part of Rescension c of *Lebor Gabála*

Chapter 4: The Bear's Battles begin.

On a flat stone there is a faint rippling pattern easily dismissed as the work of some sea creature………

Robert, shepherd and soldier

I am sitting close to the sheep settled and safe in their pens for the night. The collies lie at my feet. All is quiet on the Maen. Directly below me is where I live. My wife and children are asleep down there. The white beacon tower of the sea city can be seen from the doorway of my home. At night its steady glow gives Mima great comfort when I have to be away on the hill. She believes the lofty fire warns of danger and warns off too. I dare not share my doubts with her. It is true that Guinnion is a great strength and was in my father's day and his father's too, but these times are different. The number of raids is becoming more and more frequent. Every year, almost before I have finished the lambing, the word is out to abandon the crook for the sword. That is the way of things now for all of the Kindred. Fear comes with every dawn.

****

This narrative was generated from the two very different scenes worked upon this stone. It is much worn but with some effort a story can be distinguished. It is significant in several ways. It presents what seems to be a peaceful pastoral scene on one side (shepherd, dogs and sheep on a hill) and on the other a navy (faint outlines of crewed ships) and a military force (men with spears, some on horses) have been portrayed as facing each other. It may be a description of the military strength of a people on land and water or perhaps it is a presentation of armed land defences against hostile raiders from the sea. The overall impression given is of a rural idyll that needed to be defended. The predicament of a community seems to be communicated. This work was interesting also for the apparent absence of leaders. Was it a commissioned piece , the sculpturer charged with the remit to document a particular time in the story of a pastoral people obliged to organise a defence from sea raiders?

According to Skene (1868/ Bryce (editor) 1988) the work called the 'Historia Brittonum', the 'History of the Britons' may have been compiled in the 7th or early 8th centuries. It is thought that it was originally written

56

in Welsh. Around 738 it seems to have been translated into Latin and king-lists of the various Saxon kingdoms in particular those of Northumbria were added. Further additions were made in 823 and the version of 858 has the name of Nennius attached to it (Skene 1868/ Bryce 1988, pp19-25). Nennius was a ninth century monk from Bangor, North Wales. The 'Historia' is a collection of texts which give an account of the history of the Britons from their origins to the invasions of the Romans, Picts and Saxons. He cited a variety of sources for his work such as folklore and annals as well as the king-lists already mentioned. In chapter 56 of his *Historia* he describes the wars of Arthur. It is thought that although not considered a very reliable source of 6th century history, his naming of particular sites for these Arthurian battles suggests that he perhaps drew this information from bardic poetry. Below is one translation:

"The first battle in which he was engaged was at the mouth of the River Gleni. The second, third, fourth and fifth were on another river, by the Britons called Duglas in the region of Linnius. The sixth (was) on the River Bassas. The seventh (was) in the wood Celidon, which the Britons called Cat Coit Celidon. The eighth was near Gurnion (Guinnion) castle where Arthur bore the image of the Holy Virgin mother of God, upon his shoulders and through the power of our Lord Jesus Christ and the Holy Mary, put the Saxons to flight and pursued them the whole day with great slaughter. The ninth was at the City of the Legion..... The tenth was on the banks of the River Trat Treuvoit. The eleventh was on the Mountain Bregion. The twelveth was the most severe contest, when Arthur penetrated to the hill of Badon."

(From 'Nennius Historia Brittonum' translated by J.A.Giles circa 1841 (Parentheses Publications, Cambridge, Ontario 2000) Words in brackets are my additions.)

It is possible that this battle list was compiled in poetic form quite soon after the events described took place (Fraser, 2009, p125). I think the period for the stone documentation of the same events may have started at a similar juncture but given it exists in such quantities, may have been produced some years or decades after the demise of Arthur. The source for my understanding of the military action that involved him are based most particularly upon a number of stone maps that I have found in the ground and on the beach close to the where the old stronghold stood. Three in particular, stand out with regard to the amount of information I could glean from them. These I have called the

Emperor's, the *Glass* and the *Campaign Maps* (see <u>Appendix 1: The Emperor's Map</u> and <u>Appendix 2: The Glass Map</u> for brief descriptions of the first two). Only the last is primarily documenting battle locations that the Uotadini were participants in. The other two appear to provide contexts and narratives as well. They are recognisable as descriptions of where and how the fighting took place as well as to some extent, who were the protagonists. As with much of my stone evidence these maps and others are worn and in miniature form. As usual this made my observations difficult but by perseverance it is possible to discern figures, sometimes birds wearing helmets and carrying spears or human figures with animal or bird headdresses and sometimes military formations of men. For example, I have already mentioned a stone that depicts an attack on Guinnion/Iudeu with tiny warriors figured beside a stepped object, perhaps representing a siege machine. In addition a large cat-like creature has been sculpted into the vignette.

The cat would suggest northern attackers as this animal was associated with the far north of Scotland (Caithness) possibly millennia before the time of Arthur (Moffat 2005). 'Cat identity' may have moved south through the centuries until the animal was depicted sometimes as faintly bluish engaged in aggressive moves against the lowland Brythonnic people of the sixth century AD. Based on observations that will be elaborated upon later, I am presuming the cat was the cartographer's signifier for Pictish people (ie non-Romanised) of a particular tribe or community. However, to ensure clarity, I will refer to this signifier using both labels. This use of totemic identifiers helps in the deciphering of what the story is. From what I can gather given the extensive portrayal of birds I have found near the old stronghold and the carved battle locations in which the Uotadini were represented as men with bird heads or as warrior birds, I would hazard a guess that the people of the Lothians, at least those from the coastal lands identified themselves closely with seabirds in particular gannets and gulls (<u>Note 1</u>).

In other carved stones in which there is greater detailing of protagonists I have been able to distinguish the human features of individual warriors wearing an animal or bird head or headdress. Other examples observed of this form of tribal or totemic portrayal being deer, badger, wolf, pinemartin and horse. So far in any scene studied there has only been one figure often amongst many represented as a bear. Most frequently a bear's profile shapes a stone, sometimes the whole animal is portrayed and less often a man/warrior. The latter is distinguished by headgear that can only be described as that of a bear's head facing backwards. The maps often provide a location by creating a recognisable coastal outline on a flat surfaced stone and/or the four great citadels of the Uotadini, the Trapain and North Berwick Laws, the Castle Rock of Edinburgh as well as Arthur's Seat, have been portrayed three dimensionally making the geography clear to the observer.

The Emperor's Map stands out from all the others as having been of great quality. There are remnants of enamelling. The topography is distinctively stylised but at the same time conveys quite clearly to me the location and to some extent the history of the battles of the Bear. How do I know this? On one narrow edge the life of a particular man from childhood into adulthood has been longitudinally portrayed. The profile of a young man has been carved at the Iudeu corner of the stone and another in the diagonally opposite corner that in addition holds what I take to be a portrayal of the Northern Fife/River Tay area. There is a tinge of gold colouring still attached to these representations. Further clues to the nature of the map have been provided by the discernible, with magnification, outline of a bear, worked in specific locations on the flat surface of the stone. The positioning of the bears, I wish to argue, is deliberate and is a device to document the areas of the country that Arthur had campaigns. The sixth century map maker employed another graphical approach to delineate those positions won or held by Arthurian forces using the same colouring (gold) on them that was applied to the profiles of the young man. In other words this early cartographer had a number of graphical codes at his fingertips. As my experience as an archivist develops I am becoming aware of a number of other such devices, some of which I have understood, others not. What this coding of the land with symbols and colour seems to have provided is a pre-literate war documentation and contextual narrative and as I have already suggested, was presumably quite contemporaneous with the battles. In addition to a relatively flat map surface this worked piece is cuboid and there are five other sculpted surfaces which serve I suggest, to provide further narratives to that given by the coded map surface.

As I have scrutinised the worked stone I have become increasingly aware that there was much more happening, much more information to take on board than Nennius seems to have had. Inevitably with more information, more questions emerge. To produce in stone an accurate and unequivocal document of what happened and where, requires a knowledge of what will make the message clear. That I was able to understand a significant amount of what was being communicated should not be surprising. The people who made the stone maps shared a perception of the pictorial that was probably much more sophisticated than today. Just think of the problems you may have with the signs or instructions for furniture assembly! As familiarity with fifth or sixth century signage was important in my interpretation of the maps, some further elaboration upon the techniques used seems appropriate. Some have already been mentioned but any repetition hopefully can be borne.

The most frequently used signage was the sculpted bears. Some were represented as the whole beast and others by the distinctive head only. Clear, simple outlines were employed. There was attention to detail concerning the black nose and the muzzle which ensures there could be no mistaking the figure for any other animal. Sometimes the outline was a shadow created by some sculptural wizardry and not a straight forward carving. Zoomorphism had been employed on occasion so the human counterpart comes into focus after a blink of the eye or change of gaze. Occasionally too it is clear that a very young or youthful bear was being portrayed. This was artfully achieved in various ways such as a babe- in-arms with a distinctively bear-like visage. Sometimes perhaps the bear was made young through the use of colour and the youthfulness was portrayed using a white dye or enamel. Three dimensional bear heads and full figures were also quite frequently fashioned in iron and fixed to stone. On the Glass Map and many small worked pieces, tiny bears were fashioned onto minute plaques of a smooth orange stone. Most are so small the workmanship cannot be appreciated without strong magnification. Other minute bears are almost completely hidden in a crevice and it requires patience to spot them. Finally there are a large number of stones that were worked into the profile of a bear's head. Occasionally I have found the other side of this sort of carving the modelled outline of a dog's or baboon's profile. Alternatively there are tiny vignettes from Arthur's life story including scenes that represented the citadel of Guinnion and/or the Law. The presence of baboon representations will be addressed in the last chapter. I have already suggested that a dog or hound was closely associated with North Berwick Law. Territorial control and/or an acknowledgement of respect for a great military commander or perhaps a trace of a much earlier time may be the meanings attached to the presence of the bear's head upon these communications from a forgotten past.

With regard to the Emperor's map and to some extent the Glass Map, the varied sorts of bear signifiers used may be of further interest and conjecture. For example, does the bear that stands on the south-eastern edge of Fife indicate a great victory or a protracted series of battles or held territory that requires constant vigilance to keep? Do the tiny brown bears dotted among the crevices of the Glass Map denote a skirmish or perhaps watch positions?

Perhaps another method of indicating the Bear presence, his control or history was again the use of colour. Specifically I have observed the consistent use of a light brown/orange colouring in particular parts of a map or stone vignette. Sometimes the colouring actually etches out a scene within the zone of colour. As I have already mentioned, a white substance was used to paint and delineate the boundaries of Guinnion/Iudeu and to sculpt tiny scenes in and around the fortress.

Aside from the bear imagery there was copious use of recognisable birds such as seabirds and in particular gulls and gannets. I have already mentioned the avian 'warriors'. In all manner of other scenes on maps and other objects there was the frequent, what might be termed 'soft' presentation of the wild creatures. Because of the miniaturisation there was a less realistic detailing giving the birds cartoon-like outlinings. Birds were placed close to humans in a standing and not a flight posture. Birds seem to accompany humans everywhere. I have observed that sometimes the small creatures have been positioned at some distance from the human scenes as if they were acting as onlookers or witnesses to what was occurring. To modern eyes the identification of the people here with avian creatures was powerfully done. This ancient affinity with the wild birds of the coast may have been recognised by this traveller to Scotland many centuries after the sculptures were made:

"Fowl are as scarce here as birds of paradise. The charity of the inhabitants denying harbour to such celestial animals though gulls and cormorants abound. There being a great sympathy betwixt them."

(Thomas Kirke (1679) in 'A Modern Account of Scotland by an English gentleman'.)

Although often the detailing of what was happening on the land has been almost obliterated, the crafted outline of the coast of the Lothians is much easier to recognise. They can be compared to some of the old and modern marine paper maps in the attention given to the sand lands of East and West Lothian. The Uotadinis' knowledge of the distinctive shaping of the coast was fashioned on many flat stones. They were, of course, a people very used to viewing their territory from the sea. For a stone archivist these shapings, sometimes coloured differently or applied using another stone substance have become orientation cues helping me find my way as my eye seeks out the geography and the history. It should be noted that all these maps were recounting a history not only of battles but of other events too. Some have been crowded with characters for example, women with children, children playing together, marriages, meetings and travelling by sea.

Morris (1973) suggested that Nennius's list of the battles may have been to do with later campaigns he fought to keep at bay enemies from the north of Scotland after he had recovered the Scottish Lowlands from the Anglo-Saxons. Given that the Emperor's Map was centred mainly in the Lowlands of Scotland, stretching from the coastal areas of Angus north of the River Tay to (approximately) the lands north and east of the Lothian River Tyne as well as west across the territory south and a little north of the Antonine Wall, I am persuaded that it represents all of the areas of victorious battles recorded by Nennius as well as some detail concerning subsequent control. The Picts, enemies between the Walls and beyond to the north and the Anglo-Saxons from the south both feature on the stone map. A close examination of the early paper maps of Fife and the Lothians drawn a thousand years later (Adair 1682) and comparing them with the ancient miniature provides some interesting possibilities with regard to battle sites and more generally the areas of military campaigning undertaken by the Bear Guledig (Note 2).

In keeping with making a case for the existence and value of the pictorial, some exploration of Nennius' list of the battles of Arthur will be attempted with a view to identifying whether this remnant of what has been written about these events can be elaborated upon by the corroborations and possibly, the contradictions thrown up by the stone pictures. Much of the debate concerning the list is to do with the temporary nature of language. Place-names were changed by incomers, or were forgotten and new or altered ones took their place. On the other hand stone maps although discarded or lost for many generations can emerge with their signposting relatively intact and relevant to a physical geography little changed in one and a half millennia. Let's begin then on Nennius' list:

"The first battle...... was at the mouth of the river Gleni"

Skene (1868/1988) thought that this was a reference to the Glen River in Aryshire. Moffat (1999) favoured the river of the same name which is a tributary of the Till in Northumberland. Using pictorial evidence, I would like to put forward another possibility. This is that the *Glencorse Burn*, on Adair's 1682 map, called the *Glencors*, is the *'River Gleni'* or *'Glein'* (Skene/Bryce 1988). This burn flows through a glen in the Pentland Hills and joins the North Esk entering this river near *Auchendinny* close to the northern outskirts of *Penicuik* in Midlothian (Adair 1682). Nearby is *Rullion Green* at the foot of a hill called *Greenlaw* which was the location of a much later battle (Note 3). On Adair's earliest map (1682), a cairn (*'Kairnathur'*) seems to have been dedicated to Arthur is located on one the hills, probably the *Carnethy* the highest of the Pentlands (at 573m) closest to the course of the burn.

The Emperor's Map appears to portray Bear/Britonnic control of both sides of the Esk suggesting that the river was an important boundary for some period of time before the Arthurian battles. Close observation led to the discovery of 'busy' working on the banks of the Esk and North Esk rivers with a similar faded colouring to other sites on the map (Note 4). There are figures facing each other across the river that appear to communicate that the Esk and the Glencorse were at the centre of much military activity perhaps since the Romans came to Inveresk. On Adair's map Greenlaw was close to a pathway/road leading towards Edinburgh. This area has become part of Penicuik and the road is now the A702 (T) which exits the city and then skirts the south-westerly march of the Pentlands Hills heading for Lanarkshire and the upper Clyde Valley. North-east of *Carlops* the remains of a Roman road runs parallel for a mile or two (between the Nine Mile and Eight Mile Burns). Through time then, this route was important. It is thought to have existed in some form into prehistory as there is a chain of large, round, prehistoric burial cairns in the *Dolphinton-West Linton* area including ones on several of the Pentland summits. It is considered that these linked monuments mark out a route between the Upper Clyde Valley and the Forth Estuary. Leaving the Clyde where it meets the *Medwin Water*, the route continues eastwards following the line of the Pentlands till it veers off towards the *River North Esk* where similar cairns existed near *Roslin* and *Rosewell* (Baldwin 1985 p162)

The mouth of the Glencors is situated close to this ancient way. Watson (1926 p180) identified Glencorse as meaning *'glen of the crossing'*. This fits well with the idea that this place was a junction point for people travelling from the west overland, from the south by sea via *Esk Mouth* and north into *Manau,* the lands close to the Antonine Wall, which are present day southern Stirlingshire and West Lothian. Following the course of the 'Gleni' river would take a force through a gap in the Pentlands to *Balerno* and thence over relatively flat ground, to the site of two other of Arthur's battles. The route made for speedy access to hostilities that might be developing around the Antonine. Crucially too, rowing upstream may have been safer and quicker than running the gauntlet of any enemy held ports further up the Firth of Forth. The strategic importance of this area is further emphasised by the presence of the Iron Age fort of *Castle Law* situated close to and overlooking the mouth of the Glencourse (Note 5). In a 6th century war, control of Glencorse was vital and it makes sense that it would be the focus of the first Bear/Britonnic battle. The River *'Gleni'* or *'Glein'* was the topographic key that had to be in the possession of any military commander if he was to have some chance at winning a war in the Lowlands of Scotland. As we shall see Dear Traveller, Arthur was to return to do battle again over this riverway later in his campaign.

Battles 2,3,4,5 are four battles given a very cursory mention by Nennius. They took place

"on another river by the Britons called Duglas, in the region of Linnius".

According to Skene (1868/Bryce (editor) 1988) these battles took place 'above' the River Douglas in the old area of Lennox whilst Moffat interpreted it as meaning the area of the Firth of Forth. From my stone map observations, the river was *'Duglas'* and this refers to the little river *Dunglass* as interpreted by Giles (circa 1841) which is located at the southern border of Lothian. This would mean that these battles happened in the area that was known in Gaelic as the *Conspicuous Cape of the Uotadini* and the location of Iudeu. Aside from the Emperor's Map, I have found as already mentioned, some very faintly discernible, similarly shaped stone maps which I suggested related to some of these battles. If this is the case, at least three of them may have been located along the vulnerable coastal boundaries of Iudeu which I have posited was the present day stretch of East Lothian coastline from Aberlady in the north, to *Belhaven Bay* which lies about a mile outside Dunbar, in the south. Although it is difficult to be sure due to the stylistic presentation, the Emperor's map appears to only include territory perhaps just a few miles south-east of Iudeu. In other words at least no further than the Lothian border and the River Dunglass. According to the sculpture miniaturists, fighting was placed south of North Berwick on the *Ravensheugh Sands*; north of North Berwick on the flat lands east of *Old Battell* (Bleu 1654, NLS) (in the vicinity of present day Dirleton) and a further confrontation further inland and south of the North Berwick Law, from an enemy incursion via Aberlady Bay. All of these coastal incursions were at some of the easiest places for rapid disembarkation and movement off the shore and along wide sands with few obstructions into a coastal plain. Two of these have river mouths close by. Ravensheugh has the Peffer and Tyne Mouth whilst at Aberlady there is the North Peffer. The distinctive shapes of the sand lands were used by the sculptor to make the battle sites relatively easy to spot. These locations seem to be corroborated by the Glass Map as it has what could be termed, lines of attack drawn across its surface and some of these correspond to these areas. It would appear that Arthur was dealing with invasion or raiding forces intent on achieving a pincer movement against the power base on the Iudeun peninsula. A similar set of lines can be discerned on the Campaign Map. One could wonder why Nennius or his sources did not specifically name the battle sites as was done for all the others. Most likely it may have been that the possible repetition involved would not have suited the rules of rhyming poetry. Perhaps the reference to the 'Duglas' was a very adequate sign-posting for the southern border of 'the place of the king'. For the stone map makers however, there was no shrinking from documenting military details. They were clear that there had been at least three incursions from the sea which were fended off by the 'avian' forces from castle Guinnion/Iudeu.

The fourth battle (ie battle five on Nennius' list), in the region of Linnius may have been at the foot of Dunpender/Trapain Law, another site close to Iudeu. I have already mentioned a fight on the Ravensheugh Sands in which horsemen confront the enemy on the beach. However, there is a further scene in which a boatful of warriors has presumably managed to get through this defence. A fight upstream from the mouth of the Tyne ensues with the invaders portrayed as disembarking from a boat level with the great plateau. The engagement on the beach may have been a diversion to enable the river incursion. Warrior figures have been discerned emerging from the north-easterly edge of the plateau to confront the enemy disembarking from the winding Tyne which flows by less than a mile away. Horsemen have also been portrayed as being deployed in coming from the coast and from the direction of

Guinnion/Iudeu to intercept the raiders/invaders. This narrative of the two linked battles was found on one stone.

Four battles then appear to be centred on the defence of Guinnion/Iudeu. I would hazard that such a concentration of fighting in one area emphasises its strategic and political importance. Given that the Bear had to return later to fight near/within the stronghold (Battle 8), there seems to have been a continuous threat of losing it to the enemy. Battles 4 and 5 (or any consecutive combination) identify the vulnerability of the citadel and the surrounding hinterland to attacks from the sea, and in this part of the campaign, from the navigable Rivers Tyne (still today) and Peffer (then possibly).

Moving on, Battle 6 took place

On the river Bassas.

Skene's (1868/ Bryce (editor) 1988, p36) version of the battle location was phrased as 'above the River Bassus'. He suggested that this river was the present day River Bonny south of Dunipace in Stirlingshire because it flows near two manmade basses sited there. I have found stone corroboration of this on the flat lime stone Campaign map. On one side of this map a battle has been etched into the stone near two hills set close together and in the approximate area of the western end of the Carron River. The basses were a distinctive marker and in my view, used by a stone mapmaker to accurately site this sixth battle. It may be worth noting Skene's choice of the word 'above' as arguably it may suggest a stone map source for the Nennius battle list. The Emperor's Map seems to show several strongholds or seats of power near Dunipace where the Carron flows down from the north-west (origin in the Campsies) and the River Bonny joins the Carron. That these resided with the Britons has been depicted by the engraved and elongated shape of a bear. The engraving extends roughly the length of the northern (and southern near Denny) side of the Carron from the Denny/Dunipace area to perhaps the eastern edges of present day Stenhousemuir. Interestingly too, with her back to this shape is a similar but more feminine looking bear. The message conveyed suggests perhaps marital discord. It also communicates that the Bear had a residence on the northern banks of the Carron River (Note 7).

Examination of the Emperor's Map also provides a pictorial comment with regard to the military situation to the north-west and north-east of the Carron/Bonny confluence. There is a fierce looking cat, perhaps as I have already intimated, the totemic animal for the Picts and a singularly blood thirsty deer, totemic animal, presumably for the Caledone tribe carved in these respective areas. It appears that for some miles north of the Carron, the Bear's forces were holding back the Cats/Picts who were a threatening presence north of Dunipace and Denny and the Caledones, north of the land between Larbert and Stenhousemuir. The boggy land of the Letham Moss would have provided some defence for the Britons east of Stenhousemuir. Significantly I think, a bear has been sculpted in the vicinity of Airth on the western banks of the River Forth. It is a place with less natural defences. There will be more about this signifier later.

From my observations, the battle near the Bonny may have been an attack on a Brythonnic force coming from the west, perhaps from the fortress on the Clyde. The battle site is in the region of one of the military lines already mentioned which converge with others at the place of the final battle. Figures have been spotted north of this 'military line', heading towards it as if to attack those moving along it. With this battle, it may be that one force of the Brittonnic concerted effort against the Saxons in Manau had to turn and fight an enemy who was intercepting from the direction approximate to Torwood or further north-west. It is interesting to speculate how the western force travelled to just south of Denny from Alt Clut (Dumbarton). Looking at the rivers as transport corridors, it is possible that the Strathclyders came by way of the Endrick Water and thence perhaps part of the way by the Carron River. The Endrick rises in the Gargunnock Hills, south of Kippen in Stirlingshire. It flows south towards what is now the Carron Valley Reservoir before turning west and enters the south-east end of Loch Lomond. Old and contemporary maps record how close together the watersheds of these two rivers are. It may be that in the past in a warmer and wetter climate, a loch would have existed between the Endrick and the Carron at this point. Such a scenario would have given the ancient Britons at least a partial east-west navigation corridor (Note 7).

Battle 7 took place according to Nennius

"In the wood Celidon which the Britons called Cat Coit Celidon."

This is the Caledonian Wood which may have covered a substantial part of Scotland at one time. The location for the seventh battle from my observations of the Emperor's Map, was near Perth on the banks of the River Tay. The map shows a lot of conflict or disputed territory in what I take to be northern Fife and it is 'above' this that Arthur has been sculpted as sailing up the Tay Estuary towards Perth. Arthur has been portrayed as quite youthful but he has older men with him who morph out of his profile. One of these companions was a very elderly man with a small cap on his head and a very long beard. Either on the journey or on the boat**Error! Bookmark not defined.**, Arthur came across a Christian religious figure. Although minute, it is identifiable as a monk with a crucifix clearly visible on his chest (Note 9). Just north-east of these vignettes possibly from the Angus Glens, there seems to have been a Cat /Pictish force approaching at speed as if coming down a hill (there is a *Pictstonhill* on the southern edge of New Scone on the northern outskirts of Perth). On the map, ahead of the Bear's boat can be seen a young, dark haired woman. With slight movement, an older woman is there and the younger is mounted on a horse. Whichever way the stone is turned the horsewoman has a male companion.

What the Emperor's Map appears to be communicating was that Arthur bypassed some sort of border territory anciently fought over in the vicinity of the Ochill Hills within the present day lands of Perth and Kinross and northern Fife. Using boats he and his allies headed up the River Tay towards the heartlands of the Calidone/Deer People (Note 9). I think this impression of an earlier war documented on the Emperor's map has been conveyed in the different sculptural presentation of the battle vignette. It could be assumed that to be included in the Emperor's Map this more ancient war was of some significance to the narrative concerning the Bear. It does not seem too great a leap to suggest that in that post Roman period, there might have been a referral to the Roman occupation of Northern Britain as inevitably events of the past provide a context to actions taken in the present. I wonder whether this distinctive vignette refers to the great battle between the Caledones and the Romans at Mons Graupius. The location of this battle is unknown and there are various theories one of which is that it took place at Duncrub in Strathearn (Fraser 2009, p21) which is about 20 kilometres west of the battle site represented in stone. I will return to this later. Making the presumption that the figure of a deer within the Caledonian Wood was totemic for the Calidones, these were the people towards which Arthur was moving. In the process of doing this he has been portrayed as coming up against an army of Cat/Pict people sculpted as sweeping down towards the Britons as if coming to the aid of the Caledonians. The multi-faceted work appears to tell a story in which a young Arthur led a coalition or was assisted by older men in his campaign north of the Forth. The presence of the wise (old capped and bearded

68

man) communicates that he was well guided and perhaps came ready for a diplomatic exchange whilst the meeting and greeting with the holy man may suggest a religious justification for or Christian blessing attached to his incursion. The other shape-shifting narration places a young woman, perhaps the daughter of a Cat/Pictish queen (older woman) in Arthur's path. The male companion may be a clue to this mysterious princess as he is to be seen on other stone vignettes as almost attached to the Bear's consort. Apart from a tale of battle, it is possible that the Emperor's Map records Arthur's first encounter with the woman who would become his bride. Perhaps a marriage between the Cat princess and young Arthur was an outcome of diplomatic brokerage between the warring parties in the forest of the Calidones.

Battle 8 was

"Near Gurnion (Guinnion) castle where Arthur bore the image of the holy Virgin mother of God, upon his shoulders and through the power of our Lord Jesus Christ and the Holy Mary, put the Saxons to flight and pursued them the whole day with great slaughter." (my brackets with alternative name)

According to Skene/Bryce 1988 the eighth battle took place 'in Castello Guinnion' and 'castello' indicated that it was a Roman fort. As I have discussed already, there is pictorial evidence that a battle or battles took place in the environs of this stronghold as well as within it. In addition, several of the coastal battles may have resulted from enemy landings to the east and west of the citadel which probably had the taking of the fort as the objective. Although mostly built upon now, there is still a significant remnant of the huge fort that stood here. It lies under derelict land which overlooks the present day town of North Berwick. Standing on the seaward side of this site it is very easy to see how important the stronghold must have been in the defence of the lands bordering the River Forth. I have already cited stone evidence that points to Guinnion as Iudeu's fort on Nennius's paper list. Significantly, I think, the whereabouts of these two place-names remains elusive to writers about this period in history.

After observing a large number of carved pieces of this fort I had failed to locate any Christian signification on the worked pieces representing a battle(s) at this location. I was not too concerned as I had provisionally at least, identified it by the frequent stone rendering in white with the meaning of 'guinnion' as 'white place'. However, I eventually did find a minute scene which appears to describe Nennius' description very accurately. There in a corner of the Emperor's Map has been finely sculpted a warrior mounted on a horse with a cross on his left breast. Placed to his right can be seen the head and shoulders of a woman wearing a shawl over her head. Another look or blink of the eye and this image changes into a bear with a cross or a sword at his side and two tiny heads looking over his shoulders. Another look and I see a horseman chasing men, presumably soldiers before him. The vignette is only a couple of millimetres square, hidden from ordinary view. It may be that Nennius or his sources were very well aware of the pagan associations attached to this castle and sought to eradicate any possible doubt as to the Christian credentials of the battle with a clear literate and religious signifier. Certainly Christianity is not writ large at Guinnion but it is there nonetheless on the stone surface of this magnificent miniaturist's map. It would seem that not long after Arthur's death the Christian religion was stone-portrayed as having some part in his battles.

From early on in my observations it was evident that a lot of blood was shed over Guinnion/Iudeu. There are just so many carved portrayals of battles in the stronghold or very close to it on the shore below (large numbers), on its southern boundary or on the Law. It may be that they were recording a small number of actual events. If this was the case then the quantity suggests they were of great importance in the history of the Uotadini. On the Emperor's Map Iudeu was portrayed as having been specifically targeted by two sculpted heads. Close up to the coast can be seen the very distinctive profile of a belligerent looking male who has long loose hair with some of it scooped into a pony tail. Another of the same personage has been crafted into the representation of the ninth and twelfth battles. The other sculptured head was of a cat that had been placed mid-estuary at the front of a column coming over the water from eastern Fife. That at least one significant victory took place at this sea city was recorded by a vignette set within its walls. This pictorial consists of a young warrior/bear wearing a feathered headdress resembling that worn by Native American chiefs being greeted by a king-like image with an entourage of high status figures. The stone portrayals of battles at Guinnion often take the form of a carved scene on the flattest surface of the stone with a bear's profile providing the overall shape.

****

Last year I found a small stone sculpture in the shape of a helmeted old warrior on one side and a sculpted iron insert on the back (Note 10). I have called the warrior Auld Mur.

Auld Mur.

I first saw him on one of those bright windy days that happen so often here in this coastal place. It was well past Lammas and I was brambling on the cliffs with my pals. In the shelter of the high walls of the palace there were always the best berries. We should not have been there of course. Apart from being out of bounds to all but the military there was an extra reason for the defences to be clear of tearaways like ourselves. Everyone knew that an important young prince was coming to live in the Royal Household. In between filling up with the soft purple fruits we boys would twist our heads round to view the ceremonies in the bay below. A most beautiful ship had dropped anchor earlier that morning. We had seen many official meeting and greeting occasions before so much of our attention was on the next mouthful. Only after the welcoming entourage had made its way over the stone Brig did we get a good look at the newcomer. He was a slim youth not much older than us. Bare to the wind, his head had a thick curly thatch of fair hair. As the he drew nearer we saw that although slight in build the youth had a lithe agility, the confidence of movement of a seasoned athlete. As he approached our position we glimpsed a striking face with full lips not yet hidden by beard. Then we all gasped almost as one as we had espied, pinned to his sleeve, a whole row of ribbons of the chase. Such honours were rarely bestowed upon one so young. We knew that his horsemanship and ability with a spear had to be first class. He must have heard us as he looked up and gave a great laugh and treated us to a low bow causing a small collision amongst the dignitaries following behind. This was my first sight of Arthur and I and my friends loved him from that moment.

Of course we soon learned who Arthur was. He was the wonder child our Wise Ones had foretold would lead our people to victory. Security and peace would return to the lands of the Gwr y Gogledd.

****

Moving on…

Battle 9 was

"At the City of the Legion "

A Vatican copy of 'Nennius' notes that this was known as 'Kairlium' by the Britons and Skene argued that this was Dumbarton or Alt Clut (1868/ Bryce (editor) 1988, p39). As Archivist I have come to the view that Alt Clut was not the location for the ninth battle because it does not figure on the particular side of the Emperor's Map which details the military exploits of Arthur. The pictorial narrative that is on other stone maps seems to suggest that forces were sent eastwards from the direction of the great Clyde fort and may have encountered the Cats on the way (see 6th battle). However, the Emperor's Map has a lot to 'tell' about Dumbarton which needs to be considered because its story is sculpted on the back. What the commissioners of this map deemed as context for the Bear's battles has to be of relevance in seeking an elaboration on the narrative of Southern Scotland during Arthur's time.

I have gleaned two perhaps interconnected stories of particular note from a close perusal of the opposite side of Emperor's Map. One is the portrayal of a Roman presence at the Clyde citadel and the other is how Arthur was linked with its history. There are several pointers to this association. The first is the portrayal of a battle at the lower levels of the Rock, of legionaries crawling along the base of the massif. There are also warriors sculpted into the surrounding sea. The second is what I can only describe as a story pathway. It begins with the sculpture of the head of a young Arthur at Iudeu, which zoomorphs into the top of a sculpture of a seated old bear, which is close to an edge of the map side. The sculpture continues onto a narrow side with what appears to be a family tree. I have seen this before on other worked pieces. This one consists of a vertical line of figures, sometimes couples which continues onto the next large side arriving on the top of a representation of the Clyde Rock. I have counted about ten 'generations'. On the summit of the Rock, a meeting around a large table has been sculpted. Several totemic animal figures including a sheep have been placed around it. Seated at the head of this a large bear has been fashioned in profile. By his size relative to the others he seems to be in charge of whatever business the assembly has to deal with. He is wearing some sort of military headgear, possibly Roman, which has morphic qualities. From the size of the bear in this scene and the extent to which he configures the shape of the Rock itself, it would appear that a people who were identified with this animal, let's call them the Bear People, might have been the dominant force at Alt Clut. Close to the table there is an extraordinary linked vignette. A young soldier is being addressed by an older man who, from the ballon containing a tiny bear pictorial coming from his mouth (yes,

72

just like comic papers) seems to be speaking for the bear chairing the meeting (Note 11). He appears to be negotiating the marriage of the young soldier with a young dark haired woman, dressed in white, who is surrounded by a group of totemic figures, presumably representatives of the Northern Britons. Who she was appears to be signified by a wolf-like creature carved into her clothing. The young man from his apparel was a Roman soldier. This observation, suggests perhaps a diplomatic marriage of an important military man to a high born British woman or princess. A slight change in gaze and a Roman comes into view wearing a toga-like costume. Close to these scenes on another small side of the Emperor's Map and other worked pieces, the home territory of the Bears at Alt Clut has been portrayed as located on the western banks of Loch Lomond and the eastern reaches of Argyll.

Given the lengthy generational family tree, the pictorial generates so much more than the written word. The marriage negotiations that seem to have taken place on the great Clyde Rock were something to do with the Romans, but what? Was it a contract for peace or an agreement on some kind of working relationship which would satisfy all parties? As I have already revealed, it was a bear who seems to have been the overall leader at Alt Clut as it is the image of this animal which emanates from the mouth of the greeter and meeter of the young Roman. The map details a lineage which, taking each generation as twenty years would have amounted to perhaps two hundred and forty years or more before the time of Arthur's birth. In effect he has been represented as having Roman as well as British blood in his veins. Significantly I think, for the carved military campaigns, the latter sort of red stuff was being traced to a wide spectrum of the different cultural communities of Northern Britain. The scenes within the western citadel have been 'peopled' in the main, by native animal/bird representations suggesting that the Rock was the focus for some sort of federation or alliance which seemed to be moderated and/or led by Bear authority figures. Although not born at Alt Clut, Arthur's lineage was sourced to births and marriages within its walls, witnessed by the representatives of many communities. Alt Clut and the people of the lands to the West were not figuratively on the map, they were represented in a young Arthur placed close to the little mountain on the Iudeun Peninsula. In other words I would suggest that what was communicated was that he carried with him into the battles that had to be fought further east, the ancient shared history of Northern Britons.

With a Roman presence portrayed at Alt Clut, it might be argued that it was the 'City of the Legion' on Nennius' list and therefore the site of the ninth battle. However, I have identified from the Emperor's Map another possible candidate. There are various vignettes that originate from two tiny plaques of stone that in one gaze represent what appears to have been a fort on each of the Castle and Carlton Rocks of Edinburgh (see Appendix 1 for map description). These plaques seem to function as a historical narrative about the place that is now the capital of Scotland. For this question of location of Arthur's battle, I have to consider one particular narrative image that emanates from these miniature sculptures. Looking at the Emperor's Map lengthwise with the longest corner on the right of the viewer, there is the profile of a man with a Caesar-like laurel on is his head. Perched on top of his head and borrowing his laurel is the figure of a young woman with dark, plaited hair piled on top of her head. Now whether this alludes to Arthur and his queen or to the much earlier matching at Alt Clut may not matter too much with regards to sorting out battles. It is the portrayal of a Roman past. On the other hand it might be argued that such a vision in itself does not necessarily prove a legionary base at Edinburgh, but rather a Romano-British perception of their and their leader's Roman inheritance, nothing more. This argument may be further supported by another narrative from the same stone map, this time of Edinburgh as well as the West and Midlothian areas. It is the fashioned profile of a bear's head and shoulders, the head has also been decorated with a circlet of laurel. The map-maker has made this image presumably to identify a particular time in the career of Arthur when he had won control of these territories. He may or may not have been linking this achievement with a legionary past for Edinburgh but certainly the complexity of imagery crafted on to the tiny plaques makes clear a series of important narratives were attached to it.

After all this I would argue that rather than Edinburgh it is more likely that the City of the Legion was just a little further south at Musselburgh on the boundary of the present day capital and may even account for the Roman vignette variation in Edinburgh. Given this town's position at the mouth of the Esk the old rhyme that Paterson (1857, p20) quotes may even be an oral trace of a folk memory revealing an ancient time when the settlement was of greater importance than Edinburgh:

"Musselburgh was a burgh,

When Edinburgh was nane;

74

And Musselburgh'll be a burgh

When Edinburgh is gane"

(From 'History of the Regality of Musselburgh' Paterson (1857, p20))

The Romans built their fort on the north slope of Inveresk Hill, possibly a site for Druid ceremonies, as part of Agricola's conquest of southern Scotland (AD84) and subsequent establishment of the network of fortifications stretching from York to the Tay. A Praetorium was erected and possibly a temple of Apollo on the site of the present Church of St Michael. It is known that the earlier church of that name, demolished in 1800, had stones and tiles from such a temple and fort included in its structure. From the hill the Romans would have had a clear view of the estuary and presided over what is thought may have been a large native settlement on the lower reaches of the hill's northern slope reaching down to the shore edge (Musselburgh). Cowie (1999) posited that this encompassed at least twelve acres, twice the size of the fort and may even have been as much as twenty-five acres. The Roman harbour was at Fisherrow on the north side of the river and a road was built from there leading to a Roman camp at Sherriffhall two miles west. 'Musselburgh' is a relatively late naming. In early written records (Paterson 1857), the parish of Inveresk was divided into two baronies, 'Great Inveresk', present day Musselburgh and 'Little Inveresk', the land rising south of it including Inveresk Hill. Malcolm Canmore gifted the barony of Little Inveresk to the monks of Dunfermline. Their ownership of it was confirmed by King David 1 who also extended their lands to include all of Inveresk (1124 and 1152).

On the Emperor's Map there is what looks like a cat signifier lying at the site of the Roman harbour. Opposite on the southern shore and facing west, an Arthur signifier in the shape of a golden capped, bearded warrior has been wrought. There are the figures of men around him suggesting a fight was going on. As I have already mentioned there is a good deal of faint working around the representation of the river which suggests there was considerable importance attached to it in Arthur's time and before. There are a number of figures facing each other as one's eye 'travels west' along both banks. As you will recall dear Traveller, the Esk provided a route to the mouth of the 'River Glein' and thence through the Pentland Hills to the lands lying south of the Antonine Wall between the Carron and the Almond and Avon Rivers (see Maps 1 and 5). The Carron and the Esk were prominently fashioned on

75

the Emperor's Map. Arguably, the master mapmaker was communicating more than the latter's strategic importance when he incorporated the scenes on its banks into the pony tail of a Saxon whose head and locks form a significant portion of the Lothians north of the river. The pictorial suggests that Arthur and the Britonnic alliance were up against the Saxons who had taken control of most of Lothian including the Esk.

From such ingenious crafting it is possible to conjecture with some confidence that the 9th Battle took place at Great Inveresk/Musselburgh and that the Britons, led by Arthur, had to fight for control of this waterway because it was strategically crucial in a campaign to wrest their lands from Saxon hands. The cat on the north side of the Eskmouth suggests that there was territory in Lothian that was not Brittonnic or Saxon. Were the Picts neutral or were they opportunists throwing their lot in with whoever offered them the most attractive inducements? The latter seems more likely. Perhaps a deal was made that involved the Roman harbour or the southern banks of Eskmouth were reclaimed and its defences strengthened against Pictish or Saxon attack. The stone map has Arthur on the south side of the Esk surrounded by what seems to be the people of the settlement. That Arthur at the time of this battle held the land to the south is implied in the vignette (the warrior's head is facing north). Holding or capturing Inveresk was vital in a war in which control of the rivers was essential for successful campaigning. Facilitating the element of surprise and swift movement of men, the waterways gave a strategic advantage to those who controlled them.

Variations upon the hostilities at the Esk Mouth were to be repeated several times in the history of Scotland. I wonder whether some ancient knowledge of what exactly happened in the City of the Legion that ended in a victory for Arthur, has been left in this 13th century prophecy attributed to Thomas the Rhymer and quoted by Paterson (1857, p207), in his description of the Battle of Pinkie (1547), that took place close to Inveresk Hill and which ended in a disastrous defeat of the Scottish forces by an English army (Note 12)

"At Pinken Clugh there shall be spilt

Much gentle blood that day;

There shall the **bear** lose the guilt,

And the eagle bear it away"

(From *'History of the Regality of Musselburgh'* Paterson (1857, p207), my emphasis)

Perhaps the Rhymer from Earlston was only composing what was a known to all his contemporaries through a strong oral tradition. Reference to 'the bear' and 'the eagle' is not just interesting in providing through that tradition a time-travelling possible corroboration of what had occurred near the Esk Mouth in Arthur's time and that of the Romans' but also in how it may enable a glimpse at what were this country's narratives concerning it's ancient past. It is a glimpse that firstly flags up that somewhere in the Rhymer's collection of old stories of Scotland there was the knowledge of a history that included Arthur at the Lothian Esk which apparently disappeared from view at some point. Secondly the rhyme gives a tantalising peep at what might have been the nature of the narrative from the 13th century or earlier, about Arthur's role in Scotland's past that could have influenced Thomas of Earlston's choice of words.

The tenth of Arthur's battles was

"On the banks of the river Trat Trevroit"

There are other spellings such as Skene's 'Treuruit' and Morris' (1993) 'Tribruit'but no river of any of those variations of name has been located anywhere in the British Isles. Skene(1868/1988 Bryce (editor)pp39-42)) argued that these names could be associated with 'Trathau' with the descriptive meaning for 'shores' or 'sandy beach' suggesting the tenth battle took place on the banks of a river of estuary dimensions. Skene posited that the various names derive from *'Wreid'*, a Britonnic name for the Forth and that Treuruit alludes to the Links of the Forth south of Stirling. The Emperor's Map does have a bear signifier north of the mouth of the Carron in the vicinity of Airth as already mentioned. In addition, this particular signage is double-headed with the bear profile facing out towards the east and a king/chieftain type of head which also morphs into a bird's head with a long narrow beak, facing west, suggesting perhaps the defensive positioning at a British fort on or near an early Elphinstone or Airth castle. Opposite on the other side of the river, is the head of a young man with very structured and busy hair which appears to consist of a group of several figures. Pictorial shorthand I think, for some sort of aggressive confederaton assembled across the River Forth in the north of present day Clarkmannanshire. Around a thousand years later, the mapmaker Timothy Pont (circa 1583-

1596, NLS) recorded the western shores of the Forth from Airth to Stirling as bestrewn with fortified castles. Situated at the gateway to the north through the Gap of Stirling, the land here has been contested through the centuries of Scottish history.

Although the Links of the Forth or a little further south, in the region of the Elphinstone and Airth Castles may have been an area of potential hostilities as stone map evidence of a 'fortress bear' on the western banks of the Forth and the youth with the 'busy hair', seems to imply, I have not detected signs of a battle in that north east coastal corner of Stirlingshire. From my observations of the limestone map (Campaign Map) there is a zoomorphic head jutting out to sea on the North Edinburgh coastal line that has been fashioned from the appearance of the sand lands there. Depending upon the angle of gaze, this head looks to be that of a young bird, perhaps a gannet. Alternatively, it appears to be a frightened cat. I have settled upon the hypothesis that the fight as it has been portrayed on this map, was against the Cat/Picts who had been in possession of Edinburgh or some part of it anyway. The young 'sand bird' seems to suggest an Arthurian victory that brought a new territory (nest) for the Uotadini.

According to the stone sculpturers there were two strongholds at Edinburgh, one on the Castle Rock the other on a mount close by, probably Calton Hill. I should mention why I am fairly certain about these forts. The Emperor's map has been fashioned in such a way that it can be viewed two or three dimensionally, the latter perspective provides a topographical picture of Edinburgh as it can be seen from the coast of East Lothian (eg *Gullane Hill* or *Longniddry Bents*). The Castle and Carlton Hills can be seen clearly with the naked eye in the foreground of the immediately recognisable mound that is Arthur's Seat. Carlton hill lies less than a mile north-east of Castle Rock.

Old maps of the Edinburgh area provide a place-name on the northern coast of the present day city which is similar to one of the alternative spellings given above. The *Weirdy Burn* (Adair, circa 1583-1596) empties into the Forth near present day Newhaven or 'New Heaven' in Edinburgh (see Map 5). To the north is the River Almond which enters the Forth at Cramond and to the south, the Water of Leith. As a location for a coastal attack the Weirdy site looks promising, a good flat place to land and access to Edinburgh and the territories beyond. Perhaps the larger waterways would have been guarded and/or had some sort of populace round about. It may have been considered by Arthur and his allies as a safer distance away from the watch towers that were perhaps positioned on Arthur's Seat and the Carlton and Castle Hills. Remembering the little cat at the Roman harbour at Fisherrow it seems possible that it may have been the Picts who were manning these towers.

Today the area in which the tenth battle may have taken place is called *Wardieburn*. John Ainslie (1775) was calling that coastal area east of Leith, *'Wairdie'* and by the 19th century the shoreline that bordered it was termed the *Salt Springs of Wardie* (Edinburgh 1852, OS map). This labelling of a significant piece of shoreline as one name, I think could make the hypothesis more plausible that this particularly named battle could have taken place there. The Campaign Map may also provide greater credence for Wardieburn. According to the bear and colour signifiers on this stone (including a bear in the sea) Arthur's forces may not have been in a defending position in Edinburgh. They were, I think, on the attack from the sea to the north of the Leith area and at least an attempted landing if not a full blown attack appears to have taken place along the Wardie shoreline. It may be of no significance but with regard to the colour coding on the Emperor's Map, there is a little north sloping up from Wardie, a district called *Golden Acre*.

I am of the opinion that the Weirdy incursion was one part of the 10th battle. Perhaps it was a diversionary manoeuvre to draw some of the enemy away from what I presume to have been the Britons' main objective, the taking of Edinburgh's Castle Rock. I would argue that another possible location involved in the pursuit of this has been stone-mapped and its antiquity argued for by modern wordsmiths. This was in the present day *Portobello* and *Duddingston* areas of Edinburgh which take up the coastal lands between the northern Wardieburn and the southern Musselburgh and Inveresk localities (see map5). The place name 'Duddingston' is thought to have its origins in 'Dodin' a 12th century family name. Barrow ((1959) cited in White (1990, p13), agreed with this view but argued that 'Traverlen' was the earlier Brittonnic place-name which was historically linked to *Arthur's Seat* or *'Craggenmarf'* and *Castle Rock*. Barrow (1959) translated 'Traverlen' as meaning 'homestead of the lector'. A lector being a reader of scriptures suggests that the settlement may have been of some religious importance. By the 12th century when Holyrood Abbey was established (1128) it seemed to be acknowledged in charters that the Castle Rock and the part of Arthur's Seat closest to it belonged to the kings of

Scotland whilst the eastern portion belonged to the village or estate of *Treverlen*. *Uviet the White* owned the latter around 1090-1130.

According to Barrow, on Uviet's death, his lands were acquired by the King who gave Treverlen and its 'crag' to the Kelso monks. That the ordinary folk of the Wester Barony of Duddingston considered the lowlands and/or the slopes of Arthur's Seat as their common land was hinted at in a Crown Action in 1544 against 'the tenants of Sir David Murray (of Balvard)' who were accused of tearing down parts of the wall built by James V, that enclosed the Royal Park (White, 1990 from the Accounts of Lords of Council in Public Affairs 1501-1554).

I have found one stone map in which a fight has been documented as happening in the vicinity of present day Holyrood Park. One force was positioned on Arthur's Seat, the other at the foot of the 'crag' with defenders above them. The Emperor's map appears to show that the bear held or won the Castle Rock. Unless sheer cliffs were to be scaled any force seeking to threaten the Castle Rock would have had to approach through what today is Holyrood Park with a view to moving forward and up towards the stronghold. According to White (1990) the Travelene estate had a good deal of bog land between the Forth and Treverlen's 'Crag'. Indeed the whole of Edinburgh would have been much wetter underfoot than it is today. This makes it likely that the Bear's forces would have made for the higher ground on the easterly side Arthur's Seat out of view of the watchers on what seems to have been Edinburgh's ancient northern fort on the Carlton Hill as well as the northern or coastal slopes of the 'Crag' itself. Interestingly given the sculpted narrative, Watson ((1922) cited by Barrow 1959) translated 'Craggenmarf' as 'dead men's rock'. In the 12th century a monk referred to the 'crag' as 'Mons Dolorosus'(Barrow 1959,p4) or 'Hill of Sorrow'.

It is possible I think that the main part of the Britons' strategy was to capture the Castle Rock by landing on the banks of or rowing upstream on, the *Figgate Burn*. This water sourced to the Pentland Hills, reaches Duddingston as the *Braid Burn* and empties into the Forth at Portobello. The Britons may have either skirted Arthur's Seat on foot or perhaps the adjacent Duddingston Loch would have enabled them to move fairly rapidly inland (see <u>Map 5</u>). It seems to me Fellow Traveller, that the Figgate Burn itself may have been 'Trat Treviot', 'Treuruit' or 'Tribuit' as long ago it was thought to have been a large sandy estuary (Baird 1898). A mile or two inland it would have flowed through 'the old peat moss of *Cambrune*' (Baird 1898, p16, my emphasis) now the *Cameron Toll* area of
80

Edinburgh. Curiously given the colour signifier within of the old name for the moss, Uviet's neighbour who held sway there in nearby *Liberton* was called Malbeth (or MacBeth) 'The Bear'! (Barrow 1959, p8)

Perhaps a memory trace of the role of the Figgate in the Men of the North's struggle to regain control of their lands lies in a later name. According to a survey map by John Lawrie (1763), it was known as the *Freegate Burn*. Sculptures that I have across recently suggest that a significant number of combatants were involved in the fight on the slopes of the Figgate Burn. It may be no coincidence that in a 15th century charter from Kelso Abbey there was a reference to a large cairn of stones that was part of the boundary of the Figgate lands. Baird (1898) located this long gone feature at *Mount Lodge, Portobello* which is within half a kilometre of the mouth of the Figgate Burn. Could the cairn have been built there in memory of those who fell at Trat Treviot? The present day *Figgate Park* situated in the *Mountcastle-Duddingston* locality that features a small loch and a little green valley through which the burn flows, may be a remnant of an ancient estuary and site of a large and bloody 6th century battle.

As I have already mentioned (Battle 9) the tiny shape-shifting plaques hint at a much earlier history for the Castle and Carlton Hills including a link with the Roman period and it may be that Arthur was seeking to wrest back these former Romano-British strengths. The Emperor's Map throws up another complexity to what might have been the military and civil situation then. The two citadels were not represented in the same colour. Only the Castle Rock has been made the golden colour which I have earlier suggested may denote a site associated with Arthur. The other with strong magnification, has men at its summit whose faces have been fashioned faintly blue and feline in character. The map-maker seems to be documenting what might have been some sort of agreed coexistence between the Cat/Picts and the Uotadini after Arthur's campaign. Two citadels, two peoples with presumably their surrounding settlements, appear to have been what emerged from the eleventh battle. As I have already mentioned, examination of another visual from the same map that includes Edinburgh and an area that approximates present day Mid-Lothian, shows a large head of a bear wearing some sort of Caesar-like laurel. I would argue from this additional facet to the story told through the Emperor's Map, that this concord was managed during the period of Arthur's leadership.

A further pictorial can be detected from the 'fort plaques' at Edinburgh. It is the face of young man (Arthur I think) in warrior head gear on the golden plaque with a young woman presumably his wife holding a baby. She has been made the same blueish colour as the feline figures on the second half of the zoomorph, the implication being that she was Pictish. This vignette seems to about representing the fragility of a marriage, not between the two figures as much as between two peoples, the Britons and the Cats/Picts. Marriage through history has been used to cement alliances, gain land and power and this vignette perhaps speaks of the precariousness, the delicacy of the connection between previous enemies. The wife is given equal if not slightly greater status within the vignette as she holds her child and has a row of approving feline figures on the Carlton Hill fort close by.

Stone-mapping placed incursions from the sea at Wardieburn and Portobello with a confrontation on the slopes of the Figgate Burn, coastal-facing slopes of Arthur's Seat and possibly a further skirmish on the eastern Duddingston Loch area of Arthur's Seat. It may be these conflicts amounted to the victory required to secure the Castle Rock. Today Edinburgh is still described along a north-south axis with Princes Street and the Gardens separating the Georgian New Town from South Edinburgh where the medieval settlement grew out from the castle. Originally there was a natural trough or ravine where the railway and gardens are situated. From the stone pictorials it is possible that in Arthur's time with no bridging between the two parts of Edinburgh, a scenario in which different communities, even enemies could have lived in close proximity on the high places north and south of this topography. This may have meant that control of Treverlen including 'Treverlen's Rock' (Arthur's Seat), would effectively have resulted in the south side of the territory of 'Edin' including the Castle Rock falling to the Gwyr Y Gogledd .

The eleventh battle was

"On the Mountain Bregion "

According to Skene the location was 'on the hill called Agned' (1868/1988 Bryce (editor) p42) or Arthur's Seat and the Gwyr y Gogledd were fighting the *Cathbregyon* which he interpreted as being the Picts. This would fit well with the stone documentation I have already detailed (the fight in Holyrood Park and on the slopes of Arthur's Seat). However from stone depiction the Cat/Picts were also the Bear's opponents in at least one battle at Iudeu. If you remember there was a cat positioned midway across the Forth as if approaching the Conspicuous Cape. On close inspection the elongated form of the creature amounted to a following militia. I am of the opinion that a battle took place on the slopes of the North Berwick Law and that this hill was Agned. I have observed a number of stones which portray a fight between two forces on the Law. Those not familiar with the conical North Berwick Law may be sceptical but there are two levelled areas on the hill about 6 and 15 metres up. It can be approached on foot or on horseback from the northern and southern sides. With regards to the latter mode of ascent, it is known that an annual horse race to the summit took place in the nineteenth century and up until the First World War (Ferrier, 1980). Such an event may even be a glimpse of past times when the battle may have been commemorated in some way.

Why would this hill be a battle site you may wonder? If you recall earlier battles (ie 2, 3, 4, 5, 8) took place in which the focus was Guinnion/Iudeu. Strategically and topographically the little hill would have had its share of death and destruction. It stood as the landward sentinel before the great red castle and white palace of Guinnion. With bogland at its foot an enemy may have tried its lower reaches as a way through. From my observations of the Law itself and its crafted representations there is a lot of evidence that fifteen hundred years ago this little mountain was highly decorated in bright colours. That the Law was a vivid sight to behold then may have been remembered and documented at some point. I have already described how the Law was often featured on the fashioned story stones I have found, and some of the detailing that adorns it. What was communicated was that it had a central place in the culture of the people who lived not only here but across the lands of southern Scotland. The Hound, the Maen, the little mountain would perhaps have been a prize in itself.

That the second last battle on Nennius's list was in all likelihood again in the vicinity of Guinnion/Iudeu is revealing. Not only does it emphasise its importance but also its vulnerability. Six of the twelve battles take place in the vicinity of the Guinnion/Iudeu. In addition there is something of a pattern to the fight order, which suggests that whenever the Gwyr Y Gogledd engaged in battle elsewhere, they were forced to keep returning to defend the eastern citadel. Below is the battle order in a home/away format:

away: 1 Glencorse Burn (Midlothian)

home: 2,3,4,5 Conspicuous Cape/Iudeu (East Lothian)

away: 6 Dunipace/River Bonny (Stirlingshire)

away: 7 New Scone/Perth (Perthshire)

home: 8 Iudeu (North Berwick)

away: 9 Musselburgh (Edinburgh/East Lothian border)

away: 10 Shores of Wardie and slopes of Figgate Burn (Edinburgh)

home: 11 Iudeu (North Berwick)

Perhaps the predicament that the Uotadini faced may have been remembered by way of the Scottish oral tradition in this rhyme told when trying to distract or soothe a child using a 'dingle dousie' a lighted stick waved rapidly to form an arc of light (CSD 1987):

"Dingle, dingle dousy

The cat's at the well

The dog's awa to Musselburgh

To buy **the bairn** a bell"

(In *'Chambers Popular Rhymes of Scotland'* Chambers (1870, p21), my emphasis))

It is only conjecture but perhaps the well referred to may have been what is now called St Andrew's Well, walled up now, it is located close to the Wall Tower House (possibly the site of an ancient Iuduen boundary wall) in North Berwick. The cat and the dog may be a long forgotten reference to the tribal totems of opportunistic Cat/Picts seeking to take Guinnion whilst Arthur and the Uotadini (dogs) were fighting at Esk Mouth. Who was the 'bairn'? Well my first guess would be Arthur.

It seems clear that Arthur's battles amounted to a difficult campaign to regain and hold the Old North against enemies from within (Picts) and without (Saxons). It was a desperate time in which the Uotadini/Gododdin and their Britonnic allies fought to preserve their place in the lands between the Walls. As stone observed, a crucial part of that place was keeping and not only because it was strategically vital to them in terms of estuary control. The 'place of the king' I would argue, was intrinsic to their identity as a people. As this archive continues it may reveal why their enemies saw the island/peninsula as a prize worth pursuing again and again. The story stones seem to tell of a long forgotten history that located Iudeu at the cultural and religious centre of the lives of the ancient Britons of Southern Scotland.

Finally the twelfth battle was

"The most severe contest when Arthur penetrated to the hill of Badon"

It is thought that this battle was the victorious end to the North Britons' campaign and took place around 516 AD. Interpreting the monk Gildas who recorded the battle in his *'Ruin of Britain'* (circa 540) there may have been a few more confrontations afterwards but Badon was the most important and decisive victory for the Britons (Hunter-Mann 2001). According to Morris (1973, p112), the location of Badon was 'in the west country' and cites Bath in south-west England. However, from my study of the 'lined' stone maps I would concur with Skene (1868/1988 Bryce (editor)) who argued that the Badon Hill was actually the Bouden Hill, near Linlithgow. It is in a western territory, now known as West Lothian. The River Avon flows close by this hill entering the Forth at the southern end of what is now the huge Grangemouth oil refinery which itself is bounded in the north by the Carron River. Interestingly, on the Blaeu Atlas (1654 NLS) of this region, a little north of the hill is a place called *Baderstoun*. That the coastal land between the Carron and the Avon rivers was associated with Arthur was recorded on Pont's map (Pont 32 NLS) and the Blaeu Atlas as *Baircrofts* and in Gorden (1687), Roy (1747-55), Grasson (1817) and other maps as *Bearcrofts* near the mouth of the Avon (Note 13).

On the Campaign Map near to where the Avon and the river Almond enter the Forth south of the refinery and Cramond respectively, there are what I interpret to be military 'lines' moving inland towards Bouden. From a stone seeing perspective there seems no doubt that Boudon was the battle location as I have found several stone maps now that have lines coming in three or four directions and meeting approximately where the hill is. The meeting of the lines sometimes makes a triangle and one map without lines has a sculpted triangle, clearly I would argue, indicating a mount or hill. On another I could discern not only the outline of a bear but that of an elderly king-like figure. A clearer representation of two male figures can be discerned on the Emperor's Map and the younger is wearing what can only be described as the full feather headdress of the sort usually identified with native North American culture. You will remember that I had noted similar apparel worn by a young warrior in a ceremonial scene in the Castle Guinnion. I wonder if the older figure is a representation of Ambrosius Aurelianus said by Gildas to have led the fight at 'Badon'. The monk described the battle as a siege but gave no details as to who were the besieged. He made no mention of Arthur at all and called Ambrosius the leader of the British, which suggests that he was in overall command. Hunter-Man (2001) asks why it is that Arthur is remembered as the victor at Bouden and not Ambrosius. I would suggest that the stone narratives may point to the beginnings of an answer. The elderly presence alongside a very youthful figure is interesting because of what it may hint at about Arthur individually and of the politics of the time. He may have been of an age to shine in battle and perhaps lead a detachment of men but he appears to have been too young to be in overall command. Perhaps Arthur was important in some other way to the Britons to be stone portrayed in the company of experienced war chiefs.

As to representing who the Britons fought at Bouden the Emperor's Map I have already detailed the less than flattering profile of a warrior with large quantities of long hair some left long and hanging and some scooped up into a pony tail on top of his head. Further hair has either been sculpted into a moustache and a narrow beard or perhaps the latter was painted on his chin. This vision morphs from the battle scene and its environs. I have found no feline signposts in the vicinity, so the enemy at Bouden seems to have been wholly Saxon. I have already referred to a similar apparition threatening the Iudeun Cape and hazarded that it represented a Saxon force. Perhaps two geographically separate representations of the Saxons communicated the size of the forces that carried out the attacks on the North.

How the Campaign Map makes clear that Bouden Hill was the location of the final battle is by the placement of the other named fights along lines impressed onto stone which finally meet at this hill. It is interesting to speculate about this form of presentation. If several of the battles were won by the Britons at sites on geographical lines or routes that meet at a final siege at Badon or Boudon, who indeed were the besieged? It is possible that before the Bear's campaign, the Saxons were in control, in large part, of the Lothians. At the Rivers Gleni and Tribuit and Great Inveresk it appears that it was Arthur that was on the attack from the coast closing the door on the Saxons securing any chance of a quick escape by sea. The lines suggest more forces allied to the Uotadini/Gododdin came from the direction of Dumbarton and across the Forth from Fife towards the Avon and the Almond Rivers. Giles' translation ('penetrated') gives a sense of the focused movement of forces towards Bouden. It conveys a sense of speed too which comes with the use of the waterways and such short cuts as the pass through the Pentlands via the Gleni/Glein/Glencourse.

Guinnion was the one exception to this strategy of encircling the Saxons in that the lines on stone were from the sea north and south of the citadel. The Campaign Map has these possible routes of incursion meeting at a location just south of the North Berwick Law making clear I would argue, that Guinnion was a destination for battle and not part of the strategic preparation for the seige in West Lothian as I am suggesting of some of the other battles. The locations of Arthur's battles as mapped by the stone sculptors make sense strategically and logistically. All the other battles excepting Guinnion/Iudeu take place within roughly a forty mile (64 kilometres) radius of the final fight at Bouden Hill. Given such a small geographical area for manoeuvres and the fast and flexible use of the rivers, it is possible the campaign was undertaken and completed within one or two years at the most.

It seems from all this that working with the stone documentation brings the observer to a point of complete focus on the topography of the country. Such a form of study facilitates a stripping back of man's work on the landscape since the Bear's time, leaving the rivers, plains and hills as unmoveable participants in his long ago battles. In this way the apparently 'invisible' history and culture of the Ancient Britons of Southern Scotland can be accessed through a physical environment that was integral to how they sought to survive and make clear their presence and claim on the natural world around them.

Chapter notes

Note 1
In East Lothian today there is still recognition of the wild avian world. The Scottish Seabird Centre has been built at North Berwick and the headquarters of the Scottish Ornithlogical Club is located in Aberlady. The peregrine falcon is the region's logo.

Note 2
More about 'guledig': According to Skene (1868/Bryce1988 (editor)) the term 'Guledig' was an old Welsh name derived from 'Gulad' meaning 'a country'. It was also associated in Welsh documents with 'Gosgordd' or a retinue of around 300 horses. He also posited that 'Aureliano' was an equivalent term used by Gildas.

Note 3
The Battle of Rullion Green took place in 1666 between rebel Covenanters from the St John's Town of Dalry area (Dumfries and Galloway) and the Scottish Royal Army (2,600) led by Tam Dalyell of Binns. The Covenanters were defeated, many killed or taken prisoner and then executed. It is interesting with regard to my theory of the significance of the 'Glein' that the rebels had headed for the Pentlands. It was by the ancient pathway from the south-west of the country coming through Biggar and Pentland villages such as Carlops and West Linton that they would have most likely taken to reach the capital.

Note 4
Originating in foothills of the Pentland and Lammermuir Hills respectively, the North and South Esks come together at the north edge of Dalkeith Country Park at a place called *Castlesteads* (Ordanance Survey 1999)

Note 5
There are several other routes through the Pentlands to West Lothian as described by Crumley (1991) including waterways. Of particular note with regard to the subject of this chapter is the Lynne Water which is fed by the *Baddinsgill Burn*. Is the latter a reference to the last Bear Battle? Did the later Scots/Gaelic speakers name the burn 'Badon's servant'? In the present day there is an associated reservoir of the same name. Following the path of this burn and continuing on westwards between

the hills a walker would be close to reaching Castle Greg and the remains of a Roman fortlet.

Note 6
Interestingly with regard to the transfer of stone narrative to written document, there is a **Heads**wood about a mile south-east of Denny close to the Carron. Moving in an easterly direction *Dunipace, Denny, Headswood, Larbert* and *Camelon* (sites of Roman camps and Roman fort) are all within about a mile of each other (OSL65).

Note 7
Following the Carron River it must have been possible to go further west to *Crom Mhin,* a few miles south of present day *Balmaha* on the south-western shore of the Loch Lomond via the *Endrick Water* (Bartholomew 1912). There may have been a loch between the two rivers in the 6th century. In the 17th century Nimmo describe this place as the *Carron Bog.* Certainly, today there is a man-made reservoir between their watersheds. From my observations, the Glass Map seems to portray both military and civilian traffic on four waterways. I think these may have been the Almond, the Avon, the Carron, and the Pow Burn. There is even a glimpse of a Christian monk spotted by a crucifix beside him. North of these waters was a confrontation between some stick-like warrior figures. Given the different style of presentation perhaps this was an allusion to an earlier history of strife in Stirlingshire that may have given important context to the Arthurian battle narrative.

Note 8
There is still today a possible trace of this narrative in the *Friarton* (or *Moncrieffe*) Island on the River Tay at Perth (OS 58).

Note 9
'Deer People' is the name that I have given to the community in the Perthshire woods. The head of a deer was observed on the Emperor's Map a little north of the Carron Water and across to the east in what is now Angus. Like other animal signifiers I have assumed that it constituted the identification of a particular Northern Britonnic group.

Note 10
On the iron insert there is what looks to be pictorial narrative concerning the migration of a people to these shores. On the prow of a ship a king-like figure stands holding a cat out before him.

Note 11

My first thought was that this image was communicating or translating for the huge bear at the table in the fort on Alt Clut and I think it is the right one because it has been based on the experiential. Many months of looking at this form of communication has, I think, has made me perceptually attuned to this particular pictorial language. Later reflection introduces the possibility of other meanings such as he was greeting a bear, treating the soldier as if he was a bear or he was a bear himself. Given the positioning of the figures in the vignette and the great size/presence of the bear I hold to my first understanding of what was going on.

Note 12

Thomas the Rhymer was Thomas of Ersildoune (Earlston) who is thought to have lived in the Scottish Borders in the 13th century. Moffat (1999) posited that Thomas was a literate man of some substance who was poet and collector of ancient stories and rhymes at a time when the old P-Celtic language was dying out and there was a danger of losing the heritage of earlier times. He appears to have been a colourful character who cast himself in some of these old narratives. These and his penchant for prophesising brought about his mythic and romantic reputation within Scotland.

Note 13

Interestingly on Grasson's (1817) map near Bearcrofts are the place-names *West Candie* and *Candie* which presumably suggests that coastal Brittonic settlements were located between the two rivers. In his analysis of the source of the name *Fintray* Watson (1926) identified an earlier name associated with the town (*Cantress*) that could be traced to *Candref* which was linked to *canto-treb* which means 'white stead'.

Chapter 5: Bloodlines and the Sea Baby

Commentary from an Avian God inspired by the Emperor's Map..........
Solannie.

Dawn is coming. Soon it will steal over this magnificent feathered rock that is my home. Gana is transformed as the days lengthen and I return with the flock. Dark and desolate in winter it becomes the shimmering white colossus of the summer. Before light, there is sometimes a faint haar over the estuary which cloaks the rock and the earthling citadel, but not today. My mate will stay close to our offspring, diving for food in the channel between the Gana and the Mae, while I will head west overland.

For generations, the people of this part of the North have revered the avian creatures of the coast and I of course, as the King of all sea birds have a very special place in their hearts. I know this because all their settlements have my image placed upon them. Sometimes my cousins the snowy egret, the kittiwake and the gull are there in the carvings that decorate the forts but always, I take precedence. I am fashioned on the wood of the great gates of the citadel and upon the prows of their ships. I am metal too as these people have many forges exploiting the ore lying below their feet. I would go as far as to suggest that the humans portray themselves as Solan in their dealings with others of their kind. This level of appreciation is most satisfying and I see it as my duty as a deity to regularly scan the horizons of this, my human flock.

First is the cliff top citadel, a shining resemblance of my rocky home and I think another sign of earthling reverence. There are several ships harboured in the coves closest to the white palace and Canty and many more at the wide Goose Bay a few flaps of my wings westwards. Soon there will be much activity from here on the last curve of the estuary towards this anchorage and the ports upriver. To the east on the northern shores, the great twin beacon hills are emerging from the night, the deepest blue on a marine horizon. Oh, I am tempted to veer off course and head for the mouth of the river flowing from the tout-rich loch that lies at the foot of these bastions. After all the Sula People live there too between and at the foot of the peaks. Settlements nestle close to the edges of the loch. Perhaps on my way home I will pay this beautiful land a visit. Brown trout for tea-delicious!

Looking south again a large port draws the eye, its important buildings standing white and handsome high above the coast and the Great River of the Sula People. Rich in salmon I am tempted to follow its course. The Water and its tributaries make for the best inland causeway into the eastern and western territories. However I have to fulfil my obligations as a god and make a full survey of my domain. No shortcuts for me.

Following the shoreline I am soon circling the great fort and watchtowers of Edin and the many lochs that surround it. I have allocated these fruitful basins to kindred from the isles nearest to this nirvana. Swinging out on the river again I fly on north, north westerly. I spy ahead the familiar hooked headland. Here is the entrance to another important inland river of my subjects. A port with castle and settlements is situated there. The harbour is busy with military and merchant shipping. It is light now and I can see the earthlings going about their business. There are traders on the streets; carters loading and unloading cargo; sailors making ready for journeys and others arriving at the dock perhaps starting voyages or there to meet passengers yet to arrive. It is a crossroads this place, north, south east and west. Mostly east and west as the much of the land on this flight path is held by the Sula People and their Kindred.

There are already signs of boat movement westwards as those that had broken their journey and berthed for the night get underway. Many human settlements are dotted all along this stretch of water. The most grand has a great castle standing at the very edge of the river. Smaller fortresses lie further west and north past glittering waterfalls. I have caught a few salmon here as they return to the sea from their spawning time. Truly this is a royal river as the kings of fish and men choose to honour it with their presence. Interspersed amongst the palaces are many inferior buildings and little villages. No doubt the inhabitants of these serve the needs of the torqued leaders. Taking it all as a whole, the bend in the river is almost filled up with the footprint of man.

Watching the wakening of humankind to the endless tasks of existence is all very interesting but I have my own survival to attend to so I carry on west. Soon I am leaning into an updraft over the two pinnacled rock that stands guarding not only the land from which I have just come but also the kingdom of my cousins the Sea Eagles. I do not linger near as, cousins or not, I am a little wary of provoking them. I have glimpsed enough to garner an impression of wonders both natural and human. It is a land of many mountains in which the eyries of my brethren are well placed. In the protective midst of these heights, lies a beautiful sea sprinkled with many isles. On its banks and on every island there are castles and splendid houses. My father told me that this was a secret land in which the very oldest peoples had made their home after the ice domes receded. Being **Before Everyone** had made them the wisest too and many of their children are the guardians of the sacred knowledge of earthlings.

Veering ever westwards, I am now close to my favourite hunting waters. The People of the Sea Lochs are pushing their craft out into the new day.

****

Recently a particular sculpted and sometimes painted narrative has impinged upon my consciousness. It started with a metal and enamel artefact no more than 4cms square and required strong magnification to make out the tiny scenes. The most striking of these was that of a baby alone in the midst of strong seas, his pink white skin bright against the black waves. The baby in the blink of an eye or rather the slight tipping of the object becomes a little bear. My curiosity was obviously aroused by beholding such a scene and I started to look out for similar carvings. My searching brought results in the identification of a story that is modelled in a similar way no matter the medium used. As I have found such consistency as to the plot in this and other worked pieces, (eg battle maps; interior of Guinnion), I was fairly certain that this was a narrative worth detailing.

At the top of a hill or mountain there is the figure of a large bear. His size suggests power, that he is a chief or king. He is bent over a young woman whose recumbent position and mien suggests that she is very ill or dead. To his left is a minute court scene. Nearest to him is a male figure standing holding a little bear and from this there is the inference that the woman has just given birth. There are various figures together beside what I take to be a large crib with several little children in or around it (represented by small animals and birds). That something dreadful has happened and that more trouble is on the way seems to be indicated by the sculpting of two female figures nearby. In one worked piece this is especially clear. Standing behind one shoulder of the bear king there is a dark haired, dark clothed young woman with a veil covering all but her eyes. On his opposite side there is the brown and bulky cloaked figure of an older woman climbing the hill sometimes with the help of a large stick or staff. Aside from these figures there is another woman standing apparently watching events as they unfold. She is accompanied by a young boy or sometimes by a young horse. A ship is launched from the rock which has the little bear and the other children and a few adults on board.

Near this scene there is, in several instances, a deep groove in the stone which given the watery context could represent a sea loch. The group of children and adults are embarking again on a boat in this groove. There are figures standing at the waters edge watching them leave. The next scene is of more catastrophe as the vessel is shown as either breaking up and/or of some of the children and adults falling out. Another dramatic scene follows in which there are one or several people in a very distinct sort of water. Whether it is in coloured or uncoloured stone or enamel on stone the unvarying portrayal is of a swirling pool in which there are one or several heads in the water including that of the little bear. At least some of the children, with the baby bear, are rescued by another ship crewed by a large white bird, probably a swan. The children are taken to the apparent safety of another fortress where they are handed over to chieftain-like figures. This fortress was sometimes portrayed as being high up, above water, and between two great rocks. On one stone I detected a boat being carried over an isthmus on the children's journey to safety. There appears to be another part to this story, but to date I have seen it only on one stone and that is of a large number of mounted horsemen portrayed as emerging from the fortress that received the travellers. The implication of this vignette appears to suggest that the events described may have needed to be avenged or sorted in some way or another.

From his posture over the collapsed young woman the king was presented as distraught. Indeed this was emphasised on several stones in which his profile showed him with his mouth wide open as if giving a roar of anguish. The narrative has another twist in the form of some sort of subterfuge which appears to be the monopolising/seeking the attention of a young queen or princess by one man, part of a small group of visitors to a court. The young queen sometimes has been portrayed as a white horse with a yellow mane. This activity seems to be followed by another scene suggesting that she was assaulted by the visitor. Through the study of a variety of story stones there are a number of vignettes that seem to be linked to this theme. For example, the visitor/visitors were sometimes standing on a raised object, sometimes they have disembarked from a ship and are being welcomed by a king figure. On one flat stone the 'ship' appears to be a landmark offshore and the shape of it is remarkably similar to the natural rock arch located in the north of the *Isle of Sanda*, adjacent to which is the present day lighthouse. Sanda is situated two miles south-east of the Mull of Kintyre, its northern anchorage across the Sound of Sanda from *Dunaverty Castle*. Once a formidable fortress standing on its own peninsula, Dunaverty's known history can be traced back to the 7th century. According to Watson (1926, pp237-238) *'averty'* is derived from *'Abhartach'* or *'hUi Abartaich'* an Irish sept (Note 1)

To the front of the traveller's head there is a bear's face indicating that he was or was pretending to be, one of the Bear people. To the back however, there is what I think is the visage of a fox. This combination seems to be communicating deception with regard to the traveller's intentions and his identity (Note 2). Perhaps a clue as to where this personage set foot on Kintyre may also be another illustration of how a detail from ancient stone stories lives on in the place-names of Scotland. On the east side of Dunaverty is *Brunerican Bay* and it could be argued that this is a name that conjures up the two-faced visitor. 'Brun' may be a derivation or alternative to 'bear' by the denoting of the colour brown and 'erican' could be linked to Erc, a chieftain of Irish mythology and supposedly the father of Fergus, a figure bound up in the scant written narrative concerning the hill-fort of Dunadd in Argyll. I will return to Fergus later.

There are other vignettes such as a scene of one of the visitors alone with the Horse Queen and a bed scene where there are three in the bed, the king/chief and his wife and this interloper. There seems to be a third older and malevolent male figure in the background as if manipulating events. On one stone he is holding a strange looking receptacle cup with a spout from which emanates a vapour suggesting perhaps that it held a potion or inhalation. Looking at what seems to me to be a sequence of events, I have at times wondered if this assault took place against an already pregnant queen and that it precipitated childbirth with fatal consequences for her. It may be possible that this terrible incident which appears to be related to Arthur's birth, may have been alluded to in the poem 'The Chair of the Sovereign' from the *Book of Taliesin* which refers to him as :

"....a warrior of two authors,

Of the race of steel Ala"

(From 'Arthur and the Britons in Wales and Scotland' Skene 1868/Bryce 1988 (editor), p124).

Because there were several very clear cultural and geographical signposts to enable the conscientious stone observer to put together the context, it was not too difficult to locate where the story had been set. A number of stones feature the white feminine looking horse lying beside or close to a brown bear. In several portrayals her head (with mane) lies above and her back and hind quarters reach below the bear outline. The bear's shape is similar to the *Kyles of Bute* (the bear's feet) and the lands of *Cowal* (bear's back and shoulders) and to the north-western border of Loch Lomond (bear's head). I would suggest that the horse's recumbent shape may have been worked to represent the Kintyre peninsula as well as, possibly, part of North and Mid-Argyll. Several stones seem to indicate that apart from the Bear territory already detailed, there was a 'Brun' presence in Mid-Argyll, perhaps only representing a single settlement and its immediate surroundings. Further areas of brown were placed within the white southern equine (Kintyre) shape. Another stone quite large with a flat surface, (already referred to) seems to position a boundary (use of colour again) between bear and horse lands in what was like the upper part of the peninsula, possibly where the *River Gilp* enters *Loch Fyne* at present day *LochGilphead*. This small town lies a few miles south-east of the great valley of Neolithic monuments, *Kilmartin Glen*. The impression given in my view, is that in Arthur's time there was a mixed population on the Kintyre peninsula, some areas predominantly 'bear' and others 'horse' with a Bear held northern outpost situated close to the western banks of Loch Fyne in sight of the Bear homeland, Cowal.

The second century Greek geographer Ptolemy knew the name of the people who lived on Kintyre, as the *Epidii,* the *Horse People*. The pictorial message from the stone sculptures appears to suggest that the white/light horse was a Horse Princess/Queen of Kintyre. Kintyre, variously called *Kyn-tyr, Cantyr, Caintyr* in early paper maps, a place-name that may be linked to the meaning *'white',* or *'bright'* although according to Watson, 'Kintyre' is a direct translation of the Gaelic, 'Ceann Ti-re or 'headland' (Watson,1926,p364 and p92 respectively). The yellow mane of the horse may be another geographical identifier for the peninsula noted for its beautiful yellow beaches. There is apparently no paper reference to a community or tribe that called themselves 'bears'. It would seem that one group of northern people was identified into the future (ie the Horse Folk) and the other was not. I would suggest however, that the ancient worked stone recorded the latter's existence and something of their place in the story of the time before Scotland. Dyed/painted and sculpted work seems to have portrayed the bear and the horse peoples as geographical neighbours on good terms and that their important people had some of the leading roles in an origin story of Arthur.

I think the clue to where in Argyll this story took place is in the hunched shape of the Chief of Bears. The squareness of his shoulders and the sheerness of his sides rising above the small scenes below are suggestive of the uneven plateau at the summit of the rocky hill upon which the fort of Dunadd once stood. It's slightly lower peak sometimes serves as the court anteroom/nursery scene. Incredibly one rocky outline of Dunadd appears to be represented in the chieftain bear's distressed profile first observed on a variety of miniatures but then viewed again (from the main road and several hundred metres away), as one angle of the original emerging like a gigantic zoomorphism, the wide open mouth emitting a roar of pain across the quiet landscape. The magic of ancient imagination is as thrilling now as it must have been for the more receptive peoples of long ago.

The boat launching (often coloured an amber/brown shade) as if from the hill fort itself communicates the presence of a river at its foot. The winding River Add is a good match with the pictorial description. In the deep indent and the little audience of figures seeing off or witnessing the boat-launch that have been placed hard up against rocks behind them appears to identify the substantial and steep-sided cliffs that are characteristic of the kyles and sea lochs of Argyll.

Situated 54m above the surrounding *Moine Mhor* or *Great Moss*, in the south of the Kilmartin Glen Dunadd was thought to be the location of the fortress of the Scots Kingdom of Dalriada (circa500-850AD). At its summit is a flattish slab of stone upon which is carved the shape of a boar. The narrative stones, I would suggest, put the great stronghold further back in time. Although not situated on the coast, the River Add flows by below the great rock. A short boat journey along this stretch of water would take the children to nearby *Crinan*. Their guardians may either have set sail from there or Ardnoe Point into the Sound of Jura, presumably heading south. Alternatively they carried the boat from somewhere near the present day village of *Bellanoch* to *Loch Barnluasgan*, then to *Loch Coille-Bharr* (and given wetter climate then there may have been more water and a little less land to traverse). Thence the party would have reached Loch Sween and sailed on from there round to the narrow isthmus at *Tarbert* in North Kintyre, a place where a short boat-carrying would have taken the party into the possibly safer waters of the Sound of Bute and the Bear domain. The latter seems the most likely option as Loch Sween would have been more sheltered than the open sea and on leaving it behind the voyagers would have been many miles further away from the dangerous waters that are a few miles north of the Crinan coastline. The already mentioned deeply indented groove on some narrative stones is very suggestive of the very distinctive peninsula that shelters *Loch Sween* from the *Sound of Jura*.

I think that the artfully crafted swirling pool with the little heads caught in its vortex, a consistent feature of these narrative stones, can only be representations of the *Corryvrekan* Whirlpool. The name is thought to derive from '*Brecon's cauldron*', from the Gaelic '*coire*'- '*hollow*', cauldron and the personal name Brecon or more likely, from my observations, '*bhreacain*' meaning '*speckled*' (McKillop/Brewer's 2005). This famous natural feature is situated in the Gulf of Corryvreckan between the islands of *Jura* and *Scarba* about five miles off the Scottish mainland. At certain times the whirlpool is a formidable sight of swirling, bubbling water and the noise of it can be heard for miles around. One legend associated with the Cauldron concerns the *Cailleach Bheur* or '*old woman*' (Scottish Gaelic). The Cailleach was a mythological figure, a divine hag who represented winter and who fought to stave off the spring. She was said to control the whirlpool and decided who would or wouldn't survive it. Local people today still call it the Cailleach. According to McKillip (2005) '*cailleach*' in Latin means '*veil*' so it is possible that the dark-haired and veiled young woman behind the Bear chief was the representation of this goddess in another form, presumably of spring. The presence of possibly two versions of the same goddess could arguably have been a signposting and context-setting for the time of the year in which the events crafted took place. Perhaps it was late October/November or February/ March.

No doubt many have lost their lives to the Cailleach and there are several cairns on the adjacent headlands and coasts that may be evidence of that but there is one place-name which could refer to the drowning people featured in stone and that is *Bagh Dail nan Ceann (Bay of the Field of Heads)* on the Craignish Peninsula (Welsh and Isherwood, 2003). It has been related to a bloody battle with Vikings but I think it is much more evocative of the scene in the great Cauldron hundreds of years before when there were 'bears' at Dunadd. There may have been quite a large number of drowned people buried there. Given the consistency with which the whirlpool has been represented in Arthur's early life, (ie speckled with waves/eddies and/or heads), it perhaps was an iconic image connected with his story in the time of the stone crafters of Iudeu. Such powerful imagery may have left a trace in the place-names of western Argyll.

Another worked piece also seems to portray a community or a gathering on the banks of Loch Lomond as well as on the group of islands in the southerly portion of the loch itself. It is a convivial scene with a mixing of peoples as half there have been represented as bears the other as horses. Perhaps it was the gathering of a chief whose stronghold was by the loch. The greatest density of worked representation was on the south-westerly banks and spreading in a north-easterly direction, across the loch onto the islands and reaching landfall again perhaps, given its proximity to the islands, at present day Rowardennan. This scene also portrays the meeting of a bear and a horse. Whether this was the meeting of the chief of Dunadd or another with the white horse (princess) is not clear.

Aside from the Spring Goddess or the Cailleach there is another woman portrayed in the Dunadd vignette whom I take to be of high status and as she was accompanied as I have already mentioned, by a young boy or a young brown horse. My initial impression was that she was featured as perhaps not an altogether disinterested actor in the story. The horse was a relative, a son perhaps, for whom she had ambitions. Perhaps she herself was a Horse Princess who saw an opportunity in the death of her kinswoman. Had she influenced the decision to send the children away? Perhaps her presence tells the viewer who was destined to inherit the lands of the powerful bear figure. However, the more likely possibility I would suggest, was that she was yet another goddess portrayal in the form of *Epona*, a Celtic goddess who was the protector of horses, donkeys and mules. As such she may have been placed there in that role of providing some guardianship of any Epidi setting out on a dangerous voyage. Alternatively, other more contradictory roles for this figure as either fertility goddess or, with her horses, the leader of the soul into the afterlife may fit well with a childbirth death of the Horse Queen/Princess. Her sculptured presence may also have been communicating the likely outcome of a sea journey for a newly born baby undertaken at a time of the year when storms are common in Atlantic Scotland.

As I have said there is little variation in the origin portrayal. That it is a story concerned with Arthur's beginnings is clear not only from the use of the bear signifier but also because this birth narrative was frequently 'told' on the same stone that has the sculptural details of his death and funeral (see chapter 8). The similarities between the two stories such as how hills and boats feature in his origin and end have been picked out in stone to perhaps give a fatalistic emphasis to the life of one man. What was being communicated then and now to me I would suggest is that his was a life predestined for greatness shown in his surviving the Cauldron. There is an impression of the magical, of a life enchanted and protected for a heroic future. At the same time this was a story that began and ended in a context of treachery, danger and tragedy.

'But did it really happen like that?' you may ask. With regard to the geographical detailing, the story stone makers were evidently familiar with the topography of the area around Dunadd Fort. This was demonstrated, I would argue, in the artistic insertion of the several signposts which I have already mentioned. From studying of the maps of Argyll and Kintyre I would postulate that Loch Sween was the most likely route the boat party could have taken once they had negotiated the Add and it would have been the safest way if they were heading south or west. Perhaps Alt Clut was their destination. It would have been natural to send the vulnerable to relatives but if the eastern route was blocked by the enemy a more circuitous route may have been necessary to reach the Clyde Estuary, involving sailing round the Mull of Kintyre or some boat-carrying further south into Horse territory, perhaps at Tarbert (see Map 6). So how could they have ended up in the open sea in the Sound of Jura perilously close to, if not in, the Cailleach? The presence of the Hag and the Dark Goddess could have been signifiers for it still being late autumn or early spring and so it seems possible that poor sea conditions were being flagged up as the context for such a misadventure. All the more likely then that those sent from Dunadd would not have taken such a dangerous route voluntarily and that knowledge points to further evil being wrought at the fortress. The flat stone already referred to hints at an attack which may have only left a quick escape by the Add emerging into Loch Crinan and thence overland to Loch Sween. Perhaps on exiting Loch Sween the travellers were blown off course and north towards the whirlpool. In a later chapter further credence to this version of events will be given.

Given the geographical detailing it seems possible that some version of the stone story did take place. The death of a queen/princess perhaps after a clandestine assault, the sending away of the young and the possible military reaction from Alt Clut suggests some historical basis. Could this have marked the end of Bear rule at Dunadd? The deaths of the young may have triggered retaliation, even war. Further stone documentation may not only provoke more questions but also, hopefully, reveal some answers.

What then of the function of this origin story as a history to be passed on from generation to generation? As I have already observed, it was a fateful story, suitably heroic for a hero. Already as a baby the Bear had experience of great danger. To have survived the Cauldron must have marked him out as very special. The veneration of water was so ingrained within pre-Christian pagan religion that the Christian leaders had to keep the holy well as a focus for worship and pilgrimage (Ellis 2002). From Ellis' (2002, pp132-156) analysis of Druid rituals it seems likely that the little child that was rescued from the Corryvreckan would have been seen as having undergone the most sacred of baptisms. The inclusion of several pagan goddesses is interesting given that Arthur was thought to have been a Christian. The reason for this juxtaposition must be related to the mid- to late sixth century being on the cusp only, of cultural/religious change. Belief in a Christian god was but one of a range higher powers available to the story tellers. From my observations the baby was most frequently crafted in a white substance. That the other children were not similarly represented perhaps means it may not have been used to signify Arthur's extreme youth but that there was something else that marked him out. Was it linked to the purifying bath in the Cauldron or the whitened citadel at Iudeu or was it both? I have already touched on the religious aspect of the 'Conspicuous Cape'. As has been revealed already by the genealogical pathway of 'heads' from the Emperor's Map, he was related to the powerful at Alt Clut and closely linked to people in the eastern sea-city.

Some story stones may have been records of a further journey for the baby bear accompanied by a little girl that brings them to the east of Scotland and Iudeu. The male figure that took the children to Guinnion often resembles the one that was entrusted with Arthur at Dunadd. Sometimes with an altered gaze this representation changes into a large, long-beaked bird. With regard to what the origin story reveals of that distant time, it is illuminating. The influence of the Bear people was over a wide geographical area and seemed to include the western and some of eastern banks of Loch Lomond (see Map 6). The story conveys a sense that there was some sort of confederacy amongst the ancient North British. If the various other young children represented as different birds and animals were of different kindreds, it would appear that they were under the care of another chief. From the Emperor's Map it was made clear that the Bear king would have been related to those who controlled the stronghold between the two-peaked Alt Clut, the hill fort of the Britons at *Dumbarton*. That the death of the Horse Queen/ Princess initiated the sending away of not only the young Arthur but the other children too suggests some underlying danger for Dunadd, why else would the young be sent away, probably at the worst time of the year given the goddess presence. The horsemen that emerged from the Clyde Rock were perhaps heading west presumably towards whatever this threat was. That a perpetrator of the disaster was identified, given physical characteristics in the narrative stones, suggests that a specific person was blamed. Such detailing conveys to the observer a further sense of a dangerous dramatic tale which had many different actors working together to save Arthur and the other travellers. It is probably beyond my brief to postulate about who was blamed. Nonetheless you will not be surprised that as Stone Archivist I will shortly do just that!

This stone narrative of the tragic and miraculous beginning of Arthur's life was the stuff of legends and heroes and when you read a later chapter, was matched by an equally dramatic ending. How close the stone pictures were to the real story of his birth is difficult to judge but the sculptures had to have been contemporaneously linked with those times as they are located at a place closely associated with him. Then there is the dreadful content of the tale which is hard to believe was a fiction.

Fraser's (2009) analysis concerning the cultural/ethnic origins of this part of western Scotland, a subject of some debate, marries well with what the pictorial reveals of Kintyre/Argyll and for that matter, the other parts of Scotland stone-portrayed.

"A people do not have origins that can be pinpointed to a single moment in time or a single place. Rather ethnic identities are constructed and re-constructed, imagined and reimagined, through an ongoing process of interaction between cultural practices and cultural self-consciousness."

102

(In 'From Caledonia to Pictland Scotland to 795' by James E.Fraser (2009, p147))

The more stone narrative that I examine the more layered it seems to become, revealing something further of the ethnic evolution of Atlantic Scotland so long ago. This is partly a matter of the quantity of crafted work bringing greater variety to the story being told. It is also to do with observatory experience bringing an awareness of just how complex the physical design and workmanship wrought upon these stones has been. They are works of an artistry unrecorded and unacknowledged as yet. To know of them is to be in awe of the energies and time involved. Yet surely because of such an expenditure of effort what is being communicated deserves a reciprocal attention? I am certain there is much more to be gleaned from their study. For example with regard to language it seems clear that the strangers who arrived at the Mull of Kintyre were able to converse with those at the Horse Court but whether it was in the Q-Celtic (Gaelic) or P-Celtic (Brittonic) tongue is not. Both languages would have been spoken in the Argyll of that time with a shift to the former between the 4th and 7th centuries Fraser (2009 p148). Stone pictures seem to communicate an ethnic mix of people through the use of colour (white horses/brown bears).

Further layers to the story of Arthur's birth are to be found in the myriad of miniature context. What I have distinguished must be the more obvious signposting, revealed with the slight turn of a worked stone underlying the main portrayal. Some white adult bears have emerged into the story which may provide some further meaning to the ethnicity/status of the baby at Dunadd. In a similar vein the identity of the peoples of Argyll is made more intriguing in the appearance of an animal not known to have lived in Northern Britain, the crocodile. As this archive progresses this amphibian also makes an appearance on Lothian and Fife coasts with its great jaws reassuringly clamped together with with some sort of banding. Interestingly too I have seen on several stones a cross carved into the 'summit' of the great bear of Dunadd alongside the outlines and shapes of other belief systems.

Accepting the complexity and evolutionary nature of the identity of a people, the stone narratives can be seen as providing windows that look out into such an ever-changing process. Within any cultural artefact there is a distillation of what a community experiences. It's perceptions of the past leak into the main story which itself has to be a product of future interpretaters. To come close to understanding such communicative art is to accept the fluidity of human identity through time. The question of when this archive of birth narrative was produced may be difficult to answer but I would argue that the consistency of portrayal and the sheer quantity of it presented on an array of materials tells the observer something of the lived experience of a long gone people. It was an experience which included a common knowledge/narrative across the communities between the Walls and perhaps beyond, of the main events of Arthur's life and the production of vast numbers of commemorative objects/ souvenirs for the rich and poor. The deposition of large numbers of these artifacts on the southern banks of the Forth extends the narrative to a time when the Conspicuous Cape was seen as the appropriate place in which to leave behind the story of the Bear. Because of the frequency with which the story pictures of Arthur's birth crops up in stone it seems worthwhile to examine the written narrative associated with Dunadd. This has been gathered from the very limited amount of documentation of what was happening in Scotland of that time. Given the supposedly Christian credentials of Arthur, the monks who were the documenters in those times seem to have failed in providing future generations with much knowledge of him. This absence from record of such an early Christian figure whose origin was stone-commerated as linked to Argyll and Kintyre and not many miles south of the great monastic centre of Iona founded just over twenty years after Arthur's death (563), is intriguing. Given the number of stones portraying both a birth and a death narrative and the white bear portrayals, perhaps there was a cultic or religious influence at work. As will be revealed later there is much to suggest the development of a cult after Arthur's death. The vast quantity of stone work points to such happening. All the more curious then that so little is recorded of the life of this man. How could such a tragic tale be lost?

Many factors may have contributed to how this came about. There was probably little written documentation by the Britons themselves given the emphasis on the oral tradition. Within sixty years of Arthur's death the Gododdin had lost much of their territory to the new power, Northumbria. Over time the language (and therefore a good deal of the cultural narrative) of the Britons between the Walls would have fallen out of use. Through the centuries many records which may have held traces of Arthur's story would have decayed to dust or were destroyed in the many upheavals that marked Scotland's history. However, dear Traveller as this archive progresses the idea that there was a deliberate absence of the Bear's story from the written record of Scotland may cross your mind.

It may be worth exploring the identity of those who were perhaps linked in some way with the destruction of the Bear dynasty at Dunadd. The small traces of Arthur's life and death are to do with battles yet the attack at Dunadd has been lost to history. There seems to be no paper records found that even hint at there being a kingdom ruled from Dunadd before the Dal Riata takeover, never mind the absence of any mention of the 'Bear People' from ancient sources. There is however, the scarce narrative concerned with the founding of the Dalriadan dynasty in the land that was eventually called after their tribal Irish name, 'Scotti'. The legend is that it was Fergus son of Erc who established a new dynasty of the Dalriata of Antrim in Argyll around 498/500 and ruled for three years before his son Domongart succeeded him (Calise 2002 Regnal lists D, F1, F2, I K). Mystery seems to surround his death. According to Marsden (1997) although Fergus may have been quite old at that time, it is possible that age or infirmity was not the cause of his death. Marsden pointed to one copy of the 'Chronicle of the Kings' as having a note at Fergus's place on the king-list that stated that:

"He was killed by his followers"

(From *'Alba of the Ravens'* Marsden 1997, p45).

The usual reason for such a killing, another claimant to the kingship, does not appear to apply given his son's succession. Interestingly, Domangart's rule was short (501-506) and 'tumultuous' and the style in which his death was recorded suggests he had retired into monastic life (Marsden 1997, p46). According to king-lists and annals Domangart was succeeded by his son Comgall (Rule 507-538). However, there is a discrepancy between the records over when Comgall succeeded which may mean that his father gave up the kingship in favour of his son in 503, after only two years of rule (Note 3). The name 'Comgall' was linked to the territory of 'Comgaill' or Cowal today, the land stone-described as Bear territory at the time of Arthur's birth. After Comgall's death the kingship passed to his brother Gabran who seems to have died in 558. Comgall's son Conall mac Comgall then ruled till 576 (Fraser2009). Then the annals record that Gabran's son, Conall's first cousin Aedan mac Gabran became king/chief of Kintyre.

It has been noted (John Bannerman 1974 cited by Sharpe (2000, p53) that the *cenel* Gabran began very early there usually being several generations before a name becomes dynastic. Given his supposed role as the founder of the royal lineage at Dunadd it is odd that there was no 'cenel Fergus'. It is extremely unlikely that the formation of a new dynasty was not accompanied by death and destruction of those who came before. I would tentatively suggest that such a situation seems to have been part of the story at Dunadd but that what distinguishes it from other ancient takeovers was Arthur. Hypothetically using stone narrative Fergus may have been a disgraced figure. Could his possible killing by his own people have been to do with the drowning of the innocents in the 'Cauldron' and subsequently his name was not dynastically fitting in a time when the Arthurian story was well remembered?

Where was the bear child taken after the tragic events at Dunadd? Scouring the Emperor's Map to glean what I could about the Brythonnic territories north of the Tay, I came upon a curious scene which may provide a clue. A cloaked male figure holding a tiny bear was positioned in the Montrose corner of the map (which I will return to in the next chapter). Off the coast facing an assemblage of dignitaries has been crafted the head and neck of an aggressive-looking black horse whose lower regions consisted of the head of a young man. I can only speculate about the identity of the 'horse' but whoever he represented he must surely have had his origins with the Epidii People. In my experience as archivist the use of colour was always about conveying meaning and identity. Was this vignette a glimpse into the 'tumultuous' Domangart years which may have amounted to just two before a religious retirement and the passing of the chieftainship to young Comgall? What the scene does convey seems to be an attempt to wrest the little Arthur from the North Britons. From the many stone narratives the little Bear remained with them into adulthood.

There is further mystery concerning Comgall's story that seems hugely coincidental to that of Arthur's life details. He was heir to the lands of Cowal, the Bear homeland, and dies around the same time as the Brittonic hero. According to the records his years of his rule were 'without strife' (Marsden 1997, p51). Did he exist or was he a convenient fiction to blot out the place of Arthur and the North British influence and power in the western lands of Scotland? The lack of parchment data led Sharpe (2000, p50) to note that there was no way of knowing how the Dalriadan dynasty came to control Argyll. Stone documentation points to the importance of ancient links of blood and kindred in the Old North and possibly with regard to the tragedy at Dunadd, the lengths that men would go to claim a place within these ties. In this regard the pictorial throws up another facet to the incident between the visitor to Kintyre and the Horse Princess/Queen.

The stone presence of Arthur in the Dalriada story puts some semblance of context into what seems to be the absence of Arthur from Scotland's ancient history. Arthur was strongly connected to Argyll. His mother was from the Epidii of Kintyre, a Britonnic people. The Kintyre of those times however, taking note of Fraser's (2009) analysis very likely had an ethnic mix of people, some Brythonnic and some new and some old settlers from Ireland. The sculpted stones seem to portray a Bear Folk who were part of this mix but that around the time of Arthur the lands to the east of Kintyre in Cowal and beyond to the banks of Loch Lomond belonged to the Bear Folk. Arthur's mother may have been married to the chief who held Dunadd or his close relative, no doubt strengthening ties of kinship with the Bears of the fortress in the Great Moss. Horse and Bear Folk were on good terms. I am certain the stone workers were making clear who was the master of Dunadd. As already detailed he was portrayed as large, (often forming the whole shape of the fortress rock) aka a politically powerful figure. Could he have been the 'Mor', which in Welsh means 'sea man', who according to the genealogy table of the 'Thirteen Kings of 'Y Gogledd' in the North' (Skene 1868/1988Bryce (editor), p165) was a grandson of Coel Hen? According to this family tree Mor had a son called 'Garthwys or Arthwys' (Note 4).

What might have been the role of Bear-held Dunadd I wonder? A bear overlordship may have been a political feature of the Kintyre peninsula. The territory's socio-cultural character and/or its proximity to Ireland may have made the Bear fortress strategically important to Cowal as well as to the lands in the northern hinterlands accessible by one of the longest lochs in Scotland, the Awe. Between the southern end of this loch and Dunadd is Kilmartin Glen. Were the Bear Folk at the fortress guardians of the substantial religious site that lies within this glen?

Into this scenario came two visitors who were given access to a court and the story of possible assault, childbirth death and the drowning of innocents and miraculous survival in the Corryvreckan began. The Britonnic overlordship was presumably destroyed or weakened but the ties of blood still existed in the form of newly-born Arthur. He was brought up in the east of Scotland amongst the North British communities. From the start perhaps his miraculous survival may have engendered a sense of unity amongst the peoples between the two

Roman walls and marked him out as destined to lead them to victory. In the Welsh triads he referred to as *'pen teyrned'* meaning *'chief prince of three lands'* (Calise 2002, p180). Perhaps these lands were Argyll including Dumbarton, Lothian and as will be revealed in the next chapter, a significant portion of Fife and Angus, their potentates perhaps linked to the three branches of Coel Hen headed by Mor, Gorwst Ledlwn and Garboniaun. Already detailed were the portrayals of a very young Arthur surrounded and supported by what appears to have been a British federation who battled and perhaps arranged Arthur's politically expedient marriage in the woods of Perthshire. If there is a fit between parchment and stone the Bear must have been born around 500 AD and would have been very young when involved in the campaigns leading up to Badon in 516 AD. A few lines from the Welsh poem *'The Brithwyr'* (The Picts) in the *'Red Book of Hergest'*, which calls for a return to the time before Arthur's death at the battle of Camlan, seems to relate to the stone portrayals of Arthur of the Cauldron:

"Scenes of groaning will be seen again

And dismal lamentations,

And mischievous contention,

And the child will grow

Strong in battle, even when small."

(From 'Arthur and the Britons in Wales and Scotland' Skene 1868/ Bryce (editor) 1988, p141)

Arthur's story may have encroached further into the descendants of Fergus with Gabran who would have been around 15 years old when the bear was born. Gabran became ruler of Dalriada in 537 but it is thought that he already ruled in Gafran or Gowrie due to a marriage to a North British princess from the lands of Forfar (Brechin). Is it possible that that this marriage relates to the baby Arthur's story at Montrose? Skene (1868)/Bryce (editor) 1988/Watson (1926) pointed out that for five years before he became 'king' of Dalriada (574) Gabran's son Aedan had reigned somewhere else south of the Firths of Clyde and Forth. Further, in 596 Aedan was fighting a battle in Circhenn or Angus (Watson 1926, p113), Brittonic lands according to the Emperor's Map.

There was no uncertainty in the stone portrayals of Arthur's birth. He was crafted as a small white bear which may have had religious connatations and/or was related to his being bear on his father's side and white of the horse queen on his mother's. Did the assault on his mother directly result in her childbirth death or was there real dubiety as to Arthur's parentage? As already detailed the early Welsh literature referred to him as 'of two authors'. It may be that the annals and king-lists known to have been altered in the 12th century provided elements of truth concerning Arthur. What if 'Comgall' was actually Arthur of the Britons named in Gaelic after the western homeland of the Bear Folk? His death in 537 was one date given for the battle of Camlaan and Arthur's end. In the Brittonic or early Welsh language he was *'Artur'* the 'Bear'. The sculpted stones seem to record that he was heir to Cowal and Bute and the ancient overlordship already alluded to and sent away quickly from Dunadd with other North British children after the death of his mother. Could it be that the Black Horse at Montrose was Domongart seeking out his 'son'/son from the Britons? Perhaps he was appeased with the marriage of his son Gabran (possibly the youth at the base of the black horse (Emperor's Map), to an Angus princess? Dubiety over Arthur's parentage may have resulted in some leverage for the family who were involved in the overrunning of Dunadd (Note 5). Arthur's years of rule may have been 'without strife' if the period of his childhood is not considered.

Stone observation may provide another link in the hypothesis that 'Comgall' and Arthur was one and the same individual. In the *Senchus fer n-Alban* (Note 6) meaning the *Census of the Men of Alba* in which there is a listing of how many men could be mustered for rowing duties in the different regions/lordships of Argyll, the ruling kindred of Cowal and Bute was identified as *Crich Comgaill* rather than the dynastic term of 'cenel'. 'Crich' originates in the Old British word 'cruc' which means 'hill'. I have already alluded to representations of Arthur's death. From my research countless numbers of miniature sculptures locate the Bear's last resting place on a hill and so it seems possible that whoever wrote up the Senchus was using a more colourful dynastic term for this particular Argyll family.

If it was a given that the cenel Comgaill were direct descendants of Arthur it presumably may have had some bearing on what part this kindred played in the history of Dalriada and even perhaps later in the early development of the Scottish nation. Stone documented as related to the Epidii of the Kintyre peninsula and of the Bear Folk of Cowal, Bute and Alt Clut, placed at the head of a Brittonnic federation to free and defend lands between the Roman walls, married to an eastern Pictish princess, 'High Prince of Three Lands' and 'Emperor' too must have been an influential inheritance at the very least. James E. Fraser's book 'From Caledonia to Pictland Scotland to 795' gives a detailed analysis of the fate of the kindreds of Argyll and their Pictish, Brittonnic and and Anglo-Saxon political contemporaries in the decades and centuries after the death of Comgall.

Of a much much later time it is interesting to speculate whether evidence that there might have been challenges to the Scottish kingship in the 12th century was faintly linked to Arthurian blood ties. According to MacDonald (2002) these challenges have been a little explored area of Scottish history. He argued that the rebellions led by the MacHeths and the MacWilliams against the Canmore kings which were thought to be of no significance in fact were of a scale that would have posed a real threat. That they were dynastically motivated and strategically organised seems likely as the dates of insurrection were at times when the Scottish kings were most vulnerable. MacDonald argued that the ruthless crushing of these uprisings suggests that they were taken very seriously by the Canmore kings.

Although it may be possible to alter monastical records or annals to obscure events which may cause discomfort to the powerful at one time or another, it is more difficult to edit entire oral and literary traditions. From my observations of the stone narratives I would suggest that there was reference to the Bear's story in Gaelic stories and poetry. According to Clancy (1998) a narrative poem called 'The Birth of Aedan Mac Gabrain' written around 1060 by a Leinster poet for a Scottish audience would have been part of a large body of work about the Dalriadan king in the old Welsh and English as well as the Gaelic traditions. The royal wives of Gabran and Eochu who was an exiled Leinster king, gave birth on the same night, (Gabran's wife two daughters and the Leinster queen, two sons) and switched babies so that Aedan became son to 'horse-rich' Gabran but really was a son of the king of Leister. This 'two father' story seems no coincidence in its similarity to the 'two authors' aspect of Arthur's origin tale. As part of a tradition of narrative about Aedan it would be interesting to speculate as to the motive for this possible fudging or merging of identities. Is a changeling story about the Dalriadan king/lord supposed to enhance his entitlement to rule over the lands of the Forth and Tay as well as Atlantic Scotland? The poem describes his birth-place as near the Forth. Perhaps it was Guinnion.

What if the original narrative was the one told in stone about Arthur born around forty years earlier? As the world knows Arthur's story has gone through many permutations to the present day and it may have all started with the carved stones on the Lothian coast and the long-lived oral tradition of the North. The 10th century version would have been no different in reflecting the political and cultural facets of its time in the remaking of a hero's story in its own image (Note 7).

Arguably there were more allusions to the life of the Bear in some of the praise poetry concerned with Columba specifically. An early Gaelic poem attributed to Dallan Forgaill entitled *'Elegy for Colum Cille'* may be an example of this. As with other such poetry concerned with the enhancement of Columba towards sainthood, there was use of warrior terminology to portray him as a spiritual soldier in a comparative sense to make clear his superiority vis à vis the chieftains and warlords who were the secular leaders of men of his time (Markus 2007). However, according to Clancy (1998), this particular poem may have been very early indeed (possibly 597AD) and contains other perspectives on the saint not seen in later poetry. This 'highly wrought and often difficult poem' (Clancy 1998, p102) composed around sixty years after the death of the Bear became a treasured, much commented upon text within the Scottish church. Suspicions are raised sufficiently by some of the descriptions for a Stone Archivist to moot that Dallan Forgaill may have adapted or deliberately plagiarised an earlier work, perhaps a Brittonic bardic eulogy to Arthur, which could have been in circulation in the years after Arthur's interment. This does not seem too fantastical given the propensity of later generations to make a well regarded work their own. In the case of the early church there would perhaps have been the added satisfaction in supplanting a popular secular figure or saint with their own religious one. Some sense of this may be gleaned from following quotations from the elegy:

"For he has died to us, **the leader of nations who guarded the living'** (Verse I); 'By his mighty skill, **he kept the law firm. Rome was known, order was known'** (Verse IV) and 'In place of pomp, in place of splendour, he bestowed, **the pure descendant** of Conall ruled in his monastery" (Verse VIII) (My emphasis).

(From the *'Elegy for Colum Cille'* by Dallan Forgaill. Translation by Thomas O. Clancy in 'The Triumph Tree' (T.O. Clancy (ed) 1998 pp102-107))

There seems in these lines to be quite a direct focus upon facets of Arthur's career flagged up by Brittonic sculptors. The stones portray the Bear as overlord and leader of battles that secure a peace between different peoples. The very existence of the miniaturists informs of them living in well administered and stable societies whilst their detailed and sometimes colourful complexity stimulate visions of great wealth and imposing architecture. The reference to Columba's genealogy may be an oblique, perhaps vicious swipe at Arthur's beginnings. The case for this Gaelic elegy to have had its origins as a praise poem for the Bear seems even more likely when Columba, who was about 76 years old when he died (521-597) was in the same poem described thus:

"His lifetime was short,

Scant portions filled him" (Verse II)

(From *'Elegy for Colum Cille'* Translation by Thomas O. Clancy in 'The Triumph Tree' (T.O. Clancy(ed) 1998 p103))

Arthur of the Cauldron was to die at the battle of Camlaan in 537/9 having in all probability, not reached 40 years.

Amongst the pictorial stones of the 'Conspicuous Cape' there is a consistent story-line of intrigue, evil and tragedy surrounding the birth of a child within a great chieftain's household. There is no doubt that in Scotland's turbulent past there were many such stories in which a ruler was overthrown and the death of the innocents followed. In this one however the great Cauldron off the Isle of Jura had a prominent part. The little bear survived the whirlpool and this would have elevated him to something approaching god-like status himself. Dunadd, a fort of which apparently nothing is known before 500AD was stone-portrayed as held by a great bear chief/king. Today's archaelogists have made clear that a large Neolithic ceremonial centre lay in the landscape close by. The story stones through the use of totems and colour seem to link Dunadd to a ritual history thousands of years before Arthur's birth. The sea baby then was already special in having important relatives and in being born into such an auspicious land. His fateful place in the story of the people between the Walls was augmented further on some birth narrative stones in the mirroring of the details of his death and interment on another hill.

That such a powerful story apparently lost its place here in the 'North' or southern Scotland, seems to suggest that there may be a case for arguing that the circumstances surrounding the Bear's early life influenced what was recorded or perhaps written out of the narrative concerned with the future nation of Scotland. In such ancient times lettered documentation was the preserve of the Christian clerics. Whatever the motivations or circumstances for the absence of Arthur from written record, the lack of monastical ink matters little I think as Stone Archivist, compared to the vast numbers of people who must have visited the Conspicuous Cape to commemorate the hero's life and left behind the story of the Sea Baby of the Cailleach on the shores of the Forth. I have suggested that such an outpouring of adoration or respect for one man may have left its mark in the early literature of Scotland.

Chapter Notes

Note 1
Coincidentally perhaps, on contemporary marine maps this part of Sanda is known as the 'ship' ('Sanda' Wikipedia)

Note 2
From my observations vignette characters were usually presented as having human heads and the totemic animal heads that appear to mark their tribal/community origin was fashioned onto the back of these. The two animal-headed Kintyre figure so far is a one-off and as such suggests that the message being conveyed was not so much to do with identity but about motive. In this case what was probably being communicated was intrigue.

Note 3
The annals Tigernach and Ulster both document Comgall as having a 35 year reign, (Marsden 1997, p51).

Note 4
Coel Hen or Coil Hen was a mythological founder figure of the gene tree that linked many of the leading families of the Men of the North. He may have been one of the last Roman military commanders in the North who stayed to make the lands under his governance into a kingdom Morris (1973, p 54).

Note 5
Sharpe (2000, p55) noted that Adomnan, the 9th abbot of Iona and biographer of Columba, did not actually describe the ruling kindred of Dalriada as 'royal' but rather as of 'aristocratic descent' or 'tigerni' or lords.

Note 6
The *Senchas* is thought to have been drawn up in the mid 7th century (Sharpe 2000) and rewritten in the 10th.

Note 7
Of further interest is a reference within the Leinster poem to 'the most powerful eastern stone' which T.O.Clancy (translator and editor1998) interpreted as being the Stone of Scone (the Stone of Destiny upon which the kings of Scotland were traditionally crowned). However, stone

evidence suggests otherwise. Rather I would argue that it was the 'maen', the 'hill' of Welsh poetry, the 'Agned' from Nennius' list of Arthur's battles or just 'the Law' by North Berwickers. The pyamid stone on the edge of the plain of Lothian may have been identified in poetry four centuries after the death of Arthur. Further literary leakage from the Gaelic and old Welsh traditions that may provide corroboration for this particular topographical feature so central to many stone portrayals, will be explored in a later chapter.

Chapter 6: Over the Gannet's Bath, Arthur and the Gwyr Y Gogledd in the lands north of the Forth.

Stone Archivist

I hope I have convinced you dear Traveller, that the stone maps provide a complexity of narrative from the Uotadini. Of particular note for this chapter is the inclusion of the lands north of the Forth in Arthur's story. Those territories that I would hazard were being alluded to in the Anglo-Saxon Chronicle as *'over the gannet's bath'* (Swanton 1996, Peterborough Manuscript (975), p111). It seems very likely that the English chroniclers were making reference to the Forth Estuary as the Bass Rock is the world's largest single gannetry. Those who have taken a boat trip out from North Berwick can attest to the aptness of this old description. In the spring and summer thousands of these beautiful birds fill the sky and sea around the Rock. That there was an ancient shared story-line between the communities on each side of the river should not be surprising given that until relatively recent times rivers and estuaries must have figured strongly in the everyday lives of the majority of Scots. On the coast or inland, people knew their waterways. They had the knowledge of where and when to fish or cross or harness the flowing energy or even where to go after heavy rains to reap the harvest of what was washed down from the hills and mountains (Sommerville 1873,p31 and <u>Note 1</u>). Strategic estuary defence must have become a part of our ancestors' concerns too. From the Emperor's Map it is made clear that Fife was being fought over in Arthur's time.

Paper documentation from the North Berwick nunnery does reveal that the aristocracy and then the endowed religious orders, owned land simultaneously on both sides of the Forth. With land comes the income it generates and the employment of overseers whether secular or religious which seems to have led to individuals having roles or duties on both sides of the estuary. For example in 1380 William of Norberwik also known as William de Lundie was granted for life the vicarage of North Berwick. He also came to hold two posts as Vicar in East Fife at Crail and Lundin Links (Ferrier 1980). Had there been similar ownership and accompanying dual roles in place for hundreds of years before? Certainly such practices seem to have still lingered on hundreds of years later if the case of John Fall, member of a prominent Dunbar family in the eighteenth century, is any example. Fall, a successful merchant, managed to be Provost of Dunbar for part of the time that he was also councillor of Kilrenny (1779-1791), a royal burgh on the East Neuk of Fife (Forbes Gray 1938 and Note 2).

Aside from official positions there are likely to be other traces of social contact between the two communities that a relatively short boat journey would have facilitated. Whyte (2000) noted a significant number of people with the surnames 'Lothian' or 'Berwick' are to be found in the registers of Fife. Are these traces of a very ancient socio-cultural and political relationship between the opposite sides of the firth before the Scots turned away from the waterways as their main means of transport? Very faint paper glimpses may have stone corroboration. Indeed I should emphasise again that I have only sought out the former because of what I have observed on stone. The Emperor's Map I suggest, takes the viewer back to a time when a part of present day Fife was allied to its southern neighbour and presumably strategically important in the control/defence of the entrance to the Forth. Once again a topographical perspective assisted by stone-mapping will provide a window through which to look into the dark past navigating towards what has always been within reach yet remains unseen. Lost it seems to eyes unaccustomed to workmanship of magical intent.

By combining the topographic using the old maps and place-name research with any relevant stone work, Fife is revealed as having an interesting profile with regards to early history (See Map 7). It must be said first that the Emperor's Map representation of Fife and the coastal area of Angus is a faint shade of gold. Three districts have been more deeply coloured, two in Fife and one in Angus. At one viewing angle Fife takes on the shape of a large standing bear with his young at his feet. The presentation of this outline as an underlayer to events inscribed above it I think communicates that a people with a bear totem lived on these lands at some time distant to the main narrative of the map.

A tour of the physical features and place-names of this county and close by districts seems to provide a glimpse of a past linked to the Uotadini/Gododdin. Beginning at the mouth of the Tay River, Arthur and the Brittonnic delegation have already been identified. If you will recall dear Traveller, they were heading up the Tay towards present day Perth and were being greeted by a Christian monk. Nearby and a little to the north there was another vignette between the Britons and a Pictish feline force led by a young female charioteer with a male figure affixed to her side.

East of these scenes on the northern shores of Fife the Fifers look on to the Carse of Gowrie of eastern Perthshire and towards the estuary mouth, the lands of Angus. There, at the northern edge where the Tay meets the North Sea is one of the deeper gold areas. Its outline resembles the head of a deer and although it is only very roughly triangular in outline, I will use the shape as a convenient identifier in this archive. The triangle seems to emcompass the land adjoining Buddon Ness, called today Barry Links, as well as stretching 'north-east' of this headland to include the coastal plain of Angus reaching towards the Angus Mearns. One gaze there brought a feline high status figure to the fore.

Above the northern triangle in the 'north-east' of the Emperor's Map can be observed the profile of an amiable-looking bull on a tiny raised black plaque upon the surface of the map (ie can be seen with the naked eye). His mouth is open and tiny figures appear to emerge from it as well as a vignette of a boat journey towards the Fife coast. Look closer and the plaque is an amalgam of animal figures and with a shift in gaze, a three dimensional figure comes into sight. Strange to see on Scotland's shores, but the image is of a baboon standing on all fours looking down on a ship scene   As with other miniature sculpturing there are facets to the image which provide some details or identifiers to the person represented. In this case a sculpture has been attached to this animal's 'forehead'. It resembles a female deer (no antlers) and is a distinctive grey against the black. This additional identifier presumably makes clear his kinship links. In other words, I speculate that he may have been related by marriage or through his mother, to a people whose totem was the deer. This icon as it were, together with his sometimes bovine profile and open mouth suggests a particular location which I would hazard was Montrose and the lands between the North and South Esk Rivers in Southern Angus. The Glen Esk stag is still totemic in modern day Angus. The area in the past was home to large numbers of red deer. Today too, Angus is world famous for its black cattle. Along the Angus coastline it seems that it is the distinctive natural harbour of Montrose and 'mouth' of the South Esk that is evoked by the little black sculpture.

A hatted, blonde youth can be spotted 'above' or 'north' of this zoomorph. Perhaps it was a representation of Arthur. Beside the youth has been placed a young female cat/human in some sort of high status

118

headdress. The inference is that a marriage has taken place. Perhaps this was linked to the battle story set in the Caledonian forest. There are other crowned figures seated 'nearby','west' of 'black bull' and I wonder whether this scene was linked to an ancient inauguration site that is still remembered. This is the *King's Seat*, the remains of which is situated on the ridge out from *Dunsinane Hill, (Collace)* overlooking the Carse of Gowrie.

Another narrative strand north of the Tay seems to be in evidence in another morphic form that emanates in part from the friendly black bull. It is of a young warrior with some attendants on the corner edge of the map. The profile of an older man in white has been placed beside him. Another shape-shifting scene unfolds when, gazing at a downwards angle, the whole of this corner of the map forms into some sort of shelf on which several figures, (two high status males and several taller religious figures, (in long gowns) have been fashioned as taking part in some sort of greeting ceremony. It is a small group that includes a young white bear. Turn the stone through 180 degrees and what comes into view is a high status figure (wearing a cloak), holding a tiny baby standing some distance away but on the same 'level' with the black bull . These vignettes seem to suggest that this may be a portrayal of the the infant Arthur's story already referred to in the last chapter. Perhaps Arthur spent some of his childhood under the protection and tutelage of Angus chief(s) and associated Druids (Note 3). The zoomorphic image that emerges on the coast as the head of a dark aggressive/amiable horse with a body that is the head of a fair-headed young man seems to be part of that particular story. It may be no coincidence that there is a *Rossie Island* (from '*Hrossay*' meaning '*horse*') at the mouth of the Montrose Basin thought to be sourced to there being at one time, a Norse presence near the harbour ('Montrose' Wikipedia). Could the Viking settlers have heard the story of the little child Arthur being pursued or claimed by the Black Horse? There are more vignettes which must enlarge upon the ancient story of southern Angus but too many to include here.

More stone-gazing and across the Tay and opposite the Angus triangle/deer head there is jutting out of the north-easterly coast of Fife, the head of one of the standing bear's young (Note 4). Young bear and deer appear to be fixed in a kiss. It is also possible to see that the kiss scene amounts to two golden coloured approximate triangles with their apexes meeting. What seems to be communicated is that before the 'golden period' there had been been ties of marriage and blood between the outer estuary lands of Fife and Angus. There are faint sculpturings of tiny bears within the Fife shape. It is more obviously triangular and extends a little along the northern Fife coast from its 'westerly' base angle. This triangle appears to represent the vaguely triangular north-east part of Fife, on the northern side of the Eden Estuary roughly bounded by the *Motray Water* (see Map 7).

Beyond the Fife triangle there begins what looks to be an extensive conflict area which is to the west, north and south of it. It appears to take up what today is north-west Fife in the area of Newburgh; Auchtermuchty; the Howe of Fife and Falkland. The latter in 1745 (Moll 1745) was a substantial territory and would perhaps have included the Lomond (or Falkland) and Bishop Hills on its southern edge and the close by lands of Clarkmannanshire and Kinross and perhaps a portion of neighbouring southern Perthshire. Topographically this part of the country features the last of the Ochills which tail off into northern Fife and the Gask Ridge which is a 16km ridge of land north of the River Earn. The ridge itself has the remains of a line of Roman fortlets and watch towers which were part of what is called the Gask Ridge System. This was the Roman fortified land frontier which lay between the highlands and the lowlands of Scotland including Fife and the coastal plain of Angus. It consisted of what may have been an integrated signalling and glen blocker series of installations controlling access to the frontier areas. Woolliscroft(online 2012,p9) studying the field of view of the known remains of these, notes with regard to the Gask Ridge itself, that of the eleven known towers only two have any view to the north-east. All the others have 'superb views over Strathearn' and are designed to monitor in an east-west orientation. It seems therefore to have functioned as some sort of early warning system of incursions from this area in particular.

Like the fashioning of the ancient standing bear, the sculptor seems to have used a different form of presentation to separate off an event that took place before the campaigns of the Arthurian period. This part of the Emperor's Map is grey coloured and the sculptures which look like a multitude of tiny figures, some in twos as if engaged in hand- to- hand conflict and others, too many to detail, have been fashioned raised or proud. At one angle I thought I saw the head of an elongated grey cat emerging I would hazard from the Strathearn end of the vignette (Note 5). The overall effect is eye-catching now in the map's worn state, how much greater it would have been when the stone was fully enamelled. In amongst the scrum of activity and closer to the Fife end of the grey work, there is the head of a dark skinned man his mouth open as if caught in the moment of shouting 'Forward!' or 'Charge!' Accompanying him is the hint of a Roman soldier in the style of helmet he is wearing. On the northern edge of the the grey land, another Roman figure can be distinguished reclining in long robes beside a waterfall. This vignette placed as it is on the coast I think identifies it as Carpow, the Roman fort that stood guard at the entrance to the River Earn with a long view of the River Tay as it flows down to the estuary. Turning the Emperor's Map in such a way as to get a downward look onto the Fife golden triangular territory and it becomes a hill upon which I have distinguished another male figure. He has been presented as dressed in trousers and a three-quarter coat and sporting what looks to be a pigtail. He has been made facing westwards, perhaps looking down on the fray. Spookily enough dear Traveller, there is a *'Golden Hill'* (O.S. 59, 2000) close to the Grange of Lindores which must give some sort of view across the grey territory. Unlike the outlined bear there is no other superimposed narrative suggesting perhaps that whatever the conflict was, it had had a continuing impact on the region. It may be that what was being inferred was that the grey vignette was an important extended boundary-danger zone where conflict still took place in Arthur's time between the Romano Britons and the 'barbarians'/non-Romanised peoples. From the field of vision research of the Gask Ridge, the danger to Arthurian Fife was directly opposite, in and west of the 'grey land'.

I wonder if the grey portrayal was designed to represent the disastrous defeat of the Caledonian alliance by the Roman occupiers under Agricola at the battle of *Mons Graupius* in 83/84AD. According to Tacitus, Agricola's son-in-law, the Caledonians had their frontline 'on the plain' and the rest 'seemed to mount up the sloping hillside in close-packed tiers' (Tacitus 'The Agricola' in Yeoman 2005, p5). With the advantage of height the Caledonians were at first doing well throwing missiles and finding their mark but as they began to descend to complete their victory Agricola had his retreating forces turn and attack them from behind. The Caledonians were forced into hand-to -hand combat which unlike the Legion they were ill equipped to do. A rout ensued in which the Caledonians were pursued, ambushed and slaughtered in huge numbers, ten thousand in Tacitus' account. The site of this famous battle has never been definitively identified. However, through a combination of stone and paper map reading and etymology the site of this conflict may come into view. The root of 'Graupius' is the old Welsh word *'Crwb'* which means *'hump'* (Moffat 2005, p265). The word does not suggest the sharp outlines of our mountains rather a more rounded but still a significantly bulky height much like the Ochill Range. Stand on the edge of Airth and look over the narrowing Forth to Clarkmannanshire and you will, I think agree dear Traveller, that the old name best describes these imposing hills.

From my observations the main locus or start of the battle seems to have been in the *Lumbennie* area (Note 6 and see Map 8). This place-name is thought to mean 'bare plain or field near or on a conspicuous hill' the latter being most likely one of the surrounding Ochills which includes the *Baw Hill*. This hill may actually have been called 'Bow' as there is a Bow Burn nearby (Taylor and Markus 2010). The Lumbennies (Wester and Easter) with the Lumbennie Hill between them are a few kilometres south of the coastal town of Newburgh and the ruins of Carpow. Further place-names that point to this quiet part of Fife being the site of bloody conflict may be traced to a hilly ridge on the Wester Lumbennie farm called *'Clevitch'* which is thought to be from the old Gaelic meaning *'swordland'* (Angus Watson 1856 OS cited inTaylor and Markus 2010). Further corroboration of stone narrative is suggested in a place-name with the same meaning. *'Clevage'* (and Clevage Hills and Clevage Loch) lies between the *Water of May* and *Dunning* in Perthshire 25 kilometres from Wester Lumbennie. It is only about 5 kilometres east of one of the sites conjectured as being the battle site- Duncrub (Fraser 2009, p21). The position and distance between these two swordlands and Tacitus' description of the pursuit of the Caledonians into the 'trackless wilds' (Tacitus 'Agricola' Yeoman 2005, p7) aligns very well with the grey sculptured hand- to-hand combat on the Emperor's Map.

Returning to the Lumbennie area I would suggest that other place-names hone in on the Graupius conflict. It may be significant that there are three places called *'Colzie'* triangularly situated just south of the Lumbennie Hill with two of them on the *Glassart Burn*. I think 'Colzie' may signify a place suitable for ambush (Watson 1926,pp143 and 489) and I wonder whether this is a trace of the Roman strategy at Mons Graupius, of instigating a cordon of forces that would drive the defeated, retreating Caledonians into a trap enabling the slaughter of as many of them as possible. It is worth noting that the Glassart is also known locally as the *Beggars' Burn* in the area of the Lumbennie Hill. An alternative and not unrelated interpretation is that Colzie and *Colessie* a few kilometres east, are of the same origin (Taylor and Markus 2010) and that it is possible that this part of northern Fife was known for a particular topography, as an area of tight corners and hidden recesses. Driving there is a little like being on a very gentle version of a rollercoaster where much of the more distant surroundings cannot be seen most of time.   The association that 'Colzie' has with the topographical and ambush seems to be further remembered in the Glassart being known as the 'Calsay' as it flows through Auchtermuchty. This little town lies at the foot of the little upland area.

Another interpretation of 'Colzie'/'Colessie' given by Taylor and Markus (2010) is that it may mean 'back' or 'corner/neuk' of a *waterfall*. There is a *Fountain Wood* a little east of the Lumbennies and intrigueingly if you remember dear Traveller, the Emperor's Map situates a recumbent Roman figure beside a waterfall (possibly Carpow) on the edge of the grey battle scene. The Roman fort is about three kilometres from the Lumbennie Hill. All and all from a Stone Archivist's perspective the Lumbennie area fits well as the site for the Caledonian battle against the Romans. Whoever he was, the man in the three-quarter coat on the Golden Hill most likely would have had a clear view of the main action.

It seems likely that the killing of thousands of Caledonians was remembered in the place-naming in northern Fife. Whether Graupius was further commemorated may be considered with respect to what is known as the *Cross MacDuff*. Identified as a cross or boundary marker by the RCAHMS (1933) the remnant of this stone is situated near the pass through the hills at Whinnybank on Ormiston Hill.   From the Whinnybank there is a superb panoramic view of the confluence of the Rivers Tay and Earn where they enter the estuary of the Tay at Carpow. The cross stood overlooking the Tay about a mile south-west of Newburgh. The Whinnybank pathway leads to the very same locality as the Roman-Caledonian battle. Thought to have been placed there in the 8th century it seems possible a later generation may have erected a memorial of that event. According to Laing (1872) the monument was probably destroyed during the Reformation leaving only the base.

You may remember that in an earlier chapter I asked you to accept that the North Britons distinguished some Picts or 'barbarians' as the 'Cats'? I have already described several feline figures worked into the Emperor's Map. In studying this north-eastern corner of the map where the greatest amount of 'cat history' appears to be stone-documented, an elaboration on this concept seems appropriate. Although a people

123

known as the 'Cats,' presumably a reference to the wild cat, are thought to have lived in the far north on the Shetland Isles anciently called the *'Innse Catt'* and on the Scottish mainland in Caithness and Sutherland Moffat (2005, p213), it seems pictorially clear that the Brittonic peoples between the old Roman walls may have used the term more generically. The use of blue colouring of the feline signifiers is of further interest. It sent me on a word-search for traces of this ancient signage within the older and the contemporary Scots language and what I have found so far does appear to resonate with the meaning of *'picti'*. As already detailed the Latin term was probably from a native British word meaning *'painted ones'* and may have alluded to painted skin or clothes (Note 7). The Scots word *'bluncat'* means *'grey or greyish blue cloth'* whilst *'blunochs'*, sourced to Aberdeenshire, are *'clothes'. '* There seems to have a Fife saying, *'putting the buchloch on people'* (Whyte and Whyte 1974 .Kist of Riches ID. 36963). *'Catter'* is either a *'chief attribute'* or *'some kind of cloth'*! A *'cateran'* means a *'Highland marauder(s)'* (SCD 1987). Is it possible that the actual North British/P- Celtic word for the Pictish peoples or their warriors may be traced to word meanings from Fife and Angus to do with violence in these words *'catterbatter'*, and *'cattie wurrie'* (*'a quarrel, disagreement'* and *'a violent dispute'* respectively (SCD 1985). Could it be that these Scots words are part of a folk memory of ancient turbulent times?

Violence, distinctive clothing and the cattish habit of waiting for an opportunity to pounce on a prey seemed to be rolled into one clever devise by the ancient sculpturers to signify a community or communities of people threatening the territories of the Romano-Britons. I can only conjecture of course with regard to the etymological links but what is stone clear is that the crafts people of the 'Conspicuous Cape' represented those pressing towards Fife from the direction of Strathearn, as well as threatening East Lothian and as we shall see the southern coast of Fife, as the 'Cats'. It may be fruitful to look more closely at the pictorial and written feline descriptors that may exist. In other words the people labelled 'cats' were opportunistic hunters/raiders and were distinguished by their Romanised Brittonnic 'prey' by their own particular (blue) clothing just as tartan cloth identifies specific clan membership today. Further identifiers may have related to ethnic origin tales or widely known behaviours of an individual leader or force (Note 8).

In the 'Black Book of Carmarthen' which is the earliest Welsh poetry to have Arthurian references, and in which interestingly, given the black horse threatening Montrose and the Horse Folk of Kintyre there is a narrative called *'Triads of the Horses'*, has a poem which alludes to a *'Padul's Cat'* or *'the clawing cat'* (Sims-Williams 1991,p45). To an archivist of story stones this poem, referred to as *'Pa-gur'*, seems to be about the activities of Arthur and the Men of the North in the lands of the Forth and Tay estuaries (Note 9). The site of Arthur's 10th battle, Traeth Tryfrwyd, was referred to in the poem and according to Sims-Williams the name means *'very speckled shore'*. Stone observation brought me to the view that the shoreline of north and east Edinburgh was being held by the Picts/Cats presumably lots of them, and Welsh poetry seems to corroborate this. I am suggesting that the 'speckle' may have been an allusion to those who held the shoreline, in other words those people or forces who were distinctive in dress or appearance. Perhaps it was a word that was much used within the oral tradition of Northern Britain to denote the 'picti'. Verification of this may lie in the Scots word *'kenspeckle'* that means *'easily recognisable'*; *'a mark by which a person may be known or recognised'*. A word that is still in use in the Lothians and Lanarkshire (CSD 1987) 'kenspeckle' seems like a long forgotten link with Arthur's time and his adversaries, the blueish or greyish Cats.

An alternative interpretation as to who was recognisable comes from the use of the orange/brown dye in some sculptures of this shoreline and the coastal 'Craggenmarf' to pick out a substantial number of figures from a complexity of other outlined people. Apart from being of the Bear People or their lineage, were they physically distinguished by being red-haired? Was Traeth Tryfrwyd or Trat Trevriot (Giles's translation) named for there being a settlement with a predominantly freckled populace?

From a small number of sculpted stones that I have come across recently another connection to the poetic description seems a possibilty as when they are viewed from a few inches away they are finely speckled in appearance. A closer look reveals a myriad of vignettes giving the impression that the Edinburgh coast was a very eventful place in those 'dark' times. Was 'very speckled' a term used by the story tellers of the Old North to convey the presence of many people and events? Did these words already belong to the language of the oral tradition and were eventually carried over verbatim into early Welsh poetry?

Continuing a little longer with sixth century colouring codes, the stone signifiers may suffuse some more light behind the dark windows of 6th century Scotland. I wonder if there is room for another name for the Black Bull/ Baboon/'crested one?' From *'Dub'* meaning *'the black one'*, originates the Scottish surname *'MacDuff'* from the Gaelic meaning *'son of Dub'*. Bannerman (1993) pointed out that unlike many Gaelic patronymics 'MacDuff' (Mac-Duib) was rarely used as a first name for obvious reasons (ie it means *'son of the Devil'*). Remembering the Black Bull/Baboon of Angus and the likelihood of its high status kindred migrating south to Fife, it is surely significant that through history the name MacDuff was closely associated with those who ruled in that region as well as the kingdom of Scotland itself with a goodly number of the MacDuff kindred becoming kings themselves including Kenneth III (997-1005) ('Cinaed mac Duib'). The earls of Fife (MacDuff) and Strathearn were together involved in the crowning of Alexander III at Scone 13th July 1249. Such honours were bestowed upon nobles who may have had some claim to the Scottish throne (Bannerman 1993, pp22-23). Such a situation seems to suggest that later generations who were linked to the Black Bull of northern Angus may have come to hold very influential positions in the medieval Scotland of the 13th century. In Fife 'the law of Clan MacDuff' was acknowleged and enforced, contributing to the development of medieval Scottish society (Bannerman 1993, p21 and Note 10). Indeed this was a time when it was the practice of Scottish kings to send their heirs to learn kingship from the Earls of Fife. The Emperor's Map hints at a territory made up of several sub-kingdoms and possibly two overlordships which may have been allied to or actually representative of the power residing at Iudeu. It may be that Fife had much experience with kingly ways of doing. Could it be that the Scottish kings were acknowledging an ancient time still remembered, when this part of the country was organised, at least to some extent, into a number of coherent administrative entities?

Given the Arthurian focus of the Emperor's Map, the young man in the north-east 'angle' of the northern triangle may have been Arthur. He was fashioned with an elderly man in white directly west of the bull/baboon and the occasional glimpse of a crocodile. Montrose, the most northern coastal town in Angus is situated on the north bank of the Montrose Basin, on a promontory between the North and South Esk rivers. The estuary of the latter forms the Basin, its mud flats a food heaven for birds that is replenished twice daily by the tidal inflow from the North Sea. It is home to many Mute Swan and was once called more aesthetically the *Loch of Swans*. An earlier town was situated on the south-eastern edge of the Basin. Where the South Esk enters the sea, now the site of the present day harbour was once a Norse settlement called *'Stroma'* which means *'Tide race river'* an appropriate name given the rapidity of the water flow in and out of the Basin. Archaeological research has found evidence of human settlement there in the period 2500-800BC. Edwina Proudfoot (cited in Montrose History Society 2004) has posited that structures discovered at old Montrose may have been part of a much wider Neolithic ritual landscape in the countryside surrounding the estuary.

From a stone archivist's perspective paper maps for this part of Angus document traces of an ancient past that have similarities with the Lothian coast and Fife as represented in Uotadinian art. In particular is the presence of place-names that locate land that is *'white'* or *'bright'* near strongholds. In the case of Montrose and its environs this arrangement can be identified as focused upon the territory of *'Dun'* on the north-west side of the Basin. *'Dun'* or *'Dinne'* meaning *'fortified hill'*, is unusual in there being no other name attached. Perhaps this signified its importance to the people of Montrose and I would conjecture of its place in the oral tradition. Strategically situated on high ground close to the mouth of the South Esk, this strength on the hill may have been a very effective block to raiders coming from the open sea or from the upper reaches of the Esk itself. There is also a folk tale with a distinct Arthurian flavour that is associated with Dun called 'The sword in the Stone'! Although concerned with the time of the Crusades the story line may be closer to a 6th century Arthur than those concocted later.

Brychan or Brachan is thought to have been an Irish prince whose name may be associated with the Angus town of *Brechin* (Watson 1926, p112) a few miles west of Dun. The vignette of the cloaked figure holding the tiny baby Arthur seems to have been positioned in the vicinity of that ancient little city. Perhaps there was a kindred link there for the orphaned child for it to be chosen as place of safety when he was taken to the east of the country. A further area for Arthurian conjecture lies with one of Brychan's many progeny. From the Welsh genealogies one of his daughters, Luan or Leian became the wife of Gabran, Lord of Dalriata in Scotland from 537AD. Various ancient sources give versions (Gouerin; Goureran Goverine) of his name that appear to have been the origin of *Gowrie* (Watson 1926), the district west of the northern 'golden triangle'. Is it possible, that Gabran, who died circa 559 and Luan were the high-status couple seated on the King's Seat at Dunsinane? Was this marriage the means by which the wonder child of the Cauldron remained with the Gwyr y Gogledd of southern Scotland? Brittonnic marital links might explain why their son Aedan mac Gabran, heir to the western lordship in Argyll is known to have fought a battle in neighbouring *Circhenn* (Angus and Mearns) in 596. Aside from his relationship with the territories north of the Tay there may have been another obligation or entitlement touched on in the last chapter, that might have brought Aedan to a fight on the eastern seaboard- Iudeu.

Crafted stone and ancient poetry from the Pictish origin legends may be journeying through time together in the following verse...

"Unisnem the name of the seer; he would search for the way of favour; He was sage to their warriors, Crus son of Cirig the Weak (?) (Crus the Weak, son of Cirig?)"

(From 'Pictish Sourcebook: Documents of Medieval Legend and Dark Age History' Calise 2002, p61)

Probably there is no connection but there was an 'Ulissen' (Edward1678) which was called 'Usantown' by (Moll 1745) on the southern side of Montrose and the South Esk, near Ferryden.

On old and contemporary maps of the Tay Estuary the details of its distinctive nature in the form of extensive sand banks and shallows may hold vestiges of how the people of much earlier times may have experienced its turbulent waters. The largest river in Scotland, its source tracked to Ben Lui in the west of Scotland, the Tay has the largest output of fresh water in the British Isles, draining 6000 square kilometres of land. Of particular interest is the Tay Mouth. Here unlike the sheltered inner estuary, the Tay Mouth is subject to strong currents. On the south side the Abertay shoals combined with sand banks extend out into the estuary mouth for a distance of 6kms (Bates et al 2004). On the north coast, east of Buddon Ness and reaching out into the Tay Mouth are the Gaa Sands. In Adair's 1703 mapping of the 'Frith and River of Tay' the entrance to the estuary seems partially gated by a submerged sand bank called the 'Cross Sands' almost linking the Gaa with the Abertay features.

Heading southwards, down the eastern seaboard of the Fife triangle are the sand lands of Tentsmuir separated from the rest of coastal east Fife by the *River Eden*. The River Eden or Edin (Moll 1745) is one of two main rivers in Fife, the other being the Leven. It has its source on the West

Lomond (or Falkland) Hill and flows eastwards through Cupar, the old county town of Fife which lies at the foot of Tarvit Hill. The 'right hand' angle of the Fife triangle, possibly located at the mouth of the Eden at Leuchars, has a zoomorphic signifier which depending upon the tilt in the observer's gaze, provides at least three different images. One is the head (no neck showing) of a chieftain with a feline appearance. His headgear conveys the impression of a ruler of some sort. A slight change of gaze and the small head of a young man can be seen. He seems to be hiding or is behind something, perhaps a bush or rushes given the meaning of *'Leuchars'* is *'rushes'* from the Gaelic *'luachar'* (Nicolaisen 2001, p71). On the Angus facing side of this sculpture there is a large whiteish face with no neck and his headgear morphs into several figures. There are other figures around this hatted cat suggesting more detailing perhaps of the history of wars/migrations of the Cat People. Clearly there is much to narrate about this corner of the map. The white miniature also morphs into a marriage scene with the couple facing the Angus lands.

In his analysis of Celtic place-names and the ancient territorial division of Scotland Watson (1926, pp108-109) identified the province of Cirech (or Circhenn) as meaning 'crest-headed'. It seems that the stone pictorial of the deer-crested baboon/bull aligns with this old name. In the Pictish Chronicle *'Crus mac Cirig, Crus son of Cirech'* was the chief warrior of the Cruithnigh' (Picts). A further name associated with Angus and the Mearns was *'Gergenn'* ('Girgin') and the 'plain of Gergenn'. Watson (1926 p109) noted that in Irish the name *'Gerrchenn'* meant *'short head)'* and that there was a Gerrgenn who was father of a warrior called *Muinremur* (mac Gerrchinn) meaning *'thick-neck'.* Again I would suggest that some remnant of the stone narrative of north-east Fife seems to have been remembered long enough for it to be written down.

Close to where the Eden becomes an estuary at *Guardbridge* ('*Gherbridge*' on Gordon1642/Pont NLS) is the town of *Leuchars* (see Map 7). On the Emperor's Map it may be the location of the complex zoomorph already detailed. I would argue that what this intricate work seems to convey is that in the Arthurian period the Picts were marrying into and going on to rule within the golden (Brittonnic/Romano British) territories. Significant dynastic blood ties were being made. That such connections were stone documented must surely have signified their importance to the Northern Britons. Arguably such alliances may have been part of a strategic defence/peace-making policy.

Leaving the territory of the golden triangle behind and continuing southwards towards the south-east corner of Fife or the *'Neuk'* there are the remnants of some sort of walled defence or rampart of unknown date, called the *'Dane's Dyke'*. It consists of earthworks with an inner core of stone (RCAMCS 1933) which originally stretched for half a mile across the promontory of Fifeness.   Roughly a mile and a half south-westwards is situated the ancient town of *Crail*, (once *Caraile*, the *'car'* meaning *'fort'* Watson 1926, p369).   One sculptured miniature I have found portrays an ancient settlement at Crail which features bears and birds and several non-native species. Crail, (*'Careill'* on Gordon's map (1642)) which could mean *'corner fort'* is a small, picturesque town which has a long known history. It was once the administrative centre of a royal constabulary which it is thought extended from *Putikin Burn (Water of Kenly)* (Rennie 2008) to the *Kincraig Point*, a few miles from Largo. The town was a place of influence before the reign of David I (1124-1153) and that king had its castle as one of his residences. In the Middle Ages it was an important trading port before it was granted royal burgh status by Robert I in 1310.   The town had rights over all the ports within the boundaries of the old Constabulary right up until the 16[th]century (Rennie 2008).

The harbour, the subject of countless cards and calendars, is accessed from the town's main thoroughfare by a steep road and as it turns down towards the once busy port, there is another path that follows the wall of the old castle. On this walkway there is to the left, the high wall of the old castle and to the right, a sheer drop to the sea. On the Emperor's Map there are several figures bunched close together with bright headgear. Another stone seems to reveal a community that in Arthurian times was a royal centre as the head of a white swan has been clearly delineated in the whitened stone 'neuk'. Zoomorphing out of a surface lateral to this vignette is the form of a crocodile (jaws bound). In a later chapter I will attempt an explanation for the presence of this animal. For now I would argue that it is a pictorial vestige from a much, much earlier time that suggests perhaps that Crail was the site of a kingship or 'chair' almost two thousand years before the time of the Bear's wars.   Various totems within the vignette point to a shared history between Crail and the Fife Ness area and those ruling on the Conspicuous Cape of East Lothian long before Arthur.

Three miles westwards along the coast from Crail are a row of fishing settlements situated within a mile or two of each other. These are:

Cellerdyke; *Anstruther*; *Pittenweem* and *St Monans*, each having a burn flowing through and out into the Forth. Approximate to these places on the Emperor's Map a row of king-like figures has been fashioned suggesting the presence of small sub-kingdoms. Moving further westwards the land closest to the East Lothian coast begins some miles past St Monans where the coast line becomes more sharply indented. Adair's (1684) map has a settlement called *Ardross* (Watson p496, *'height of cape'* old Welsh *'rhos'* means *'heath'* or *'moor'*) but he also marks the inland area in this way too so perhaps part of it was known as the *'moor of promontories'* as there is (east to west): *Elie Ness*; *Kinlargoness; Rindon* (from rind top/point or rhyn point/ promontory) Watson (1926, p495)) and *Kingcraig*. Adair's map also documents the pilgrimage route across the Forth which seemed to include other landing places in this area apart from Earlsferry. The promontories end at the curved eastern part of Largo Bay in which the town of Largo is situated.

The *River Leven* the other main river in Fife empties into the Forth west of *Largo Bay*. This river has a good number of tributaries some of which can be sourced in old maps to the many lochs or 'beths' or bogs that characterised the topography of the county in the period prior to the agricultural and industrial 'improvements' of the 18th century onwards. More than a thousand years before due to a warmer and wetter climate a greater degree of wateriness must have existed. Travelling by the rivers must have been the norm. The Leven is some sixteen miles long and is the only outlet for Loch Leven which lies within what was Kinross-shire (now part of the administrative district of Perth and Kinross). In past times, due to its 300ft downward flow from the loch, the river had many mills along its banks. *Leven* comes from the old Celtic river name *'Lemona'* which transformed into Gaelic is *'leamhain'* meaning *'elm water'* (Watson 1926). The name of course suggests the river was tree-lined, perhaps within a forest and many of the surrounding place-names provide an inkling of how watery and wooded central Fife may have been in the time of the Bear's battles.

On the north-west side of Loch Leven, are the already mentioned Bishop Hills, their slopes forming a valley with the two Lomond Hills. According to Moll's map (1745) these hills were the *'Lomonds of Falkland'*. A plateau of around 350 metres in height lying between these two beacon hills was occupied in the Iron Age and traces of stone fashioning are still evident. The extinct volcanic peaks are a distinctive feature on the northern horizon for those living on the southern shores of the Forth

Estuary. Close to these hills and bounded by the River Eden a few miles north and the River Leven a little south lies *Falkland* and *Kettle* which includes what must have been quite an extensive wood. So we have come full circle Dear Traveller and returned to the raised and grey coloured part of the Emperor's Map.   Place-names may help to corroborate my interpretation that a big Roman battle took place there and that in Arthur's time it was a dangerous borderland, or debatable land. According to Johnston (online access 07/05/12) *'falk'* may be Gaelic in origin from *'faile'* meaning *'peril'* or from *'falaichi'* meaning *'to hide'*.

Moving my gaze a little 'south' on the Emperor's Map within what must be approximately, the territory bordered on two sides by the Eden and the Leven there have been fashioned bear heads. The largest of these appears to be in the eastern region of the Eden Valley. There is a large bear's head facing eastwards approximately in the centre of Fife. A little 'south'of this a seated chieftain figure appears in trouble from the variety of faces behind him and most significantly, the neck of a languishing/dying swan lying over the arm of his chair. There are also faint outlines of other smaller bears. Clearly I think Arthur and his forces were involved in a conflict in the central lands of east Fife, an area of rolling hills and fertile plain today. There is a 9th or 10th century poem called 'The Fall of Rheged' which is thought to have been amongst the last of the Old Welsh literature written in Northern Britain (Clancy 1998 p152) which I think might be associated with this contested territory. The poem concerns the death of North British leader Urbgen or Urien (modern Welsh version) of *Rheged* and harks back to the heroic times of the Men of the North. Here are two extracts:

"A head I bear in my hand's hard grasp: Bountiful lord, he once ruled a land; Prydain's pillar-head, it was removed."

and...

"This hearth, a hen scratches it: Hardship could not harm it

 While Owain and Urien lived,

This pillar, and that one there,

More common, once, around them War-band's revels, and path to reward".

(From *'The Fall of Rheged'* (9th or 10th century). Translation by Joseph P. Clancy in 'The Triumph Tree' (T. O.Clancy (ed) 1998 pps: 154; 157 respectively))

'Pillar' was a term for a great warrior or leader in this tradition of poetry and it is used as such in the first extract. In the second however, use of the word seems to relate to something in the landscape. There are known to have been six stone circles and twenty one standing stones in the Fife, Kinross-shire and neighbouring Clarkmannanshire (RCAMCS 1933 and Note 11). There are also place-names which identify stones standing in the landscape. Fife is recorded as having three places called *'Pitcorthie'*. According to Watson (1926) this name is from the old and mid Gaelic *'coirthe'* meaning *'pillar stone'*. On Gordon's (1642) map there was an *Easter* and *Wester Pitcorthie*, although it seems, according to the 1933 Inventory that only the former stone exists, a mile or two north of Inverkeithing in Dunfermline parish and two east of the River Leven in the parishes of Carnbee and Kilrenny (see Map7). Could it be that the 'pillars' of the Welsh/North British poem refer to these same stones? In the 'Book of Taliesin' there is a poem called 'Ercwlf', Welsh for 'Hercules' which I suspect may have been a praise poem for Urien's son Rhun. Rhun is thought to have been a religious man and the poem refers to Ercwlf as 'chief of baptism'. In the poem there is a reference to the 'four pillars of equal length' edged with gold that

"Will not dare a threatening,

A threatening will not dare"

(From 'Arthur and the Britons in Wales and Scotland' Skene/Bryce 1988, p120)

These words seem to be another reference to the Arthurian-linked territories within the Pitcorthies of southern Fife and may place one of Urien's kin in Fife.

I have already mentioned the crafting of 'magical' 3-dimensional effects in cup-fashioned stones. From my observations these had a commemorative function, displaying the features of loved ones. The cup markings on the Fife pillar stones were described as 'scattered indiscriminately', (RCAMCS 1933, pxxxi). I would like to argue that such a distribution may mean they were fashioned on site whenever there was loss of life nearby. I am positing that such stones, which had a much earlier significance, were perhaps brought into use by later generations involved in deadly conflict. There are examples of place-names linked to stone elsewhere in Scotland but with regard to the military movements signified on the Emperor's Map, is it possible that these particular poetic and sculpted works were focused on the same remembered history of the Men of the North?

West of the Leven is more indistinct but my visual impression is of a mix of 'heads' - cats and bears. However, there is no doubt of a Cat/Pictish presence south-west of the Leven Mouth as there has been sculpted a very large cat figure lying as if half under the edge of the land. Why in such a position you may wonder but this is a coast which is dotted with caves hence the place-names Pittenweem, *East* and *West Wemyss* or 'Weems' (Blaeu 1654) 'weem' being P-Celtic for 'caves' (Watson 1926). The stone cartographer was being very specific it seems in pinpointing where the Cat/Picts were during the Arthurian campaigns. Such a location and stone presentation suggests they may have engaged in guerrilla attacks upon the inhabitants of southern Fife, west of the Leven, in the area of the Forthridge Muirs and the river valley of *Strathora* or the *River Ore*. In this vicinity there are the modern day towns of *Cowdenbeath*; *Cardenden*; *Lochgelly*; *Ballingry*; *Kelty* and *Lochore*.

Of further significance in piecing together what was happening in Fife in Arthurian times, there is on the Emperor's Map a small golden coloured plaque of zoomorphic figures situated in the west part of the Forthridge Muirs. It seems to represent a district that included the plateau on which the present day town of Inverkeithing stands and the hill town of Dunfermline about three miles further north, delineated in a slightly darker hue. The amalgam produces a kingly profile that faces westwards with a smaller scene below of a high status couple with little children including a little bear. The vignette stretches eastwards along the coast. The outline of the latter resembles the head of another crocodile with its jaws bound. The same creature emerges from the king at Dunfermline. Remembering the white sculpted scene at Crail and the accompanying crocodile, close connections with the East Neuk such as ties of blood from very ancient times, seemed to be flagged up. With a slight change of gaze the darker part of the plaque becomes a magnificent miniature bear facing eastwards. A further scene at Dunfermline that includes a tiny chiselled enclave to one side of the plaque is of a young boy, presumably Arthur, facing a dark haired man. These portrayals seem to infer that the baby- and boyhood of Arthur was centred in this part of Fife

134

Anyone who has looked over the garden wall of the old Friary Hospitium of Inverkeithing could imagine the strategic power of holding this rock. A protective ridge above it in the west (*Castlelandhill*) and the *Ferry Hills* to the south with the Forth and a wide open view on its eastern edges must have made these heights a great prize. The people on the plateau would have overlooked the *Forthridge Muirs* and the *Keithing Burn* which flows into the Forth at the town's natural double harbour. The narrowing estuary between the Fife and West Lothian coastlines as well as the roughly mile long stretch of water between North and South Queensferry seem to have been important crossing points more than five hundred years before a ferry was sponsored by Malcolm Canmore's queen, Margaret, if my interpretation of the Emperor's Map is accurate (Note 12).

Inverkeithing has an ancient history probably earlier than the fifth century saint, St Erat or Erhad or Erthad who is known to have been baptised by St Ternan and had become a missionary to 'the heathen Picts' (Ora et Labora 06). In Inverkeithing there is a well named after him close to the old parish church. The various names associated with the saint are thought to be dialectic variations of St Yrchard. Up until the early twentieth century Inverkeithing was made up of two parishes, Inverkeithing and Rosyth. Before 1164 it was Inverkeithing rather than North Queensferry that was linked in records with the ferry passage across the Forth. On paper its beginnings were not greatly documented. It had been a burgh before 1159 and when William the Lion granted the town a charter (between 1165 and 1178) he was only confirming what lands and powers the burgh aldermen already had. What is particularly significant with regard to the strategic position of the plateau is a further charter given to the town burgesses with regard to demanding toll.

"to draw toll, customs, and all dues pertaining to the burgh, between the water of Leven and the water of Devon and between the middle of the Forth and the large stone standing beyond the mill of Ell horth (Milnathort)"

(From 'The Story of Inverkeithing and Rosyth' Stephen 1938, p15)

This may, like the earlier charter, be a trace of the ancient influence of Inverkeithing in post-Romano times. This was the land bounded by the *Moss Morvin* (Gordon, 1642) (Morran today) on the east side of the Forthridge Muirs, a marshland that may have been a good deal larger in wetter ancient times given the many burns as well as the tributaries of the River Ore and Loch Leven documented in the 17th century. The burns and bogs and 'damp' places named on early maps flag up the difficulties for any enemy incursion. In addition, according to the Emperor's map there was some sort of coastal fort to the west of Inverkeithing that would have been perhaps some defence against raid. It seems likely that this part of West Fife had an ancient landscape that demanded guerrilla tactics from any enemy. The position of the cat on the coast seems all the more significant. Interestingly rising above *Loch Ore* is *Benarty* Hill thought to be named in commemoration of Arthur. Once a year on its flat summit, before the increased amount of fencing reduced their numbers and importance, shepherds and their families from all over Fife and neighbouring counties had a festival lasting several days (Chambers 1870).

Dunfermline was once the capital of Scotland. Malcolm (III) Canmore, King of Scots (1058-1093) had his residence there. His second wife Queen Margaret, a Saxon princess was to become Scotland's only royal saint. She founded a Benedictine priory in Dunfermline and promoted the pilgrim route to St Andrews by giving free passage across the Forth. Her son David I built the great abbey of Dunfermline. From the 11th to the 16th century Scottish royalty were buried there including Robert the Bruce. King Charles I was born in the royal palace close by. The stone map sculpture suggests a much older history than the times of these well known historical figures.

There may be written corroboration of the Arthurian pictorials of Inverkeithing and Dunfermline which corresponds with the former's area of influence in medieval times. In an Irish source there was a description of a place called *'Comgellaig'- Comgell's (for Comgall?) place or hollow* (Faclair.com) that was described as being between the 'Ochil upland' and the 'sea of Guidi'(Fraser 2008 p10 citing W. Reeves 1864 and A. O. Anderson 1908). It is a description which fits well with the territory stretching from the River Devon over to the north-east edge of Loch Leven (Milnathort) that was subject to the levy-raising powers of the burgesses of medieval Inverkeithing. If Comgall was Arthur of the Britons, which seems quite likely from what could be deduced from the Sea Baby narrative, the multiple vignettes from the stone map appear to give a more specific location for his home in West Fife- the lands close to and including the heights of Inverkeithing and Dunfermline.

A few miles further up the Forth is the *Torryburn/Crombie* part of the Fife coastline which, according to the Emperor's Map seems to have been part of the strife in and close to the Ochills already detailed. This portion of the map is also grey and has raised sculptures fashioned on it which seem to progress out into the Forth as if crossing to Edinburgh and the West Lothian lands opposite. Above Torryburn are the *'Tuilyies'* or *'Tollzies'* (Scots for *'fight'*) which are four standing stones: one cup-marked grey sandstone and lying south of it three whin stones positioned in a triangle. Locally the site is thought to the burial place of chiefs after a battle. From the stone map there seems to have been several possibly Uotadini/Gododdin/Gywr Y Gogledd friendly fortresses in this area as well as what is today the Clarkmannanshire coast a few miles further upriver.

The most detailed depiction is in the form of another seated chieftain-like figure west of the Inverkeithing/Dunfermline area. This zoomorphic sculpture, depending upon the direction of gaze, changes into: a bear and a young boy standing beside him; a bear; the beak of a not particularly friendly bird (raven/crow family) or a young deer. I would suggest that any interpretation of the alternating imagery would most likely relate to military alliances and the threat of conflict. The youth could have been another representation of Arthur. The crow may have been a tribal totem or perhaps a signifier of the prospect of battle and consequent carnage that this bird represented in old Welsh poetry. That is all I have been able to distinguish excepting that the background colour implies that this was a fort or base of an ally of Arthur and the Men of the North that is surrounded by signs of an inland threat. Continuing along the northern coast there are another two chair sculptures. The location of one seems clearly stone-signposted by the shape of the river and the mouth of another river to distinguish a Brittonnic fortress at present day *Tullibody* at the entrance to the River Devon. The other may be a little south of this at *Alloa*.

There are so far in my observations, several other stones apart from the Emperor's Map which appear to include Fife and neighbouring districts in the story of the people on the cliffs of Milsey Bay. Observing these prompted me to look closer at this area in the eclectic fashion essential it seems to find corroborative traces of darkened sixth century Scotland. This involved the perusal of ancient poetry, etymology, snippets in historical texts that meant little without stone-garnered knowledge. Old maps and tiny hints from an oral tradition that lingers on in the memories of some resulted in my view that the lands north of the Forth were the locus of a good deal of 'dark history'. In particular the history of events and places linked to Arthur and the 'Men of the North'. I will air my little collection of what I would term 'nudges' towards such a conclusion.

It has already been mentioned that in the medieval period, the Priory of North Berwick had lands across the water in Fife. Charters concerned with its administration reveal hints of Arthur in the names of these. In the 'Procuratory of resignation' 12th January 1587/1588 Margaret Home, the last Prioress, gave up the North Berwick Priory 'lands of Monthryve, **Athernis**, Grange in the sheriffdom of Fife' to the Crown to be then given to her aristocratic kinsman (GD110/20, NAS). Interestingly Watson (1926) in his analysis of the place-names with 'monadh' identified 'Monthryve' ('Malthrif' in same charter) as not following the word development of others which are linked to the Gaelic for 'hill'. The English version of it is 'Montrave' but 'Monthryve' was 'Mondthryve' and 'Cotton of Mondthryve' in the Blaeu Atlas 1654; 'Mathriue' before 1228 and 'Matheryue' before 1177. He used the Priory land charters to illustrate that 'mont and 'math' were related because they were linked to the same place-name, either **'Athernin 7 Mathriue'** or **'Atherny and Monthryve'**. He suggested that the 'math' might be a derivation of the Brittonic for 'mad-tref' or 'good tref' (Watson 1926, pp402-403). I think this interpretation may assist in identifying places that were linked to Arthur's life story, that were particularly named to signpost their place in the dramatic narrative attached to the hero. Interestingly on Pont's map of Argyll, Kilmartin is 'Kilmath'.

Three further Fife 'monts', Montquey, Monturpie and Montquhanie in the parishes of Aberdour, Largo and Kilmany respectively (Taylor 2004, pxxvi Introduction to 'Celtic Place-Names of Scotland') may also represent further traces of Bear history/influence. Perhaps they are the etymological equivalent of the stone bear signifiers of Arthurian battle sites! Taking my conjecture further, I have begun to wonder whether the Motray Water, the river that appears to have been the landward border of the Fife golden triangle, may be another one of this group of names. In other words according Watson's analysis, it would have been the 'river of the good settlement' which would fit well with the likelihood that the overlordship or reguli (subkingdom) was perhaps sacred in a religious sense as well as associated with Arthur's story. Interestingly too there is a 'Montreathmont' Moor in the parish of Barry (the golden triangle on the north side of the Tay) which if one follows Watson's interpretation (Watson 1926, pp357-359), would suggest the meaning 'moor of the *good settlement (or homestead) hill'.* The representation of Arthur as linked with sacred places will be explored further in the final chapter.

East of Montquhanie and about a mile south-east of the village of Kilmany which lies on the banks of the Motray Water there is an area called *Forret*. This is a Scots word and means *'forehead'*. It does not seem a coincidence that fifteen hundred years ago this district was stone-mapped as adjacent to or *before the head* of the young bear (Fife golden triangle) that was fixed in a kiss with a young deer (Barry, southern Angus). Could this be another trace of stone (pictorial) knowledge of the story of Fife on a contemporary map? (OS59)

The lands north of Montrave extending towards the Craigrothie and Ceres Burns and Scotstarvit Hill that lie south of the Eden River, with Ceres, a town recorded as being the site for the ancient mustering of men for war close by in the east, have an interesting name that may hold an Arthurian trace. Today these lands are called *Struthers* but in 1392 it was referred to in a land deal as *'Uchterutherstruther'* (Note 13). Consulting Watson (1926), this may translate as *Uther's High Strath*. Alternatively, can *'uchter'* be sourced to the personal name *'Uchtryd'* which can be found in the early Welsh poem the *'Mabinogion'*?

'Uchtryd Varyf Draws', (of the Cross-beard), would spread his red untrimmed beard over the eight and forty rafters which were in Arthur's hall''.

(From 'The Celtic Place-Names of Scotland'Watson (1926, p367)),

That there is an Arthurian and Gwyr y Gogled connection with this area of Fife is a hunch worth pursuing, particularly as Padel (2008, p234) noted that a place called *'Kelli wic'* was referred to as a residence of Arthur in Welsh poetry (Note 14). Adair's map (1684) has a *'Kellola'*, *Kellie Law* and a *'Kellie'* estate close by and interestingly this land lies between the pillar stones (Pitcorthies and Carnbees) already referred to. The Blaeu Atlas (1654) recorded that north of Kelly Law was *'Kings Muir'* on which there is a *'Chesters'* the name given to early fortified sites (Watson 1926). There was close by, *'Pitarthie Castle'*.

From my interpretation of the Emperor's Map, Fife and Southern Angus were very much a part of the story of Arthur and the Northern Britons. The miniature sculptures seem to communicate an ancient historical context to what took place there in the sixth century. The pictorial narrative reveals a range of momentus occasions and places of consequence. Because of all this I have formed the opinion that the location of the mysterious Brittonnic kingdom of *Rheged* may have been located somewhere in these regions of Scotland. This name is found in the praise poetry of Taliesin concerned with the already referred to North British hero Urbgen or Urien ap Cynfarch, king of Rheged who was portrayed as carrying out campaigns with his contemporary Gaullauc, son of Laenauc in Manau and Gododdin (ie today's east and central Scotland including East Lothian) as well as in a place called 'Aeron'. The latter may have been the isle of Arran and/or the lands of Aryshire. If the poetry is considered to have a historical basis then these men were fighting Anglo-Saxon settlers and other British kingdoms in the late sixth century. This was an era when the Dalriadan lord/king Aedan mac Gabran and the English leaders Theodoric (nickname 'Flamdwyn' 'flame-bearer') and latterly, his nephew Aedilfrith were pressing eastwards and northwards respectively. This would make Urien still active in the 590's as King Aedilfrith reigned from 592AD (Fraser 2009, pp126-127) and campaigned in the period thirty to fifty years after the death of Arthur. In some of the poetry Urien is portrayed as elderly, for example the 'grey haired lord' in the *'Battle of Gwen Ystrad'* and white haired in *'The Warband's Return'* by late 6th century poet Taliesin (Clancy 1998). This suggests that he may have been a child or young man in Arthur's time.

I can't helping wondering whether the four high-status children placed on the ramparts of Guinnion were not representations of the future four kings that were said to have fought the Anglo-Saxons in the last third of the sixth century: Urien, Guallauc, Riderch (of Alt Clud) and Morcant. The last name is intrigueing given the island status of Iudeu/Guinnion as in Welsh it means *'sea circle'*. Could it be that Morcant was the heir to the stronghold there? (Note 15) In Taliesin's poems Urien was named variously *'Urien of Yrechwydd' 'Ruler Supreme' 'Golden king of the North, High Lord of monarch' 'Rheged's defender' 'Lord of Catreath'*. He leads *'the men of Catreath'* at the Battle of Gwen Ystrad and is 'true leader of Christendom' (in poem 'The Battle of Gwen Ystrad' Clancy (1998, p79)). I will explain the relationship between Catreath, Gwen Ystrad and Urien later but for now the last description as a champion or defender of the faith may be enough to plant the seed of an explanation of why there is so little recorded of this North British king. Was such an interpretation of the man merely confined to a poet eulogising his patron or was he more generally recognised in this way as a fighting the 'Angles' who at that time were pagans and possibly other North Britons who may have lapsed? By the end of the 6th century it is thought that Aedilfrith, king of the Bernicians ruled over most of the lands in which Urien may have had influence or control. That history was rewritten to suit the new power is to be expected but the absence of such 'Men of the North' from the annals of religious houses and the writings of Englishmen (Clarkson 2010) seem significant given the supposed Christian credentials of Arthur and possibly the four kings that came after him.

Bede lauded the role of the Northumbrian dynasty in the development of Christianity in England that followed this time. However if the North Britons' story was well known, embedded within the oral tradition of the people between the Walls and beyond, and the quantity of narrative stones seems to point to such a scenario, it is likely, I would argue, that some of the prestige and possible achievements that came with the Romano-British Christianity of Southern Scotland may have been acquired without due acknowledgement by the Anglo-Saxons. A certain amount of mirroring of the ways of the vanguished enemy may be uncovered perhaps with some knowledge of the pictorial art of the Men of the North.

From the honoured descriptions of Urien he may have been heir to Arthur's role. He seems to have been fighting in the same vicinities of the twelve battles of the Bear. Clarkson (2010, pp76-77) notes that Taliesin writes of Urien fighting many battles but only three sites can be identified for certain 'Manau, Rhyd Alclud and Cellawr Brewyn' the last meaning 'huts' outside the boundary walls of 'Brewyn' which may relate to Iudeu. Given what stone-work has revealed about Arthur's involvement in Fife is it not likely that Urien also had cause to fight there? Not only that, could he have been from those territories? No English writers including Bede mentioned a place called 'Rheged' despite Urien's many battles with the Saxons. In his praise poetry Taliesin referred to the military campaigns Urien and his sons undertook. It is thought that he was writing in the late sixth century and so seems to have been giving not only an artistic but also almost a first-hand account of events. That is not to say his poems can be considered as accurate historical detail but with the knowledge that their purpose was to praise or eulogise his master/lord, which is how a wordsmith would earn his living in those times, it is possible I would argue, in the people and places referred to, to glean some information and clues concerning this North British chieftain.

According to Clarkson (2010, pp68-71), the opinion of historians that Rheged was somewhere in the Solway or Carlisle area is based on very little solid evidence. After studying in stone the historically busy regions of Angus and Fife the latter still called 'the Kingdom' by its inhabitants, I think it is possible this mysterious kingdom was located there. I have noted a compartmentalisation on topographical lines within the Emperor's Map not only concerned with strife but also with regard to the division of Fife into small sub-kingdoms. This importance of topography with regard to the boundaries of early kingdoms of the North seems to marry well with the meaning of 'Rheged' as the *'district or river opposite to the forest'* as posited by Rollason (2003, p87). From the place-names it seems possible that Fife was at one time well endowed with woodland so the forest alluded to would perhaps have had to have been quite significant in proportions in comparison. The forested territory that lay beyond the bog-lands north and south of the River Eden (Howe of Fife) seems to make sense of 'Rheged'. This 'forest' could have included the tall tree country of Perthshire, the forested heights of the Ochills and Falkland Wood. Stone signifiers, place-names and the Gask Ridge research finding of an east-west orientation all seem to point to this mysterious kingdom facing the big wooded area north and west of the rest of present day Fife. Was Rheged the less wooded portion of Fife or perhaps it was the golden land bounded by the Motray Water which included the northern coastline as far as Balmerino? (See Map 7). From the Emperor's Map Arthur and the Britons were involved in defending the territories south of the Eden all the way to the coasts and west of the Leven, the Forthridge Muirs as well the coastal edge towards Clarkmannanshire. It is within these territories that some of the battles of the 'Men of the North' including those of Urien may have taken place.

With the stone maps and Taliesin's poetry giving a sense of a history not very distant from Urien's, several clues come into view regarding these battles. Already noted are the lands of Aitherney and Mathruie as described in the documents from the North Berwick Priory. In Taliesin's poem, *'The Battle of Argoed Llwyfain'* four districts were referred to:

"Fflamddwyn came on, in four war-bands

Goddau and Rheged were mustering,

Summoned men, from Argoed to Arfynydd"

(Translation by Joseph P.Clancy in 'The Triumph Tree'T. O. Clancy (ed) 1998, p85))

And the poet has Urien's son Owain replying to the 'Flame-bearer's' demand for hostages in the negative and Urien calls for his men to raise a 'shield-wall on the mountain' and to head for the enemy. Now it may be that the incursion by the 'flame bearer' began at the Levenmouth as the river is closest to the shortest crossing of the Forth at Earlsferry. As the Anglo-Saxons were coming from Northumbria or probably East Lothian they would have approached from the east or south by sea. 'Argoed' means 'on wood or near wood'. As there was likely to have been a goodly number of woods in Fife, there may have been many 'Argoeds' including 'Llwyfain' which is 'Leven' meaning 'elm'. The Leven to the Elie/Ardross area of Fife would have been the likely water borne entry or landing site respectively, into the heart of central Fife. This presumably means the battle may have taken place close to what was a wooded area by the river Leven or eastwards a little along the coast towards the shortest crossing between Iudeu and Fife at Earlsferry/Elie. The latter would place the Saxons on 'moor of the promontories' (Ardross area) near the lands of Kilconquhar pronounced Kinuch-her and within the already mentioned pillar land (Easter Pitcorthy a mile or two north-east).

Interestingly with regard to raising a 'shield wall', according to Mc Farlane (1906) 'east of Pittenweem' there was a white rock called 'the Shield'. Studying the old paper maps I think I have located this a little inland and east of Pittenweem. It is situated on the southern bank of the Dreel Burn and is still known by this name. On the northern side of the Dreel lie the lands of Kellie already referred to. Could this naming be traced to the exploits of the Gywr Y Gogledd? Was Taliesin commemorating their efforts to defend an Arthurian home territory? That the coastal Leven and Ardross areas would have seen battles between the Saxons and Urien seems very likely from another Taliesin poem called 'In Praise of Rheged' which tells of a falling off of resistence amongst the Brittonic kings (in Fife in my opinion) to territorial incursions:

"Leader feckless, Idon was abandoned' and

Llwyfenydd saw lords tremble

In public defences at Mehyn"

(From 'In Praise of Rheged'.Translation by Joseph P. Clancy In 'The Triumph Tree' (T. O.Clancy (ed) 1998 ,p86))

Urien, the 'renowned trampler' leads the way in going on the offensive. At the very beginning of this praise work is a trace of where the Saxons were confronted by Urien:

"They moan facing sword-blades and spears;

Men moan underneath round shields.

Greedy the white gulls' cries in **Mathreu**"

(From 'In Praise of Rheged'. Translation by Joseph P.Clancy In 'The Triumph Tree' (T. O.Clancy (ed) 1998, p85) (my emphasis))

I would hazard that the 'Idon' referred to may have been Iudeu and the Conspicuous Cape. Perhaps the 'feckless leader' was Morcant. There would be good reason for the Fife Britons at Leven to be worried given the short crossing from North Berwick. It seems possible 'Mathreu' was the 'Mathriue' referred to in the Prioress of North Berwick's paperwork for the giving up of the church lands in the 'sheriffdom of Fife'. Called *Montrave* today this place which consists of an estate and hamlet lies just 6 kilometres north of the town of Leven. Stone-mapping, early literature and legal documentation may have pinpointed the raiding destination for maurauding Saxons and was where, at least once, Urien succeeded in defeating them. A destination that would also seem to have had a past linked to Arthur (remember, *Athernin*)

A swift, surprise attack on the territories between the Leven and the Eden could also have been attempted near Levenmouth given the old map and place-name evidence of bogland further up the river (Note 16). The Leven may have been wider at one time with a significant amount of wetlands on each side of it. This route into Fife's Britonnic heartland with a sizeable river and perhaps woodland cover may have been a favoured site for Saxon raiders. Note too the allusion to the threat of battle at *'Mehyn'* which was perhaps today's *Methil*, situated near Levenmouth on the west banks of the river. The poem referred to 'Llwyfenydd' which is another place-name meaning 'elm'. It is thought to have been Urien's home territory. Perhaps it was a particular domain within an overlordship that was Rheged. My hunch is that Llwyfenydd described an area very close to the Loch and River Leven. Given the gradient from the loch to the coast it would have been a fairly speedy row down-river to confront Fflamddwyn (see Map 7).

Aside from Leven Wood there is still today a district on the north-west of Loch Leven and the West Lomond Hill near Strathmiglo, that is called *'On*

Wood' or rather *Urquhart* (*Leden, Nether and Upper Urquharts*). This name is derived from the word *urchardan* with Scots and Gaelic derivations from the Welsh 'ar' that is 'on' or 'near' and 'coed' meaning 'wood' (Watson 1926, pp95 and xxiii). I am fairly sure of this as on several old paper maps there is a district named '*Urchart*' (Meuros 1780); '*Urquhart*' (Dorret 1751) and '*Wrwhart*' and '*North Wrquhart*' in Blaeu (1654) that lies a little north-west of the Lomonds. I would suggest that this district was the Argoed that men were 'summoned' from against the Saxon incursion at the coast.

'Arfynydd' means '*the region against the mountains*' (Clancy et al 1998, p348). It seems likely that this was a reference to the lands against or close up to the Ochills range of hills. From the Emperor's Map this may have approximated those lands described as under the control of the aldermen of Inverkeithing, in other words the territory between the waters of the Leven and the Devon and as far as Milnathort on the north bank of Loch Leven. 'Argoed to Arfynnydd' then would have been a substantial territory from which to draw men.

'Goddau' means '*trees*' or '*forest*' and Falkland Wood, given its proximity to Loch Leven and the Lomond Hills one of which may have been the 'mountain' where Urien's shield wall was to be mounted against the Saxons, is a candidate for this district. As already mentioned according to Johnston (e-book) 'Falk' may be Gaelic in origin, from '*faile*' meaning '*peril*' or '*to bathe or bath*' or from '*falaichi*' '*to hide*'. Given the proximity of Falkland Wood to the 'grey swordland' of Arthur's time, Owain's 'Goddau' may have been the wood that lay within this dangerous boundary territory. The 'Bath' association also seems to be valid as in old Welsh poetry Owain was called '*Earl of the Basin*'! (Thomson 2008, p160) This moniker may be topographicaly corroborated by a place-name within the Falkland area. On the south side of the River Eden, Falkland Wood seems to have extended into *Kettle*. This is a parish bounded by the Eden and a large peat moss (Ainslie 1775) which over a millennium ago was probably a loch from the number of surrounding place-names that relate to boggy/wet ground including a '*Loch-end*'. Today, there are two small reservoirs located there in the *Carriston* area ('*Karreton*' Blaeu 1654). In Scots one meaning for 'Kettle' is 'a large cooking pot' (Scots Dictionary, 1987), in other words a cauldron or basin perhaps. Close by on the north side of the Eden lies the *Howe of Fife*, by its name a low-lying stretch of territory (CSD 1987), bogland until relatively recent times. I would suggest that these names denoting the existence of an extensive area of wet land in central Fife may link Owain mab Urbgen to this part of the country. The memory of danger, possibly water-borne could have lingered on in this children's riddle:

"As I gaed to Falkland to a feast

I met wi' an ugly beast-

Ten tails, a hunder nails,

And no a fit but ane.

Answer- A ship"

(From *'Chambers Popular Rhymes of Scotland'* Chambers (1859, p110))

Surrounded by water, bog and wood even a thousand years after Arthur getting to this place was a trial. When the presbytery at Cupar was asked by King James VI to convene at Falkland (1611) they refused for the reason that

"Falkland could not be approached in winter nor after rains in summer"

(Reproduced from www.fiffhs.org/maps/stats/falklandstats.htm)

Difficult to access it must also have been easier to defend. A clue to what in particular might have been guarded can be found in another interesting place-name that may also link Fife to Urien is *Freuchie*. Today it is a small town lying a few miles between Falkland town and Kingskettle. From Watson's analysis *'freuchie'* means *'current'* and was applied to *'the shallow places where the water ran swiftly and was fordable'* (Watson 1926, pp349-350). The lord of Rheged was also known as 'Urien of the echwydd', or 'Shepherd/Lord of the echwydd'. *'Echwydd'* is Welsh for *'a flow of water, a tidal current, a cataract'* (Watson 1926'p156, cites Morris-Jones). It is possible that Urien may have been associated with the control/defence of a ford, an important place in a time with few bridges, and the one at Freuchie may have been of some strategic value as a crossing point.

As already mentioned it has been assumed that this particular title attached to Urien was an allusion to the Solway Firth. However, this was posited because Rheged was thought to be somewhere near Carlisle. Given that 'Aeron' is also linked to the war-leader, the Solway may be the 'echwydd' in question. However, with stone narratives revealing the Fife lands as host to the Bear's battles and a matched place-name

146

(Montrave/Mathriue), Freuchie seemed worth considering. However, before I came across the significance of this little place I had identified a more probable site that lies within the bounds of the Emperor's Map. This site is so spectacular a giant water feature and perhaps linked to an important settlement, that I include it here. It is situated in the *Blebo* (meaning = 'meal') and the aforementioned *Strath of Uther*, a possible Arthurian heartland in East Fife, reached long ago no doubt from the west via the River Leven and the Ceres Burn and from the east by rowing upstream on the Eden. This 'echwydd' lies within the *Dura Den Wood*. Dura Den is a three kilometre wooded and deep gorge through which the Kame Burn, (upstream it is the Ceres Burn), with waterfalls flows towards the confluence with the River Eden and thence the few miles to the Eden Estuary. Is it possible that Urien had a role in guarding this particular part of East Fife? From the place-names close by there may be a hint at ancient settlement and strife too. For example: *'Cassindorat'* (Blaeu 1654) perhaps *golden wall or fort* (Watson 1926p199); *Cassingrey*; Duncarrow Law and another *Tolzie* (a fight/ battle) situated close to *East Pitcorthie* (Gordon 1642).

Passing through Dura Den on an extremely wet day may provide some idea of how watery this gorge was in the Bear's and subsequently Urien's time. Through the dense vegetation there seems to be the remains of ancient sculpture work along its rocky walls. Faint colour wash, indented angled stone and small plaques situated proud on surrounding rock hints at a place of significance for an ancient people. Studies of the woodland itself have uncovered traces of an ancient elm wood (Woodland Trust). A sand stone of deep yellow is distinctive to the Den and some of it seems to have found its way, in sculptured form, to Iudeu on the Conspicuous Cape. I have begun a small collection of this unusual stone. It is to be remembered that observation of the Emperor's Map suggests that Arthur fought in this part of Fife. Dura Den as an important cultural/religious and fortified site surrounded by the fertile lands of Blebo would have been worth fighting for in Arthur's and Urien's times. I will return to puzzle over the possible location of Urien's echwydd later Dear Traveller.

A little south from Blebo on the East Neuk of Fife at Crail, location of the 'corner castle' there is perhaps a connection to Urien's Rheged and to his other son Rhun or Rum. The east bay of the village is called *Rome Bay* pronounced locally as *'room'*. Perhaps this name is a trace of Rum Map Urbgen recorded by Nennius as being a religious man. Crail is the place on the Emperor's Map where there has been sculpted a group of what I have described as 'bright-head' figures. The inference seems to be concerned with the Christian Church. What is known as *Constantine's Cave* at the north-east end of the Dane's Dyke less than two kilometres away may also be a link with the dark-age Christian past of the lands between the Walls.

Of further interest concerning ancient boundaries in East Fife is the territorial focus of what is called Legend B, which is one version of the story of how the relics of St Andrew were brought to Pictland by a bishop called Regulus (Taylor 2000). Regulus and his party landed at the then named Kilrymont (present day St Andrews) previously called Muckros, and travelled north meeting the Pictish king Hungus at Braemar. A church named after the saint was established there and similarly when Hungus went with Regulus to Kilrymont he sponsored the setting up of an Augustinian priory beside that of the church of the Culdees, St Rule, on the north side of present day St Andrews Bay. Cogent to our theme dear Traveller was the extensive parish given to the new Priory of St Andrews:

"..from Largo on the Firth of Forth northwards by way of Ceres to Naughton by Balmerino on the Tay"

(From 'The Coming of the Augustinians to St Andrews and Version B of the St Andrews Foundation Legend' Taylor 2000,p116)

Naughton, near Balmerino, lies about three kilometres north of and within the Motray Water 'triangle'. The western boundary of the new church jurisdiction seems also to have included the ancient battle field represented by a the east-facing bear fashioned onto 'Mid Fife' in the Strath of Uther and the lands of Dura Den and Kellie. In other words from a stone Arthurian perspective, most of the lands east of the River Leven including the golden territory bounded by the Motray Water.

From my observations Fife and coastal Angus were an integral part of Arthur's story in what may have been a peripatetic childhood. There are signs too that some of his experience as a warrior took place in the strife within Fife. Stone narrative provides a layered history of Fife that begins with the Bear Folk holding the land and at some point making an alliance with the Deer People (Caledonians and others perhaps), across the Tay. One layer on and it was important to record a Caledonian/ Roman battle that perhaps began near Newburgh and encompassed the central part of the Ochills. I have conjectured that memories of that terrible event

148

provided some of the context for how peace was maintained in an Arthurian Fife in what may have been a semi-siege scenario. Contributing to this view was the portrayal of the Picts as nipping at the edges of southern Fife and the east-west orientation of the Gask installations. Watchfulness must have been a priority in the post-Romano era. The grey land or area of 'barbarian' incursion or threat of it seems writ large on the Emperor's Map and perhaps Brythonnic Fife marriages were part of a defence strategy for a region in the frontline. In the final Arthurian layer such dynastic knot-tying appears to have taken place including that of the Bear himself to a princess emerging from the hills a little north of Perth.

It seems that in Fife at this time there were a good number of small fiefdoms (reguli). The largest distinctly marked territory was directly opposite a similarly signposted region in Angus across the Tay Estuary. Fraser (2009,p129) asked why the North British lands came under so much threat in the latter part of the 6th century and I suggest that the years of peace that the Uotadini and the other North British peoples enjoyed after Arthur's campaigns came to an end with his death. I would argue that the examination of the stone maps suggests how fragile the peace was. As already detailed the importance of the genealogy of Arthur linking him to the western Bear and Horse Folk as well as the eastern estuary peoples and his dangerous and miraculous baptism were stone-recorded. So too was his extreme youth in battle. His very existence quite possibly brought into focus the shared identity of the peoples between the old Roman Walls.

That Fife and Angus featured prominently in Arthur's story is made stone clear. Born in Argyll he appears to have been brought up in the east, stone narrative placing him as a baby in Brechin/Montrose in Angus and as a child in West Fife. He seems to have returned as a warrior to the territories of central and eastern Fife. From these findings I looked for traces of what part the people of these lands had played in the final decades of Brittonnic control in the eastern lowlands of Scotland. A study of place-names in particular was fruitful, even for an amateur thanks to the stone narratives, in the linkages that could be made to old Welsh poetry concerned with the 'The Men of the North' in particular the documentation of the Prioress of North Berwick. In the process something more about the identity of the sculpted Cats and the location of the battle of Mons Graupius emerged from stone observations. Perhaps a less 'dark' Fife and Angus may help to explain the later history of the people of these regions. Those who lived north of the Forth quaintly called the 'Gannets Bath' by their Saxon enemy (Swanton 1996, Peterborough Manuscript (975).

Chapter notes.

Note 1
Mary Sommerville (1873,p31) recorded in her diary that whilst visiting her aunt in Jedburgh there was a thunderstorm after which the Jed Waters began to rise: 'The people came out with pitchforks and hooks to catch the hayricks, sheaves of corn, drowned pigs and other animals that came sweeping past'

Note 2
An already documented location for any close communication and strategic unity between the northern and southern coastal communities was at the Broad Sands west of the North Berwick in the parish of Dirleton. From there is the shortest distance of water, about eight and a half miles from East Lothian to the western end of Elie Bay at Earlsferry. I have already given details with regard to the medieval pilgrimage route that was sponsored by the Earls of Fife. A boat journey was the quickest and probably safest way to reach more northerly sites of veneration. There seems to be some confusion as to whether that ferry point was situated near the present day harbour or in the area of the Broad Sands. The latter was referred to (Ferrier 1980) as the likely alternative due to there being a 'Ferrygate' ('way to the ferry') on the western outskirts of the modern town. Perhaps given the location of the motte, the medieval church and hospital near the man-made promontory between the town's two bays (West and Milsey Bays), these pilgrims did embark for Fife from the former whilst the beautiful indent that is the Broad Sands west of the Eil Burn may have been the place of a much earlier ferry. Indeed I am being persuaded by stone pictures that this location was very closely associated with an altogether different pilgrimage which I will detail in a later chapter.

Note 3
Although not recognised as such there is what appears to be a sacred Druid site close to the town of Montrose.

Note 4
The ancient topography of this part of Fife may have provided some of the landward boundary to the triangle as according to Pont (Map54 NLS) the earliest known cartographer of Scotland there was a large loch straddled diagonally across the Tentsmuir that had Leuchars Castle and a place called *Fasedmond*(?) at its southern and northern shores

151

respectively. It is only remembered on later maps in the place-name *'Rhynd'* (can mean a *'junction of two streams'* Watson 1926, p495). Pont has this loch as the receiver and discharger of two rivers which are sourced to a 'Swan Loch' a little to the west. He also documents several other small lochs in the area. By the time that Gordon maps Fife in 1642 (Gordon and Bleu 1654), there seems to be no large loch in the midst of Tentsmuir but vestiges of it are the two waters that flow into the *Lindow–burne*. 'Leuchars' according to Nicolaisen (1976,p71) comes from the English plural of the Gaelic 'luachar' meaning 'rushes', which could be further trace of the general dampness of this part of ancient Fife and may have served to separate it out from its neighbours. Water runs off the hills to the west of Tentsmuir to form the *Motray Water* and enters Eden Mouth. It may have been a substantial waterway in the Bear's day. The territory bounded by the Motray Water includes the Tentsmuir, Tayport and Balmerino areas of North East Fife and there is another 'Brunton' near its source in the Mountquhanie and Hazelton Walls area.

Note 5

What seems to be another place-name trace of the stone pictorial is *'Claw Walls'* sited at the foot of the Lomond Hills (Ainslie map 1775). A clue to where the threatening cat force was from may lie in Simon Taylor's (2004, pxxvi Introduction to Watson's Celtic Place-Names) analysis of the place-name Blairfetty in Blair Atholl parish, Perthshire. He sources it to the earlier *'Blairquhatti'* and the Gaelic for 'cat' (chat-).

Note 6

Besides the stone-mapping my attention had been drawn to Lumbennie because Herman Moll (1745) on his map of 'The Shires of Fife and Kinross' had written the place-name *'Dump'* locating it north/north-west of Rossy Loch, now drained. I thought that perhaps the map-maker mistook the letter 'h' for the letter d' from some earlier map. I conjectured that these two letters as they would be formed in the handwriting of 16th century Scotland could have been confused. There is however a *Demperston* in the same vicinity on other maps (Blaeu Atlas 1654; OS58).

Note 7

The blue colouring of the 'Cats' whether on skin or clothes would have been sourced to the woad plant. Interestingly, according to Martine (1890/1999) the area bounded by the Peffers in East Lothian was long known as the 'Woad Isle' because the plant was widely grown there until relatively recent times.

Note 8
Upon the metal insert that is part of the 'Auld Mur' stone (Chapter 4) has been fashioned what appears to be a migration story that features a ship and its passengers one of whom stands on the prow holding out from himself a cat.

Note 9
There are references in this poem to 'Edinburgh on the border' which is (from stone observation) the Lothian Esk and presumably refers to Arthur's battle at the City of the Legion (ie the Inveresk/Musselburgh areas). Other place-names referred to (Sims-Williams 1991, pp40-45) are *'Celli'* or *'Kelli'* which was perhaps the *Kelly* and/or the *Gelly* areas of Fife; *'Vain'* called *Vane* and pronounced 'vain' today, which lies on the south-eastern edge of Loch Leven; *'Tryfrwyd'* which I have argued was a reference to Arthur's 10th battle on the Wardie and Portobello/Duddingston shores; *'the vultures of Ely'* I would suggest referred to the little town of *Elie* on the Fife southern coast which was recorded as *'Ely'* in the 17th century (Blaeu 1654) and *'Elly'* in the 18th (Dorret 1751). There are still many 'vultures' in the centre of this town in the form of a large rookery. Earlsferry at Elie Bay was the northern port for the medieval pilgrimage across the Forth (from North Berwick) en route to St Andrews.

Note 10
'In 1384 the earl of Fife was described as 'capitalis legis de Clenmcduffe', 'chief of the law of Clan MacDuff' Acts of the Parliaments of Scotland, ed T Thomson and C Innes (Edinburgh. 1814-1875) in Bannerman(1993, p21)

Note 11
Some examples of these are: the *Orwell Stones*; the *Stones of Lundin* at Lundin Links, said to have had 'ancient sepulchres' found 'near them' (RCAMCS 1933, pxxi); a cup-marked standing stone at Torryburn; a holed stone at Craigs farm north of Dunfermline.

Note 12
The name of Queen Margaret became attached to the ferry crossing in 1164 when King Malcolm granted the monks of Scone and their staff free

passage at the 'Queensferry' (Stephen 1938, p128). Interestingly it was thought that the settlement at the present day North Queensferry was originally sited to the west of the Ferry Hills at a loch there (Stephen 1938).

Note 13
RCAMCS (1933) p54 'Sir William Keith the Marischal exchanged with Sir William Lindsay of the Byres, the lands of 'Uchterutherstruther' and Wester Markinch in Fife for the barony and castle of Dunnottar, then belonging to Lindsey who had married Keith's daughter. Thereafter the former place, generally in the shortened form of 'the Strother' or 'Struthers'....'

Note 14
In 'Culhwch ac Olwen' and the Welsh Triads (Padul 2008).

Note 15
I have already detailed you will recall, that positioned near to the group of princelings was worked the figure of a young man fashioned along evil lines. Perhaps this was a representation of Mordred who was linked to the Battle of Camlaan in which he and Arthur were killed.

Note 16
Interestingly is the situation of Markinch, Welsh *'march'*, meaning *'horse'* (Watson 1926). A *'peninsula or island of horses'* on the east bank of the River Leven and close to present day Lesley (but previously called 'Inchmartine') may hint at a coordinated transport system for our ancestors! Close to Markinch is a 'Brun-ton', perhaps a trace of the coloured stone signifier for bear or it just means 'Bear settlement'.

Chapter 7: The Bears of the North

That Arthur was known to many as the Bear seems obvious if the stones are studied. He is from my observations, more frequently portrayed as this great animal than in his human form. Until recently I had assumed that the representation was purely down it being Arthur's given name. In hindsight I realised I should have made the link of Arthur as part of a people known as 'bears' sooner given how easily I accepted the Uotadini as sea birds and some of the Picts as cats for example. My only excuse is that prior to coming across the story of his birth and consequently looking more closely at the Clyde Rock, Arthur was a bear alone amongst a whole aviary of figures. My writing about the stone archive of the pictorial has tended to some extent, to follow the order that understanding dawns. After all, the pictorial narrative was generated from the people who lived or visited here hence the large number of stones that relate to this part of present day East Lothian, the citadel and the Law figuring most frequently. Gradually, through this immersion in the local I eventually began to distinguish a sculpted geography that situates stories some distance away. Now the narrative has brought me westwards again to the great fortress of Alt Clut.

I have until now referred in passing to the great Rock of the Britons. My observations concerning this stronghold that stood on the north side of the River Clyde at present day Dumbarton are mainly based on the Emperor's Map with a small input from the narrative origin story. I have referred in passing to the other side of the former. As I have already recounted, the map maker made a deliberate link from the story of Arthur to the past. The genealogical pathway takes an observer back to Alt Clut perhaps more than two hundred years previously. A much closer look at the modelling of the Rock reveals a bear standing on all fours on a bird figure that resembles a ptarmigan. The former is much the greatest part of the structure. As I have already described, it was from his size in relation to all the other creatures around him that conveyed that it was a bear who dominated the decision-making in the fort in those earlier times (Note 1). As birth narrative stones seem to reveal that he also had kindred in charge at Dunadd many generations later. I began to wonder who these people were. Then I distinguished the faint outline of the figure that was shown straddling across Fife. As detailed earlier, there is thought to have been a taboo in the use of the word 'bear'. Here in East

155

Lothian with regard to the pictorial use of the bear to identify the warrior and leader Arthur of sixteen hundred years ago, there certainly was no taboo. This perhaps is not surprising given that he was the protector of the people living in this part of present day Scotland. But what about the people he was kindred with? Were they known by their contemporaries as a fierce war-like people or was the bear totemic for them like the wild cat was for the people who lived in the far north of Scotland or the deer for those who hailed from the Central Highlands/Angus?

From the stone-told story of the sea baby Arthur it has been made clear in my view, that at the time of Arthur's birth and probably centuries before, the bears of Uotadini art, controlled a significant portion of present day Argyll (Cowal, Bute and Mid-Argyll), and had influence if not overlordship of the Kintyre Peninsula. One particular stone portrays their settlement on the banks of Loch Lomond, particularly those situated on the south western banks and on the islands that splay across the loch from there northwards towards the east side of the loch and what is now Rowadennanan. Through its portrayal of Arthur's genealogical pathway, the Emperor's Map identified bears as a dominant presence at Alt Clut two to three hundred years before his death in 537 or 539. A closer look at the narrative scene on the back of this map appears to show the importance of the Clyde Rock and the Bear People in not only Arthur's story but to all of the people in the north of Britain for many generations before that. My reasons for coming to this view this are two. Firstly, on a stone map (Emperor's) with only two large surfaces, one is devoted to Alt Clut and its environs. Secondly, many narratives that centre on the Rock seem to take its history and the origins of the North British peoples much further back in time.

The narrative linkages mapped to Alt Clut, provide I think some hint of the sheer scale and complexity of the oral history that must have been passed to succeeding generations of the ancient peoples of the North. Perhaps historians or folklorists or both may be able to recognise some fragment of the stories being documented. I can only record my observations for now. Even this task is daunting given the number of images that appear and disappear in the smallest of movements to the stone. Images such as:

Faces of men in various nooks of the bifarcated rock; women standing at the table I have already referred to (Chapter 4); bears of various dimensions; a horse; different species of birds including the ptarmigan, I have already mentioned, which has a standing bear resting on it's back; a

156

veiled woman, perhaps a goddess; Roman soldiers crawling round the base of the Rock; groups of people; faint vestiges of structures between the two hills of the Rock; a boat carrying a little bear is greeted at the base of the Rock; long canoe- like boats in the foreground; bears with a wolf nearby.

Aside from the history that has been located at the Rock another narrative can be distinguished. On the top of Alt Clut close to the Roman soldier/British princess scene, (see chapter 4), another genealogical pathway has been fashioned. This time the line of figures progress back over onto the next side which from the distinctive 'bear brown' colouring and shaping signify from my observations, a bear presence. A seated bear is discernible at the edges of what I take to be Loch Lomond. Minute king, wolf and bear figures are within this. In a corner there are two holes which appear to represent caves with some ornamentation around them and what looks like a bear family outside. There is a procession of older bears heading towards Alt Clut. There are other figures in animal and human form of which one of the latter appears to be wearing a feather in his hair, pushing his head into the Loch area. What seems to be conveyed is that raids by other peoples spurred a migration of the community from along the edges of the loch to seek out the safety of the Rock. There are other chieftain-like heads to see by way of the digital eye. The whole collection of vignettes suggested to me that the lands of Argyll and West Stirlingshire were home to a very ancient people who were cave dwellers. Their history according to the Emperor's Map, shows warriors in rampaging mode to the north of the caves. Danger has been effectively portrayed as coming from outside and from within. At some point in time possibly more than once, the people of the loch made Alt Clut their refuge and eventually their seat of strategic power.

A trace of the Bear Folk seems lie in this extract from the 12th century 'De Situe Albanie' (quoted and analysed by Watson (1926, p226) concerned with *Drumalban* from the Gaelic *Druim Alban* that means the *'ridge of Alba'*. Alba originally was a name applied to all of the island of Britain in an ancient past when the highest mountains would have been snow covered, but through time came to be identified only with the lands north of the Forth and Clyde isthmus. 'Drumalban' refers to the mountainous range that would have been seen from the Atlantic by early voyagers. It lies mostly in Cowal and northern Argyll, the territory that is stone documented as a homeland of the Bear Folk (Chapter 5). The extract referred to Fergus mac Erc as

"...the first seed of Conaire to become king of Alba that is, from the mount Brunalban to the sea of Ireland and to Innse Gall. Thereafter kings of Fergus' seed reigned in Brunalban or Brunhere up to Alpin, son of Eochaidh"

(From 'The Celtic Place-Names of Scotland' Watson (1926, p226).)

Watson concentrated on the 'ere' as meaning Ireland as he was discussing the topic of Irish names found in Scotland and suggested a spelling error for the 'brun' part, positing that it was more likely to have been a Welsh word (bryn = hill). Stone-gained knowledge interprets 'Brunalban' just as it is spelt 'Brun-Alban' meaning 'Bear Alba' or Bear Scotland. The name of a mountain ridge corroborated by the pictorial seems to confirm the location of an ancient Bear Folk living in Atlantic Scotland before the coming of Fergus. The reference to 'Brunhere' could represent how Atlantic Scotland was known after the Dalriadian dynasty had become dominant in Argyll or perhaps there came to be an interchangeability in the use of the two names that was due to the mix of peoples between Kintyre and Ireland.

Returning to my earlier question as to who the Bear People were an ancient British people comes to mind. They were the 'Atacotti' which means 'oldest inhabitants' and the miniature figures walking away from their caves may represent such a people. According to the sparse written materials, this tribe or kindred were thought to have lived in the north west of Britain, in particular, the Hebrides. However, a contributer to Blaeu's Atlas (1654) (possibly a David Buchanan or a William Forbes of Innerwick) whose work was not included in the Atlas, had this to tell about these people:

Referring to Lothian he wrote:

"Once this region formed part of the territory of the Attalini or Attacotti, who inhabited that whole stretch of land along the sea between the Tyne and the Forth...."

(Translation by Ian C. Cunningham reproduced from the Blaeu Atlas website http://maps.nls.uk/atlas/blaeu)

This description aligns well with the Emperor's Map which appears to mark the south-eastern boundary of the Bear's story with the East

Lothian Tyne River that enters the North Sea at Tynningham. It also identifies these eastern Atacotti with coastal East Lothian. The first reference to these people was in the 4th century when they were described as being part of the 'barbarian conspiracy' that overran Roman Britain in 367 AD (Cassel 2005).

I have several reasons for linking this long forgotten people with Arthur's history and the bears of Atlantic Scotland, Lothian and Fife. Very little is known about the Atacotti and a similar fate of obscurity has befallen the Bear People. According to Morris (1973), the name 'Atacotti' is neither Pictish nor British in origin. Near the end of the fourth century the Romans found this tribe living close to the Scots and the Picts. This arguably, could only be, at that time, in a relatively discrete area, that of present day Argyll and Loch Lomond. The meaning of the name, 'oldest inhabitants' suggests an aboriginal people, which corroborates with the stone map documentation that seems to take the human history of Loch Lomond and the surrounding lands of Atlantic Scotland, back to an ancient, but remembered time when a people represented in stone as bears, may have dwelt in caves on the banks of the loch. Interestingly according to anthropologist Joseph Campbell bear worship was a common feature of prehistoric societies Cultures such as that of the peoples who lived on the lands of what is now Finland and Siberia saw the animal as representing the spirit of their ancestors ('Bear' Wikipedia). That the stone pictorials portray totemic and 'human-bear' narratives suggests a deep connection with this animal that was still important to the Northern peoples of Britain in Arthur's time. Maybe the use of the bear was the pictorial signifier for their ancestors. In my view the 'dark age' art provokes several strands of thought that seem to link the bear signifiers to the oldest inhabitants including the Atacotti. One of these relates to the portrayal of bears in the Arthurian narrative. Bears were fashioned as in positions of authority long after for example, their place in the ancient story of Fife. Were these people represented as bears somehow identifiable with the oldest people of the North?

A trace of an indecipherable language (apart from personal names), was found on Ogham stones in or near Pictish territory that were carved in Irish Ogham but were not in origin of the Irish, Pictish or Welsh languages (Morris, 1973). Thinking about this, I have remembered the unusual portrayal of the interaction that took place between two people on the Clyde Rock (Chapter 4). A Roman figure was being addressed by someone who seemed to be speaking for a bear. It may be that it was

Old British or Gaelic that was being translated for the Roman visitor or one of these enunciated a little oddly by the huge seated bear on the Rock. Alternatively what if it was a different language altogether, one that did not originate in any of those known to have existed in North Britain of that time? Remembering the bear iconography found in the east of the country indicating the apparent bear overlordship/influence of the strategic estuary lands of the Forth and Tay, the Bear Folk may have roamed over large swathes of Scotland, building their settlements and sacred places thousands of years before the coming of the Celts.

How ancient were these inhabitants I wonder? The Emperor's Map makes them very very old indeed. So far I have omitted to mention the most suprising vignette from the banks of Loch Lomond. Not only are there 'bear' cave dwellers but close by there is a procession of unclothed and hirsute figures heading away from the caves towards Alt Clut. It could be argued that the covering of a thin layer of hair over the bodies of these people was a signifier for nakedness. However, I have previously discerned a blue skinned warrior near the mouth of the River Carron who apart from his dressed hair was not wearing much if anything yet was not fashioned with surplus hair. Given this it might be concluded that the hairy portrayal was a distinguishing feature which prompted me to question whether these people were modern human descendants of a remnant of a much older and distant evolutionary relative such as the Neanderthal people who are thought to have been still living in Ice Age Europe 120,000 to 35,000 years ago (Note 2). Remembering that this portrayal was crafted around one and a half thousand years ago this possibility seems incredible but given the hairy portrayal, may be it should be a consideration. Could it be that the history and appearance of another people, perhaps a little different from the other indigenous native peoples including the Celts (who may have come to the British Isles around 700BC), somehow came to be documented upon one of their beautiful and ingenious works of miniature art. How would the sculptor know about these people if their ancestors and/or their art were not around to tell their story?

Certainly it is now thought that the Neanderthal people had the ability to speak. Research (BBC 2005) suggests that a combination of a shorter and wider vocal tract with a bigger mouth and airways than the modern human would have produced a much higher pitched, big and rasping sort of voice in the male of the species. With this in mind the translation scene on the Clyde Rock is yet again worth some reflection. Could the bear at this great western stronghold have had problems with enunciation? Evidently the other Britons there understood him. It is known that the Romans valued the Atacotti as fighting men recruiting them into their army including the Imperial Guard. For the latter posting perhaps a difficulty with speech may have added to their employability?

Whoever these hirsute people were on the banks of Loch Lomond, the ancient Britons understood them to have been an older people who identified with or worshipped the bear. They were sculpted close to the Bear Folk and as already detailed from the Emperor's Map, bear history and influence extended right across central and eastern Scotland. Their totem images were hewn into the landscape from Kintyre across to East Lothian and northwards to Angus and the Mearns. A portrayal of historical integration seems to have been made between the earliest peoples of Scotland and those who came after, epitomised in the origins and career of Arthur as a great warrior. I would suggest that the stone narrative was designed to make clear his authority to lead a Brittonnic confederation. A unity through ties of blood amongst the northern peoples seems to have centred upon Arthur's life. Through him the communities of the North could go into battle together and negotiate dynastic marriages as commemorated on the Emperor's Map.

As I have said, the stone evidence suggests there was an epoch of much violence and threat from non-Bears to the cave dwellers by the loch. According to the Emperor's Map, the history of later generations with 'bear' blood in their veins appeared to be a period of communication and cooperation and at some time dominance over neighbours. This is evoked by the large bears sitting atop both Alt Clut and Dunadd with the former outlined in the shape of the Rock as well as in charge within its fortress. The vignette with the Roman soldier/civilian portrays some sort of Britonnic alliance with a spokesman who appears to consult and translate for a large bear seated at the head of a table at the Dumbarton Rock. Such relations would most likely include intermarriage. From the origin story you will recall dear Traveller, that the sphere of influence of the Bear people of Loch Lomond (in the late 5th/ early 6th century when Arthur was born), encompassed lands in Argyll and Kintyre. The great Bear king who sat atop Dunadd had had a wife/daughter-in-law who seemed to have been a princess or queen of the Horse Folk. Her son, Arthur, was represented as a little white bear rescued from the Cauldron and taken to the Britons at various locations on the eastern seaboard.

Traces of 'bear' can be found on the map of present day Scotland. Place-name research may uncover many more particularly if the stone colour signifier for bear is taken into consideration. As you will recall, light brown or orange hues were used to pinpoint a bear presence. Perhaps the many *Bruntons* on the maps of contemporary Scotland may be the etymological equivalent of such a colour range on ancient sculpted stone. A well known trace of Arthur (and therefore the Bear Folk) lies in the Arrochar Alps just north of Ben Lomond in the form of Ben Arthur. Although not the highest peak amongst the Alps, (884m), this is a triple peaked, very distinctively shaped mountain. Known more often as the 'Cobbler', Ben Arthur dominates the landscape. It is one of the few hills in Scotland that requires a rock climb to get to the top. The summits consist of 'a leaning pyramid', 'a flat-topped table' (the true summit) and 'an immense overhanging prow' (McNeish 1999, p32-33). The overall effect is supposed to resemble a cobbler at his last but I suggest that this mountain was called Ben Arthur for the more stone–obvious reason that it stands high over the old lands of the Bear Folk of Loch Lomond. With regard to the appearance of the mountain either the peaks coincidentally achieve the effect of a recumbent crowned head (ie. the central peak and real summit), with attendant sculptures on each side or the Britons chose this particular mountain for its potential as a memorial to their hero and perhaps even worked a little of their magic on the rocks. 'How could this be?' seems an understandable response. However, the stone sculptors of sixth century North Britain have form when it comes to working at height (see next chapter) and they would shape the natural to their desire with minimalistic flair. According to mountaineers, reaching the top of the 'table' is relatively easy involving access through a 'narrow window' (McNeish 1999). To a stone archivist such a description sparks off a tiny suspicion that a man-manipulated route designed by memorial builders may be what is in evidence.

A visit to Kilmartin Glen provided some corroboration for a Stone Archivist that Arthur's origin story 'told' in the east was claimed and owned in the western Kyles. Kilmartin Glen, situated in Mid Argyll is a very special place holding as it does many traces of people living there during a period of 6000 years. Over 800 archaeological sites and monuments are located in the glen. A linear cemetery of burial cairns, groups of standing stones and the five thousand year old stone circle at Templewood lie in the landscape. Two hundred pieces of rock art, sometimes called 'cup and ring marks' on rocky outcrops of metamorphic stone have been recorded in the Kilmartin area. Although not definitively dated these pictorial works are thought to be over three thousand years old. One of these at *Achnabreck* is the largest decorated panel in Britain (Beckensall, 2005).

From a stone archivist's perspective some of the rock art of Kilmartin, are maps. They are what I would term kindred story maps. I have been able to get to those sited at *Kirkmichael Glassary* and Achnabreck in the south eastern part of Kilmartin Glen. From my small exposure to these sculptures I recognised the use of manipulated depth in the grooved stonework on the panels. They are not as fine or minute as those of the Uotadini but then they are very much older. The same principles of observation apply. For example, focus on one cup with several rings. Look at eye level so you might need to get close to the ground to do this. Focus in further on the cup. There you should spy a figure or head modelled into the depth of the cup. Keep focused and move out slowly and you will discern figures or heads stylistically modelled into the groves. I am speculating that the central 'cup figure' is the head of an extended family that is represented in the surrounding circular grooves. I would speculate that sculpted lines to other cups and rings are about blood lines and events that provided connections to other families and individuals.

From my observations in East Lothian of grooves and cup sculpting on stone the purpose of these appears to be to introduce depth and three-dimensionality to the work. Frequently I have come across a stone which is covered in cup marks. With close examination a figure or a head can be seen fashioned into the base of these. A careful look at the edges of these indentations is often rewarded with some sort of sculpted scene. Even more surprising than these finds are the very flat cupped stones. Put them at eye level and look across the cup bestrewn surface and there before you are a whole group of 'pop up' figures! Sometimes the cups are very small but still the craftsman has engineered detail. The effect comes from a very clever use of depth, shadow, colour contrasting bits of rock and perspective. It is truly a stupefying, magical sight.

Archaeologists have found that how Kilmartin's 'Valley of the Dead' looks today was a result of an ongoing process of modification to suit the belief systems and associated practices of succeeding generations over thousands of years. From my opportunity to view some of the monuments of Kilmartin, traces of the Britons of the 5th/6th century left their mark too. Their presence in the glen can be found in a pictorial narrative that is an echo of what I have identified in East Lothian. The best example of this that I have found that can be seen with the naked eye was on the lower rock panel at Achnabreck. At the bottom of this there is a golden/sand coloured boat shape. From my experience with origin stones this, I think, is an Arthur/Bear signifier. As I have detailed in Chapter 6, a deep golden/orange coloured boat-shaped mark was one way in which the boat that carried the little baby Arthur away from Dunadd was represented. Perhaps it is no coincidence that this marker was placed on this particular very ancient panel. From Achnabreck there is a wide-angled view of the seas that surround the lands east and west of Kilmartin Glen. To the west, in clear view, are the Sound of Jura, Scarba and the Gulf of the Corryvreckan. From this place then, the miraculous and dramatic story of the Bear's earliest adventure may have been told with the actual topographic backdrop in plain sight.

There are other traces of art and other stories etched onto the landscape of Kilmartin Glen. I visited Temple Wood a place with two circles built at different times, which are thought to have been the focus for ceremonies including burial for over a thousand years (Beckensall 2005). When in prehistory use of the site ended, the later circle was dismantled and cobbles were used to fill it. No mention is made of these stones being worked. From what I could see with and without the digital gaze there were small sculptures set into the stones. These sculptures were not cup and ring but something closer to what I have found in East Lothian. Perhaps then each stone is an individual commemoration of someone lost or maybe it was a communal expression about a single event. Beckansall (2005) referred to two excavated burial mounds in Northumberland (Weetwood Moor and Fowberry), which have no cists or any sign of burial but many decorated cobbles were found on the ground where the mounds would have been and the antiquarian made the allusion to these cobblestones as being brought to the burial sites 'like wreaths to a funeral' (Beckansall 2005, p19). This reminds me of what I have interpreted as miniature cairns that I have found in East Lothian. On the underside of each cairn stone of the few that came loose there were tiny carvings, of animal or birds. Coincidentally Beckensall (2003) reports that at the Westwood site those stones that had not been disturbed had 'motifs' on their undersides!

Ri Cruin is a cairn in the central part of Kilmartin Glen. Of the three burial cists found there one is described as having seven 'pecked axes' Beckensall (2005) on its west facing slab. A closer look at the 'axes' reveals miniature figures of people and birds as well as larger sculptures surrounding them. From my limited access to the work there are larger figures linked to the 'axes'. At first I thought I was looking at a fishing scene, with seven nets being cast. The figures in these nets however, suggested people and possibly their totems were what were being dispersed. It would appear that what was being communicated was a sowing of humanity. Perhaps this pictorial was an origin story of a people, or seven kindreds whose heirs were related to the monument builders

Observation of the small, particularly those works that are similarly shaped to the great Neolithic and Pictish symbol standing stones prompted another closer inspection. I have already suggested that one or perhaps two Pictish symbols relate to the possession of magnification or pinhole technology. A consistent feature of the columnar shaped miniatures that I have come across is the sculpture work rendered on the narrow edges of these. Sometimes there are vignettes but most frequently there appears to some sort of listing fashioned in the form of a series of profiled heads. The impression created is of a pictorial history dated as it were by the passing on of rulership from one carved head to the next. From the example of the miniatures, the slanted tops of many standing stones may hold the vestiges of totemic animals linked to the story of commemoration. Of course, Traveller, I know I am being very presumptuous in making these assertions about carvings that have been much studied and discussed. Crucial to my self-declared authority on the art that I have found, is an acceptance that the Uotadini and other peoples of North Briton were fashioning and decorating using magnifiers or pinhole technology. To create such miniature work extremely fine tools had to have been employed. Hopefully one day the implements used may be found. In the meantime these wonders exist.

Aside from place-names and sculptured totems, further traces of 'bear' may lie in a study of Scottish surnames. Keeping in mind that the origin of the Scottish clans is not so much to do with genealogy rather than that of the political and social upheavals of Scottish history in which possessing a particular name may have led to death or great privilege (Plean and Squire, 1994, p13), clan names, their heraldry or mottoes may be the source of some insight into ancient history. Originally people would have been known by their personal names. Through time surnames evolved from these and other sources. From the former, in Scotland the Gaelic 'mac' meaning 'son of' was a development away from the use of one name. In the latter instance, surnames originated for example, from place-names, occupations or personal characteristics (Whyte, 2000). Some examples may convince you dear Traveller that there may be some worth in searching for the vestiges of a very ancient time in the given names of the people from the lands of today's Scotland.

A trace of the oldest inhabitants may emerge by some happy chance such as this detail found by Watson (2002) on exploring the burial ground of the MacDiarmids of Glen Lochay. *Cladh Da Bhi* he discovered was the cemetery solely for those MacDiarmids who were styled as 'roghail', royal. The other clan branch was called '*bhusach*' or '*black mouthed*' and none of them were buried there. This may have just been a referral to a long-forgotten betrayal or kindred falling-out. Alternatively, remembering that there was something of a taboo in the use of the word 'bear', might this have been a faint trace of the Bear People? The black muzzle of this creature was frequently displayed in stone work here in East Lothian.

The clan of Arthur, the *Mac Arthurs* are one of the most ancient in Argyll. An old Gaelic couplet about them is interesting not only with regard to their distant lineage but its allusion to the Scottish royal dynasty:

'the hills and streams and Macalpine but whence came forth Macarthur?'

(from '*Scottish Clan and Family Encyclopedia*' Plean and Squire (1994, p417)).

Looking at the lands close to Loch Lomond there were the *Galbraiths*. The name is composed of two Gaelic words, '*gall bhreatnaich*' which means '*strange briton*'. This could be interpreted as the result of some point in time when a Briton had migrated into a Gael inhabited area and as he was a stranger he was given this name. Another hypothesis I would suggest is the possibility that this Briton may have looked or sounded a bit different due perhaps to some inherited characteristic from the ancient community on the banks of Loch Lomond. The Galbraiths were once an influential family in Lennox, the Galbraith clan chief had his castle on Inch Galbraith in Loch Lomond.

The surname *Matheson* is an Anglicisation of a name which may have had several Gaelic forms. According to Black (1993 cited in Plean and Squire,1994) this surname comes from the Gaelic '*Mic Mhathghamhuin*' meaning '*son of **the** bear*' but also posited is another interpretation, that of 'son of the heroes'. Such a name seems to be a memory trace of the

'Men of the North' commemorated in the old Welsh poetry. Note too the use of the definite artcle. According to Whyte (2000) those Mathesons who claim Lochalsh (north-west of Lennox) as their homeland, were known in the Gaelic as *'Mac Whathain'*, collectively as the 'Mathanach' translated from the Gaelic as 'son of bear'. The heraldry of the clan chief includes two brown bears each collared and with golden crowns (Plean and Squire, 1994).

As already detailed, in the distant past the colour brown was associated with 'bear' so perhaps the surname *'Brown'* or *'Broun'*, the second most common surname in Scotland today and linked to the Lowlands, needs to be included in this trawl for traces of Bear. It may in fact be a direct translation of the Dark Age stone signifier. Usually thought to be a nickname and related to hair colouring, which seems strange in itself given the preponderance of people with brown hair in this part of the world, it might make more sense if there was a long forgotten identification with the Bear Folk and/or an allegiance to Arthur and the 'Men of the North'. Another perhaps related interpretation (Black (1993) cited in Plean and Squire 1994) posits that the name may be connected to the highly regarded *'brehons'* or *'brieves'*, judges trained in the laws of Celtic communities. I am reminded this time of the great bear at the head of the table on Alt Clut, his dominant position suggesting an ajudicatory role. The Highland name *MacBrayne* is also considered to be linked to the brehons. As already detailed, the portrayal of the baby Arthur as a white bear hinted at his possible connection to a religious belief system that linked the Atlantic west of Scotland with the whitened estuary lands of the Forth. If Arthur was related to the highest secular leadership as well as to the Druidic, he was a special and perhaps unique figure. Such a child, born into a time when the lands between the two Roman walls were under threat would have been cherished for such origins (Note 3).

Well dear Traveller, I expect your tolerance has been tested with this chapter. Hopefully, at the very least, I have convinced you that I might be on to something in my search for the Bear Folk of the North. Finding Arthur and coming to understand the level of regard with which he was held in the time of the Uotadini/Gododdin makes any crafted stories or motifs linked to his bear representation important to pursue. Connections made to this long gone man may help us glimpse the wider culture and history of all the oldest peoples of Scotland and other parts of Britain and Ireland.

****

Mae again

When so long ago I began my apprenticeship I was assigned two mornings in the week to Alan the Curator of the Memory House. I learnt all the ways of storytelling and the many, many verses concerned with the stories of our people. The Memory House stood on the banks of the Fairy Burn, on the dunes close to the low road to the city. It was a single story building of red sandstone with a yellow tiled roof and shuttered windows. I had been told that in the past at high tide the house and its garden became an island as the sea joined the Fairy Burn and crashed towards the embankments of the King's Causeway. By the time I came to this place, the sea had fashioned a high dyke of sand on two of its sides and the sharp marine grasses held the House tight to the land. Further shelter from the elements was provided by a mass of wild white rose bushes that had grown up tall and spread along its walls. It was a peaceful place very different from the all day hum of the Reciter's Hall.

Alan was a small man and very old. He wore the draperies of the bards. A long auburn beard, a little faded with age was matched with a thick thatch upon his head. Very proud of his hair, I think, as I never saw him lift up the hood of his cloak. Like all the bards Alan talked a great deal, about the past of course and I was glad just to listen. I think looking back at that time, I see now that he was the main reason for my allocation to the Memory House. So much more can be remembered if told by someone who can graft together two sorts of memory, one of the head and one of the heart. Peering into the event-strewn past Alan would recall the memories of those who witnessed or took part in a piece of our history first hand. To make these stories as true to those witnesses was the responsibility of the Curator.

Our people are gifted hewers of the rich and diverse stone of the shore lands and spend a good deal of the quiet winter time creating hard aide-memoires of their personal and community history, their expertise an inheritance of the many generations that have lived here. So much knowledge has distilled down to our time passed on in the lengthy apprenticeships of the Guilds. Over many generations, the wealth of Iudeu had drawn the very best craftsmen from all over the land. The Guilds had emerged from the increasing sophistication of the work produced in such an artistic environment. To prevent a storm of jealous recriminations amongst these bodies, Bard Alan was very careful in how he went about commissioning for the Memory House.

This diplomacy would mean sometimes that I would be left on my own. Mostly when this happened he would set me some recitation work to do. There was a whole section of the House devoted to the chiselled lists of kings and queens, births, deaths and battle dates. I did not much like this part of my duties but I persevered as I knew that my master would test me when he returned. There were other times however, when he would let me choose a piece to study while he was away. Almost always on those occasions when I had swept the floors and dusted the exhibits, I would take, very carefully of course, one particularly beautifully enamelled stone from the huge map drawer. Bright with creams and pinks and soft yellows and a sprinkling of quartz and gold, it shimmered as I carried it through the dark recesses of the House. By the window that looked out onto the burn I let my eyes explore every niche and shadow. It seemed incredible to me that so much beauty and mystery could be contained in an object that fitted easily into the palm of my hand. Bard Alan had explained that this exhibit was both a map and a history of High Prince Arthur and all the peoples of the North. The Lands were cut and shaped into minute dimensions and their stories given expression in tiny scenes.

After many years I was to become Curator. It was not to be for long because the Dark Time came. War and plague brought ruin, death and destruction to my people. I hear that the house is all but gone now and its contents taken or scattered. Sometimes when I am put outside for a good airing I see myself in my mind's eye sitting in that rose-sheltered garden reciting the stories of the Ancestors.

****

Chapter Notes

Note 1
Perhaps not coincidentally there is a Ptarmigan Hill on the north-eastern banks of Loch Lomond.

Note 2
Neanderthals were an early form of the modern human or homo sapien. The first trace of Neanderthal Man was discovered by quarry workers in 1856 who unearthed bones in the Neander valley, Southern Germany. From that time there has been much scientific debate as to their evolutionary relationship with modern humans. One theory, 'the recent African origin' model (Stringer 2011) postulated that the earliest human, Homo erectus who originated in Africa, evolved into Homo heidlbergensis in Africa and Europe (whilst surviving on in Indonesia and East Asia). Heidlbergensis lived in Europe and Africa 600,000 to 300,000 years ago. About 600,000 years ago (calculated as 'the deepest split in the Neanderthal lineage' (Encylopaedia of the Human Genome 2003, (online) Wiley) based on the study of three Neanderthal's genomes to give a 50% probability) these homids are thought to have undergone another evolutionary change with those north of the Mediterranean emerging as Neanderthals and those to the south, in Africa, becoming Homo sapiens. The DNA technology of recent decades has impacted dramatically on the research into the origins of man and genetic data on man's ancestors. Genome comparisons between the Neanderthal and modern humans on different continents suggest rather than a replacement process taking place there was some degree of interbreedinging. As a result it is thought that 2.5% of the individual genomes of the people of Europe, China and New Guinea may be Neanderthal in origin (Springer,2011)   Other research has found more evidence of H. sapiens interbreeding with a species related to the Neanderthal which gives weight to the idea that both species may have lived alongside each other.

Note 3
There are other Scottish names, too that may have a trace of the story of Arthur and the Bears of the North. For example, the MacKenzies are thought to be related to the Mathesons and in Gaelic the name means '*son of the fair bright one*' (Plean and Squire 1994, p226), which brings to mind some of the sculpted representations of Arthur. The MacKay Clan

which in Gaelic is *'Macaoidh'* or *'son of Hugh'* are thought to be traced back to Celtic royalty. Spookily the clan badge is a bulrush. Remember the young man behind the rushes (Leuchars) in Fife?

Chapter 8: The Painted Hill

"Heaven's haven, longed for land's home

Woe is ours from yearning and ceaseless sorrow"

(From Verse 17 'The Gododdin' B Text. Translation by Joseph P.Clancy in The Triumph Tree (T.O.Clancy(ed) 1998, p73))

Inspired by the countless and tiny worked little mountains:

Just after dawn when the dew of early spring was still heavy on the grassy slopes of the Heugh, a white robed figure emerged from the palace through a small door to the side of the great ramped gate. This was Morvyn, Master of Public Works and project manager for the building of the tomb for the Bear. Outside the fortress he turned right taking the narrow path that ran alongside its walls. Tall in his youth, he was now well into his middle years and his bent shoulders betrayed the hard labour of his career as a mason. Possession of a spine worn down into awkward rigidity, gave him a tentative gait. Only the horses in the wide meadow saw him as he hurried on about his business holding his cloak close to his body away from the soaking vegetation that bordered the path. It was half a mile to the foot of the slope and as he walked he mulled over the minutae of the project.

He had been given two seasons to complete the commission which in any circumstances would have been too short a time. That one of those was a dark and stormy winter, had required a strong hand on a very tight work schedule. When so much men and materials had to be moved up and down such a great height, the dry autumn was a gift from the gods. It had been frenetic and exhausting but before the last leaves were blown from the rowans his team had fashioned the decorative exterior and cored out a rough space within the little mountain. Over the winter the hewers of stone had smoothed out the small cave-like tomb and created a dais for the sarcophagus to rest upon. He had organised the workers into two teams doing two or three day shifts at a time to make the best use of time and weather. His reasoning for this was that the climb could be very dangerous and cutting down the number of trips would reduce the chance of accidents. As it was he had lost his good friend and foreman Edar who mistook a tussock of grass for solid ground. Down on terra firma he had overseen the commissioned design work for the interior. The sarcophagus sides were crafted through the winter and a replica was made too in case of breakage in transit.

His thoughts turned to the task ahead. Today he was to inspect the work on the interior. The best painters and colourists had been busy on the walls of the tomb for many days now. He was hoping that he could sign them off soon so as to give sufficient time to clear the debris of labour and make a start on the approach to the tomb. Much attention to detail would be required to ensure a smooth ascent for the cortege. He was liaising with Munn the Master of all Ceremonies who was in charge of the funeral arrangements. Seven days now before the official viewing. He was so engrossed he didn't hear the sounds of activity or notice that he had reached the edge of the camp until he almost stumbled into one of its storage pits.

Annoyed with himself, he covered his awkward movements by turning and shouting for Cibno. An answering call came from the depths of a large tent nearby. It was one of the bothies erected for all the workmen. Warmed by coal braziers, these structures had been very necessary shelters for the men to rest and refuel before going back to face the freezing winds that scoured the sacred Hill. As Morvyn moved forward, a young man emerged out from the entrance of this structure. Cibno was one of the many goffers on the site, tasked as couriers ferrying messages between base camp and those six hundred feet uphill. He had one other duty and that was to organise the carrying of the Master of Public Works when he needed to get to the heights of the tomb. Following behind him was another youth who was putting on a thick wool cap as he moved away from the bothy. From the wooden board he had under his arm Morvyn knew this was to be Cibno's helper. Holding the board through the little slots on each side the two young people lowered it between them. Morvyn proceeded to sit down on it and placed his arms on a shoulder and back of each carrier. Clasping their free hands together and against his back, Cibno and his mate set off up the slope.

The 'arms' of his chair were strong after a night's sleep and with only three rests Morvyn was at the entrance to the tomb. The door was shut as it was still very early. He bent down and turned the mechanism and the door opened inwards with his small push. 'Good workmanship' he muttered approvingly. Instructing the couriers to wait for him, he entered the chamber. He was pleased with what he saw. The murals depicting the life of the High Prince were magnificent and looked almost completed. The sides of the carved stone casket had been hauled up the slope unscathed and had been wrapped in blankets until the painting was over. The floor would be cleaned and polished last. Stepping outside he looked at the paintwork done on the little carved wall to the left of the doorway. Bright little faces arranged totem fashion grimaced back at him. Standing a little back he checked on the progress made on the whitening work to the Hill itself. It was being renewed and the crisp northern light, gave a sharp, bright outline to the giant double-headed serpent that the masons had fashioned to drape the sides of the slope. Already from the ground the effect was magnificent. Sometimes bird-like in appearance and for so long the protector of the people, the great worm's fiery coils arranged in a sinuous embrace around the summit of the little mountain were going to give shelter to their greatest hero in his long sleep.

****

The only lettered record of the Bear's death is to be found in the annals of the Welsh (10th century Cambrian Annals): *'The Battle of Camlaan, where Arthur and Medraut fell'* (Morris (2002/1973) p140). This was about 22 years after Badon, in the year 537 or 539. These appeared to be years of peace with the rule of law in operation, which the Brittonnic coalition with the young Arthur at its head had secured for the lands between the Roman Walls. From the Emperor's Map he was styled as a Bear wearing the laurel crown of a Roman Emperor. As the previous chapters have revealed, the stone artists of the Uotadini were not remiss in recording and (naturally) celebrating Arthur's career. However, I have so far come across very few narratives concerned with Camlaan. Those that I suspect relate to this battle and the reasons for it have been difficult to interpret. One stone so far in my investigation seems to be directly related to context-setting this fateful time. On one side the pictorials suggest that Arthur was absent from Northern Britain. Four or more king figures dominate the plaque-like stone. A minute and painted zoomorph throws off a variety of scenes that involve a male and a female figure. Not in any order, there is a marriage, the two figures lying together and a queen seated on a throne with a male standing behind her as if talking in her ear. On the opposite side of the stone there is another tiny morphic that appears to be a seated and solitary male figure.

In contrast to this sparcity of account there are numerous portrayals detailing that Arthur was laid to rest inside the little mountain, the *hill* of old Welsh poetry, the *'Ponti[fs]kraig'/ 'Ponti[fe]raig'* of medieval documentation and the *Law* of present day North Berwickers. Where else indeed would his people place him but in this great northern pyramid, near the locations of a significant number of his battles and from the pictorials, the ancient focus of worship in the times of the 'oldest inhabitants'. Through the millennia to his lifetime it had been a place of kings and priests. The stone narratives suggest that those who held the citadal here had strong links to the story of his childhood and youth. From the numbers found, miniature representations of this 'Eastern Stone' with the dead hero interred at its summit were made in their many thousands. There appears to be no doubt that this hill had a special place in the lives of the ancient peoples who lived in this part of Scotland. As already detailed its surfaces and outlines were never left undecorated. Birds, hounds, bears, baboons and the occasional serpent were commemorated. It acted at different times as a sacred ritual site; a massive totem of a people; a grazing ground; a watch-tower; a high status burial place and most importantly for this archive, as a tomb and memorial to a man who, according to the stone pictorials, lived and died a hero in a time lost to the world of the written word.

As usual all my knowledge of where Arthur lies comes from the story stones I have found. As with other events in the life of the Bear, these can be identified initially by the particular stylised form that they take. There are variations (Note 1), but the main presentation is of a flattened pyramid shape, slightly extended on two corners, which has a highly specific set of carvings on its sides. These relate to the physical features on the Law. Sometimes in addition, some detailing of the activities related to Arthur's funeral has been fashioned. Starting at the foot of the hill, there is usually some sort of procession approaching the rock. A cortege with a recumbent bear being carried on a stretcher-like object can be seen climbing the hill. One very small sculpture shows a row of four horsemen looking on at such a scene. Today, a narrow road with cultivated fields on each side is the approach to the Law. A little further up the small stone pyramid a distinctively shaped crevice has been made in the stone which on close inspection is occupied by figures. Sometimes this crevice has been coloured differently from the surrounding stone. Sometimes one or more robed figures have been fashioned from or within this niche.

Crossing the burn that flows past the car park there is then a gentle incline and where the track levels out a small clearing can be seen sheltered by two sheer cliffs set almost at right angles to each other.

One is at a slight angle to the massif. The walls of these heights are brightly coloured and to a stone archivist at least, it is obvious that the work of man has been wrought upon them. There are shades of caramel, grey, pink and violet as well as white and the occasional patch of blue. To the naked eye the medley of colour wash is random presenting nothing that is whole and coherent but cast a digital gaze upon them and there is much to ponder over. There are vestiges of painted animals, birds and men. From my observations this was a sacred place. Facing south west, much of the wind that blasts the coastline is avoided. Walking into this space brings an immediate calm, a sense of refuge from the vagaries of weather and the high walls provide a grotto-like quality. This place equates to the niche on the miniature stone hill that give a glimpse or a shadow of a mysteriously robed figure. A Druid presence is communicated and it is not difficult to imagine the little clearing as a ceremonial space.

The miniature procession extends past this place and a scene of activity is sometimes portrayed with figures on the sides of the pyramid. Occasionally there is a row of important looking figures situated two thirds of the way towards the summit. On some stones there are people hauling up the slope some sort of litter with a bear lying on it. Frequently placed at the very top there is the figure of a recumbent bear on an indented ledge. Very occasionally I have seen sculptural detailing of a small entrance. Sometimes if examined carefully a tiny cross and in one instance so far, an ankh, the Egyptian symbol meaning 'life' or 'immortality' (Budge 1925, p315) has been scored on the vertical wall that holds the image of the great creature (Note 2)

Walking past the cliff shelter there are more colourful rock faces, which I would argue, clearly represent an outdoor gallery of murals, despite the many outcrops of vegetation that are sprouting from them. These murals are not painted pictures in the modern sense but like the miniature story stones, were a skilful use of what nature has shaped already. The artists who created these decorations made the most of the jagged and the indented. Two of them are of particular note. I will detail these in the order that they are to be seen on a walk round to the grassy south- facing slope.

The first is an unusually shaped slate gray rock ten feet or so high. On the sculpture more than partially hidden by sods of couch grass, is a boatful of travellers and I wonder whether this represents a well known place in the landscape of the route taken by the rescuer(s) of the sea-baby Arthur

176

in the journey taken from Atlantic Scotland via Loch Lomond and the Endrick Water towards the kingdoms on the eastern seaboard. I have already referred to the likelihood that in the 6th century the Endrick and the Carron were linked by a large loch near Fintry. The rock resembles, I think, the rounded ripple of a low pressured fountain, in which the water forms a continuous sheet as it descends. Looking at it I am reminded of the description of a waterfall at Auchenlilly on the Carron River in the Temple Denny area, a few miles upstream from Dunipace (Nimmo 1770). Some boat-carrying at Auchenlilly would have got the travellers to the calmer waters at Dunipace. All this is conjecture but the parish of Denny with place-names such as *Temple* and the *Darrach Hill (Hill of Oaks)* as well as the already mentioned Bear settlement (bear couple, see Chapter4) on the Denny bend on the Carron Water, could have been an important Druid domain and stop-over point for the travellers stone-recorded as having journeyed over the Clyde-Forth isthmus. Watson (1926, p256) noted that there was a place of offering or sacrifice called *Offeris* near Denny that was 'in the barony of Herbertshire'. The name Herbert is from Old German and means 'army bright' (behindthename.com).

The second stone mural is much more obviously a work of human art. In rich tones there is a very complex composition of the convex and concave that uses the full height of the cliffs. Sharp cut edges and ledges present images the significance of which, have long been forgotten. Like the miniature stone narratives these are stories being told from the past to whoever now cares to look. Once past the galleried/terraced area the grass slope itself is just that, with one solitary tree on its lower reaches. There are however a good number of large stones strewn about, some have faint carvings. There is a public footpath about two thirds of the way up to the summit. From my observations of miniatures, the slope has a number of high status burials beneath the swathes of nettles, thistle and long grasses. Above the painted and carved gallery there are signs that many of the cliffs and rocky outcrops closer to the summit were painted white. Anyone who has taken a walk to the top of the hill will have noticed the patches of whitening but perhaps has attributed them to some kind of rock- loving plant. Occasionally on a bright morning after a damp night you might discover that you can sometimes glimpse how these vestiges give the hill the faintest luminousity.

As well as adding more detail to the circumstances concerned with Arthur's death and funeral the pyramidal structures and others may provide an insight into the cultural *mores* of that time. One sculptural form in particular prompts a sense of closeness to the lived experience of people here on the Conspicuous Cape. Most affecting is a sculpture series of a bear curled into a stone alcove of some sort, which sometimes has inserts of metal on its surface. The figure of the bear has been fashioned from a red/brown material, usually clay. Tiny carvings around the alcove appear to portray events in Arthur's life. Lying, curled up, in a sleeping pose perhaps implies that the hero and saviour was not viewed as dead but in hibernation. The child-like exterior of this worked piece belies the serious narrative wrought in miniature. If there is a rationale for this and there may be none, it only being a contemporary interpretation that a contradiction exists, then it might be simply down to story-telling. The little curled up bear could have been a focus for telling the little ones about Arthur. In addition perhaps the miniature work may have been the 'magic' that made the object special and in some way worthy as a piece of art that represented the hero's story. Although it is unlikely that the owner of such an object would have been able to see the small vignettes, what was important most probably was that he/she would have known they were there and would be, as long as it survived. Hidden from ordinary sight the magical story would remain intact even after memory of it had been extinguished.

Another small crafted series relates to the bringing of Arthur dead or dying, by boat to the sea citadel at Iudeu. From the Emperor's Map, the Bear fell at a battle in the vicinity of Camelon (now a district of the town of Falkirk), which is located on the south side of the River Carron almost opposite what, according to the Emperor's Map may have been his main power base at Lairbarr/Birmatt/Stenhouse (Blaeu Atlas, 1654) or modern day Larbet. A minute vignette on this map suggests attempts to treat his injuries were done at Lairbarr/Birmatt or a little west of there and he was taken onto a boat on a nearby burn or river a little north of the Carron (Note 3) which eventually brought him to the River Forth and thence onward to Iudeu. Again there is a consistency of content in this group of narrative stones. The story begins at the base of the stone with a barge carrying the mortally wounded Arthur docking near the foot of the Law. Sometimes there are white garbed bearers involved in removing him from the vessel. One stone I have observed has these white figures, which I take to be Druids, not only at a quayside but placed as if to flag up the route the funeral cortege would take to the summit of the Law. As he is taken aloft towards the citadel a technique which I will call 'thoughts and dreams' has been employed. This involves the crafting

178

of vignettes in a more elongated way as if they have morphed out of thin air. It is a method still used today where smoke or undulating images, for example, signal to modern imaginations that there is going to be something more 'out of body' about to happen such as memories from the past or a day dream. There has been a careful choice of medium which accentuates this effect. Smoothing out a part of the wavy variegation on a particular shell and carving vignettes in an upward direction into this manipulated area is an example of this technique. What the vignettes seem to represent are portrayals of important points in Arthur's life such as his marriage. The overall impression for the observer is that the artist has been bent on conveying visually, the hero's dying experience. It appears that the dramatic method of 'seeing all one's life flash before you' employed in contemporary culture has a very long pedigree.

Usually in a stone portrayal Arthur is shown being carried in the direction of the citadel and then the next visual is his journey up the Law via the elevated sacred grotto and past the already detailed gallery. Although his upward progress to the summit of the little mountain was his ultimate destination, he of course must have spent some time in the citadel. All the pyramid stones have his cortege coming from that direction. I have come across a few stones now which suggest something of what happened to him within the palace on the sea cliff. As I have already mentioned in a previous chapter, in the north-western corner of the palace grounds there was a rounded meeting place. On one stone this round takes on more depth, appearing to be composed of several levels of seating and depicted in the centre is Arthur's body on a litter. The land that approximates this space today is a steep earth slope.

Other stones which portray the exterior sea-facing side of the citadel sometimes highlight the natural cliff as protruding out in buttress fashion. There have been alterations to the land close to this monolith of stone. There is a golf course and a sewage plant built into the hilly incline in front of it so this natural feature may be less obvious than in the past. Scratched or carved onto the miniature representation are some interesting images. Cloaked and hooded figures can be discerned working on the Bear's body which is laid out on a table. There are signs that possibly a sort of mummification process is portrayed as there are tube-like objects featured. In some way so the narrative goes, Arthur's body was preserved in a subterranean chamber within the stronghold. I am quite certain that there was and that there still is such a place. Find the path that leads to some steps which hug the side of the monolith. To the left at the turn in the stairway, there at the base, where the rock meets the lower grassy incline there is a perfectly formed arch-shaped drain-hole!

Although I was amazed to observe what looked to be a mummification being performed I was not completely surprised. As you will have noticed as this conversation has progressed the stones seem to have preserved a narrative that involved the images of animals usually confined to much more distant lands. The crocodile and the baboon were revered and associated with the gods of the Ancient Egyptians. The procedures carried out on the Bear's body may, it seems, be a trace of a knowledge remembered and passed on through many centuries. The following children's rhyme may be another fragment of a memory from this past:

"Arthur o'Bower has broken his bands,

And he's come roaring owre the lands;

The King of Scots and a' his power

Canna turn Arthur o'Bower"

(From 'Chambers Popular Rhymes of Scotland' Chambers (1870p184))

Incredibly this little lyric seems to reveal much about the power of Scotland's oral tradition to pass memories of a long gone time into the mouths of children. The nature of the hero's tomb and possibly of his mummification (bands) would have been knowingly or unknowingly called out over the generations. The rhyme also conjures up a sense of the threat the legend of Arthur, the Christian hero, may have been to a later Scottish king.

In the folklore of Wales, Cornwell and Brittany long before a medieval literary tradition had contextualised a chivalric setting for the life of Arthur, there was a strong belief that the Bear was not dead, only sleeping and that he and his men would come again and fight for freedom. Words from 'The Verses of the Graves' in the 'Black Book of Carmarthan' may be a poetic corroboration of the stone pictures of Arthur's vertiginous resting-place. After many verses in which quite often the location of the grave of a named warrior grave is given, there are these lines:

"Truly did Elffin bring me

To try my bardic lore

Over an early chieftain

The grave of Rwvawn, too early gone to the grave

The grave of March, the grave of Gwythur,

The grave of Gwgawn Gleddyvrudd;

A mystery to the world, the grave of Arthur."

(From *'Arthur and the Britons in Wales and Scotland'* Skene/ed Bryce (1988) p146 (my emphasis))

I have already mentioned that on some stones which portray the tomb of the Bear, there are other graves lower down. The occupants of these seem to have been of high status. In other words this verse may allude to the grassy slope of the Law. I venture to note too that there might be a play on the name of *'Elphin'*. Though there was a Welsh prince of that name who legend has it rescues the baby Taliesin (Mc Killip, 2005), *'Elphin'* according to (Watson, 1926, p125) means *'rock peak'*. The great Celtic etymologist also referred to the *'Elphin'* in Roscommon Ireland (with the stress is on the second syllable rather than the first) written in Old Irish as *'Ailfind'* which translates as *'white rock'*. These meanings seem very close to my earlier observations of the Law (Note 4).

My interpretation of the use of the word 'mystery' relates I suggest, to the magical intent of much of the sculptural work of the Brythonnic artists. Using the fuller descriptive meaning of this word in the context of the poem there was in/on Elfinn, a grave that was 'beyond all human knowledge to explain' or 'artfully made difficult' (Chambers, 1985). That the precipitous location and crafting of the tomb must have been a wonder of the ancient world makes the line of poetry cryptic but informative as well. There are other literary allusions in early Bardic Welsh poetry that appear to corroborate the stone representations of the Bear's tomb and its location. Again from *'The Brithwyr'* (Picts) in the *Red Book of Hergest* which is thought to refer to the period after the battle at Camlan...

"True it is, deliverance will come

By means of the wished-for man.

May he throw open the White Mount,

And into Gywnedd make his entry!"

(From 'Arthur and the Britons in Wales and Scotland' Skene/Bryce (ed) (1988, p140-141))

These lines combined with the earlier physical observation of the top section of the Law and the interpretation of 'Elfinn' would seem to have been a reference to the tomb of Arthur.

The language of this poem is of resurrection, almost creating a secular parallel to that of the Christ story of cave and stone. I have to say that it jars a little with the gentle animalistic/Pagan portrayals conveyed in the sleeping clay bears or the decorated Law with a little bear sculpted into a niche at its summit. The written word was the preserve of the elites of a community and would presumably reflect the greater influence of Christianity upon their sphere.

Returning to Dallan Forgaill's peom 'Elegy for Colum Cille' for what I would argue was an oblique Gaelic reference to the funeral at the painted hill there is no sign of soft sentiment. Rather there seems to be a clear dismissal of the tears wept over the death of Arthur. The wording is comparative. The death of Columba was being contrasted with another's. Someone who was also linked to Atlantic Scotland that Forgaill called 'Niall's land'. This Niall was a legendary Irish king called Niall of the Seven Hostages. According to Forgaill Columba's demise caused

"No slight sigh from one plain"

(From 'Elegy for Colum Cille' (Translation by Thomas O. Clancy in The Triumph Tree (T. O. Clancy (ed) 1998, p102))

I suggest that the plain referred to was coastal East Lothian and the grieving was over Arthur's death. Intrigueingly Forgaill deemed it necessary to diminish the death of Arthur 60 years before, in his glorification of Columba.

Again as illustrated earlier, there appeared to be a need to insert into the praise poetry the Bear's story hard against Columba's stature as a Christian leader. It was presumably part of that tradition with regard to Columba, of using secular images to enhance the attributes and actions of the religious man (Markus 2007). Arguably however, it was more than that given the disparaging language meted out with respect to the

182

High Prince of Britons and those that mourned his passing. It seems very possible that such words, thought to have been written within the decades after Columba, was in part at least, a response to what may have happened in the eastern lands of the 'Men of the North' after the death of the Bear. In particular the story of Iudeu/Guinnion and its people after the great hero had been sealed into his tomb. The suspicion is from Dallan Forgaill's words that 'the slight sigh' was an event of some ongoing significance to the work of the Columban church. So significant that vicious poetical swipes at Arthur's story were undertaken. It is interesting to speculate as to whether such language was representative as to how the Arthurian legend may have been belittled and eventually written out of Scotland's ancient history. Nevertheless if this important Brittonnic narrative can be glimpsed in early Welsh and Gaelic poetry it may also lurk unrecognised in work written in any of the other languages (English, Norse, Latin and French (Clancy 1998, pp6-7; Gillies 2007;Robinson and O'Maolaleigh 2007), that were spoken over the centuries in what became Scotland.

With the coming of Christianity it is quite possible that the Druids of this place would have taken on board the new religion. Some of them, according to Beresford-Ellis (2002), would have become priests themselves as well as continuing to function as the intellectual class of the community.   Remembering the large number of white garbed 'monks' receiving the dying Arthur Iudeu was probably a major centre of learning, culture and worship. From the stone narratives, some of the Druids here were involved in the preservation of the knowledge of past events and presumably in the artistic and technical understandings of generations of stone, wood and metal craftsmanship.   As already detailed, commemorative stones sometimes display a small cross on the outside wall of Arthur's tomb alongside the ancient symbols of belief from millennia of settlement. Sometimes too there is a figure in a brown habit close by. Interestingly in keeping with the concept of there being a mingling of Pagan and Christian themes on some of the commemorative stones that represent the two hills that marked Arthur's birth and death (see Chapter 5), the monk on Iudeu's sacred mount is matched by the view of a brown cloaked hag figure on the heights of Dunadd (Note 5).

Crucially in addressing the question about the fate of Iudeu, the existence of huge numbers of sculpted miniatures should figure most prominently. It seems no exaggeration to calculate that there has to be many, many thousands of such artifacts.   Such large quantities of decorated material concerned with the life and death of one person has to suggest the possibility of the development of a cult of Arthur after 537/9. Arguably, this massive amalgam of tiny pictorials in stone found on the Iuduean Cape is the tangible evidence that puts vast numbers of people at North Berwick in the centuries after his death. Their existence suggests a level of veneration of a secular figure, albeit a Christian one, on an epic scale. The consistency in the design of many of these miniature memorials seems to point to them being produced by particular master craftsmen and presumably, bought by pilgrims either as keepsakes or as votives. Some stones suggest that there were particular memorial or veneration sites associated with their hero in and around North Berwick at which perhaps, these 'magical' stones were placed (Note 6). Such a major centre of pilgrimage would have been known to everyone in North Britain and beyond.

Lambert de St Omer, a French monk and chronicler who in 1120 made this comment as a passing reference to a place that closely resembles the stone portrayals of Iudeu/Guinnion:

"There is a palace of Arthur the Soldier, in Britain, in the land of the Picts, built with various and wondrous art, in which the deeds of his acts and wars are seen to be sculpted"

(Cited in Moffat (1999, p192)

If this was a correct assertion the implication could be that the citadel on the cliffs contained this place of memorial and was still being visited five hundred of years after Arthur's interrment. A palace full of art that lauded Arthur the warrior and a painted mount which is now invisible to modern eyes would have been locations that many would have been drawn to. Perhaps in the years after 537/39 there developed a specific religious focus upon one of the various shrines that would have been situated around Iudeu It will be remembered that the eighth of Arthur's battles, (in which the Saxons were defeated and driven out of Guinnion), detailed by Nennius was given a Christian aura in the reference to Mary, mother of Christ.

In the 16th century a 'Charter of Confirmation' of 'two tenements of land' by George Home of 'Lundeis' (GD158/271, NAS) was drawn up in favour of his grandson Alexander Home (GD158/271 NAS) (Note 7). There was a reference to *'a croft pertaining to the Alter of the blessed Virgin Mary'* in the eastern lands outside the burgh boundary of North Berwick already detailed in Chapter 2 as the site of the citadel. Except for the allusion to *'the old Temple-house of Rhodes'* in James Grant's (1867) book 'The White Cockade' set in the time of the '45 Jacobite Rebellion, I have found no other mention of a religious site on the eastern edge of the town and wonder if this may mean it was of a greater antiquity than those of the medieval priory towards the west end of North Berwick and the church at the harbour (Note 8). Such close proximity to the scene of a battle descriptively ornamented with words concerned with the same saint makes it not impossible to make a case for there being a connection across the centuries between the site of this 'croft' and Nennius' description.

The stone narrative commemorates and celebrates an ancient past in which the Law or 'Maen' was the focus. A variety of gods were venerated represented by outlines of bear, baboon and hound. Those of the earliest settlers added to or subsumed into the belief systems that came with subsequent migrations. The arrival of new peoples was it seems from my observations, sometimes stone-recorded for posterity. For example, one story seems to show a memory of the first settlement at the coast here as on the cliff-top promontory (at Milsey Bay) where today there is a rough parking area. Another 'tells' a story of a Bear People greeting visitors from boats and the marriage of a Bear 'princess' to one of those strangers. A further intrigueing feature of this scene was the diminutive height of the Bears compared with the 'human' newcomers.

As already detailed at the beginning of this book, the Romans' name for those who lived here was *Votadini*. Watson's (1926, p28) interpretation of this was that this meant *'support'*. Given the pictorial narrative concerned with North Berwick I am inclined to think that this meaning related to the symbolic/religious importance of the Law to the ancient people of the coastal lands of East Lothian and beyond. From the portrayal on the Emperor's Map the little hill was given great prominence within the stylised 'landscape' of what is today east central Scotland. It surely was 'that powerful eastern stone' of the 11th century poem 'The Birth of Aedan mac Gabrain' (p182, 'The Triumph Tree' T.O. Clancy translator). If this was the case it seems possible that the Votadini/Uotadini could have been the 'praise people' or 'pillar/column people' (Roget 1962), those who upheld and honoured and gave offerings to the gods that were painted and carved upon the sacred hill (Note 9). A memory trace of it as a place of worship and pilgrimage was I would argue, written down in 15th century land documents in the word *punt* which you will remember I posited was from the pre-Latin Osco-Umbrian word *puntis* meaning *propitiatory offering.*

I am reminded at this point of two lists of names of islands of North Britain recorded in the 'Ravenna Cosmography', an 8th century list of place-names examined by Lethbridge (1954). Both lists are thought to have been taken from the itineraries or sea maps of the Romans that named islands that were ports of call for ships sailing in the waters of Northern Britain. There have been difficulties in identifying these due to the effects of multiple retranslations. One list is thought to relate to ports on the Western Isles as they were referred to as being 'in that western ocean'. There is less certainty as to the location of the other islands described as 'in another part' and were named as *'Magnancia; Anas; Cana; Atina; Elete; Daroeda; Esse; Grandena (or Gradena); Maiona; Longis; Eirimon; Exosades where precious stones grow'* (in Lethbridge 1954, pp143-144). What drew my attention to this list initially was the translation of *Atina* as meaning 'duck island' as I had noted on one stone map there was what looked to be an island close to the western shoreline of the 'Conspicuous Cape' that was fashioned as a green duck! Give this I would suggest that Fidra may have been the island that the Romans documented as 'Atina'. Perhaps *Maiona* was the *May Island* whilst *Cana* may have been *Gana*, (in my view the name for the Bass Rock as referred to in the 'Gododdin') as it means *'White Island'* which corresponds well with the whitened gannetry in the Forth. With regard to the Uotadinian holy hill and environs which would have been an island surrounded by 'bright water' (ie the Peffers) an interpretation ascribed to *Grandena* as *'Hail Island'* may suggest one ancient name for Iudeu. This appellation appears to identify most closely with the auspicious nature of the Iudeuan Cape and the people of coastal Lothian. A further nudge towards this conclusion will become evident later in this chapter.

Long before the Christian Arthur was sealed into its painted hill, Iudeu was a place of pilgrimage, a place of the gods. So such an honour for one man must speak volumes for his standing amongst the Gwyr Y Gogledd. It is interesting to speculate as to what else such an action could reveal about those 'dark' times. Arthur almost always stone-identified as a bear, an animal that may have been the ancient god or totem of the earliest peoples on the Cape and across Scotland, was also parchment-portrayed as a champion of the Blessed Virgin Mary. This linkage of hero to ancient pagan belief and contemporary Christian saint may have been an important part of some sort of narrative management that enabled an eclecticism of belief to exist. In the early Christian Church there was a focus on the Virgin which became cultic. Of later times I wonder how much the cult that grew around Arthur's resting place was treated as an opportunity in the pursuit of a greater following for the Celtic Church. Certainly I have begun to suspect that shrines to Mary, Mother of Christ may have existed close to the scenes of Arthur's exploits. I have come across several possible examples of this. The one already mentioned, the Altar of the Blessed Virgin Mary which appears to have been close to the boundary of the old citadel and that of the Burgh of North Berwick. Such a location coincides well with the Emperor's Map portrayal of Arthur having the image of the Virgin at his shoulder in Iudeu and with Nennius' description of the 8th battle. It is tempting to posit that the Welsh monk's portrayal of this battle in such iconographically Christian terms places this altar in Iudeu at a very early 'dark age' date.

This association between Saint Mary and Arthur made me wonder whether there were other similar places of commemoration. I suspect that the perilous journey of the wonder baby who survived the Corriewreckan was marked and linked by the early church to the saint. There is for example, the sprinkling of the place-name *'Kilmory'* meaning *'cell'* or *'church' of Mary'* in Atlantic Scotland. In particular with regard to the dramatic flight of the children from Dunadd, the ruined township of *Kilmory Oib* is of interest. The settlement lies near the banks of *Loch Coille Bharr*. This loch from my stone observations (see chapter 5) may have been on the baby Arthur's route towards Loch Sween. In Kilmory Oib there is a cross slab that stands at the western end of a well with the water flowing through a stone tank. On the side facing the well (and east) there is an incised cross and on the other facing outwards and westerly there is a cross with what appears to be a sun, moon, birds and various animals (Christison 1904; Campbell and Sandeman 1964; Fisher 2001). It seems possible does it not, that such a dual representation of the symbol of the Christian religion may suggest a time when Pagan and Christian belief systems were both prevalent and memories of the story of the Bear's tragic start to life were fresh?(Note 10)

With regard to the battles documented by Nennius it seems possible that the area of Duddingston called *Magdalen* may be another long forgotten trace of an Arthurian inspired shrine. On John Speed's (1610) map of the 'Kingdom of Scotland' this part of the Lothian coast was called Vrŷston which seems to be a shortening of 'Virgin Mary's town/settlement' (Note 11). On Bellin's (1757) map of the 'Golphe d'Edinburgh' it was called

'*Madlinton*', yet another name linked to Arthur in 'mad' meaning in Old British 'good' ('math' in Scottish Gaelic). Present day Magdalen lies close to the eastern edge of Duddingston and the heights of Arthur's Seat, the location of the second part of the 10th battle. On Pont's map of East Lothian (Waterston 1958) there is a *Myrylam* a mile or two south-east of North Berwick Law close to the Peffer Burn and scene of one of the earlier battles recorded by Nennius.

Another example may involve the land in the already referred to 16th century land document of the Prioress of North Berwick as '*Aithernin 7 Mathruie*' (in Watson 1926, pp402-403). That in the Christian religion the number 7 was symbolic for the 'Joys of Mary' (Hicks 2012,p51), does appear to suggest that a shrine to the Virgin may have been located near Leven/Largo and perhaps, as portrayed by the Emperor's Map, Arthur was associated with the area in a battle situation and/or in some other way. I would suggest that another reference to this connection between Arthur and the cult of the Virgin Mary may be found in the Welsh poem '*The Chair of the Sovereign*'. This poem from the '*Book of Taliesin*' that contained the already mentioned allusion to him being 'of two authors' also referred to Arthur directly by name and ascribed a 'scriptural number' to the hero (in Skene/Bryce 1988, pp124-126).

The mix of hero and the mother of Christ must have led to a powerful and distinctive amalgam of belief in that 'dark' distant time. Arthur's story always stone portrayed using Pagan signifiers may have enabled the old ideas and ways of worship to mingle with that of the Christian saviour. A Christianity formed from this and guided perhaps by the Druids of the great pagan hill would as time passed, I suspect, have made some in the Christian church uneasy about Iudeu with its ancient story and location of the 'mysterious' grave of Arthur who was a Christian but secular figure. The messianic language found in old Welsh poetry concerning Arthur arguably had to have originated from this place. The crafted 'sleeping bears' seem to resonate with a belief in his eventual return to his people. As the principal writers/scholars of the period, it may not be surprising that there is no monkish record of a place of pilgrimage to old Iudeu on the Conspicuous Cape.

Moving on in time I would hazard that the painted hill with its sleeping hero remained a sacred and iconic place for the Northern people between the Walls. Wars, loss of lands, new migrations and languages were to obscure this but as everyone knows dear Traveller, the past leaves a calling card on future events in the sense of influencing what actions are taken and in the way they are recorded afterwards.

In 634AD, almost a hundred years after the death of Arthur, Oswald king of the Bernicians invited the religious community on Iona to establish a daughter house on Lindisfarne another tidal island once called *Medcaut* situated some sixty miles south of North Berwick. The Columban bishop Aedan was given the task of setting up a new missionary church on the island. It is thought that one of the purposes of the Lindisfarne community would have been to take charge of already founded Brittonic churches of which there may have been a number including Melrose (Fraser 2009, p170). Fraser (2009) posited that one of the reasons for the Bernicians increasing their control over Lothian around this time may have been to do with protecting the preferred pilgrimage route from Iona to Lindisfarne. This route seemed to involve disembarking at Aberlady and continuing on foot southwards to Lindisfarne (*'St Aidan's Way'*) The stone acquired knowledge that there was most likely already a very well trodden path to Iudeu a few miles away makes for interesting speculations.

Was Iudeu included in this protected route or was it avoided and if so why? Was Lindisfarne set up as a replacement or in competition with Iudeu? Could it have been that Lindisfarne was envisaged as the Bernician/Northumbrian alternative to the painted hill and the clifftop citadel so much part of the identity of the Northern Britons of Southern Scotland, the enemies of Oswald? What part if any, had the Christian church in influencing this king to sponsor a religious community on a site that was topographically similar to the Conspicuous Cape but with none of the Arthurian and concommitent Pagan associations ? Perhaps Iudeu became a protected place, the equivalent of a world heritage site of modern times, remaining untouched for centuries because not even the most ruthless of enemies would dare to desecrate it? Over time several scenarios may have existed that might provide a meaningful answer to some of these questions.

It may have been that the pilgrims would have been heading for Iudeu. Most of the village of Aberlady lies just outside the Iudeuan Cape on the western side of the Peffer Burn that flows into the Aberlady Bay. This water you will remember dear Traveller, long ago formed a continuous and tidal division of the Cape from the rest of the East Lothian lands. It was an ancient topographic feature which may have made the village a border place, a gateway into a territory perceived as sacred. Perhaps once they had visited the site devoted to commemorating the life of the Bear the pilgrims carried on with their journey by sea from the bay below the old citadel, a safer mode of travel than by foot to Lindisfarne. It may have been that when the Northumbrian kings were in control of the Cape the pilgrims were given safe passage across the sea plain and on towards monasteries in the Tweed valley. But why would they need to do that unless visiting Iudeu and the sea around it was forbidden at some point? Alternatively if viewed as 'the competition' then perhaps the pilgrims' route did avoid Iudeu. It has been discovered that a large cross of the Northumbrian church used to stand in Aberlady overlooking the bay. The decorative fragment found resembles another at Abercorn on the West Lothian coast. Perhaps like much earlier stones in the landscape, these were territorial markers for a Northumbrian diocese that included most of East Lothian with the exception of the Iudeun Cape.

Fortunately the carved pieces from the Conspicuous Cape continue to generate questions about Arthur and the federation of peoples that he led in defence of the lands between the Roman Walls. I have argued that stone narratives suggest that due to his origins, Arthur may have been chosen because he was the ideal candidate to keep such a coalition intact. What happened in the decades after the Bear's death however, was seemingly impossible to discern. The Bear's story was over and may be there was, not long afterwards, an end also to the production of the beautiful and sophisticated pictorial art. As I have said the past informs the future and so it has been with the story of the great hero. Facets of such a big narrative inevitably shoot glimmers of light upon what came after.

Quite recently one particular worked stone came to my attention that led me to look all the more closely at place-name meanings and the fragments of paperwork that hold traces of what may have happened at Iudeu in those years after Arthur. I call this artefact 'White Lands'. It is a red stone with small 'workings' on it but these appear to be too worn to interpret. However there are six of what I would describe as 'compartments' that have been distinctly whitened and extend on two edges of it. I have already referred to the white painted representations of Guinnion and given the ancient crafters' penchant for colour coding, this stone made me wonder whether in this case, it was signage for a single identity of people/kinship/political control, along the coastal lands of Lothian. It reminded me of the 'land of Gwanannon' in 'Wann' referred to in 'The Gododdin', the already mentioned poem or rather a collection of poetry to be found in the 13th century 'Book of Aneiran' about a failed military expedition by warriors who set out from Etin(Edinburgh) for 'Catreath' and met their deaths at the hands of Saxons and others.

In his analysis of the setting for the poem, McDiarmid (1983) suggested that 'wann' may be linked to the Welsh for 'white' (ie 'gwen'). It is thought to have been written down around 650AD (Clancy 1998) and probably was composed at least fifty years earlier within the North British oral tradition. This would date it to a time when there was thought to have been almost continuous strife between the Uotadini or Gododdin and the Saxon settlers who were moving into Lothian as well as between the different kingships within the Brittonnic territories of the North. The event itself might be narrowed down to around 590-595AD when the occupation by the Saxons was relatively recent (McDiarmid 1983). That most of those named are unknown has lent weight to the case for this work to have been created close to the time of the event. McDiarmid argued that rather than Catterick, the usual interpretation of 'Catreath', the location of the battle must have been much closer to Edinburgh and on the coast. He cites John T Koch's theory that the Battle of Gwen Ystrad was linked to the Catreath event. This battle was also immortalised in the secular praise poetry of the late sixth century. The poem, 'The Battle of Gwen Ystrad' attributed to Taliesin, places Urien at the head of 'Catreath's men'. 'Gwen Ystrad' is Early Welsh for 'white strath' or 'holy strath' (Watson 1926, p344) and is another place-name that perhaps signposts an Arthurian cultic connection.

The 'Gododdin' is made up of two separate texts copied by different scribes who each had different earlier works in front of them (Clancy 1998). I followed Clancy's (1998) advice that the best way to gain a sense of this poetry is to read it as a whole, not picking out particular wording. The latter exercise came later. The result for me is an impression that Catreath and its environs were in the hands of an alliance of Picts, Gaels and 'pagans' or Saxons and that the Gododdin and other native Brittonnic kingdoms had sent the equivalent of a special forces unit there to wrest the territory/fortress back into Gododdin hands. They found a numerically superior army at Catreath. Not only that, it seems there may have been treachery within their own coalition as well as another army arriving by boat which may have created an ambush situation. There is frequent mention of a *'ford'*, with the

191

Gododdin meeting and clashing there with the enemy. The fighting also takes place close to the sea. In addition there is reference to the Britons attempting an assault at coastal clifftops as some of them end up falling to their deaths 'head long' into the 'depths'. There is a great sadness over the loss of the warriors albeit conveyed in blood and gore descriptions. Longing and grief too are expressed with regard to Catreath itself suggesting that it was an extremely important place for the Britons. A further, possibly not unrelated feature of the poetry is the apparently contradictory portrayals of assault and defence as their military purpose.

From stone observations there have been many battles within and and close to the boundaries of Iudeu. I would argue that this was a place much desired by many over millennia who looked for fertile land at their backs and the advantages of the sea before them. By the sixth century there was much more to covet or destroy. As already detailed, a goodly proportion of the Bear's battles were sited on the Conspicuous Cape. Aside from the stone maps, another distinctive stone portrayal has emerged which located a battle as taking place very close to North Berwick Law. A large force has been fashioned as if moving forward on a broad beach towards the lands to the west of the hill. Sands, warriors, the distinctive shape of the Law and the delineated area worked on it in which a little bear sleeps, are notable features. Great consistency in how these were positioned in relation to each other no matter the size of the stone, aided the identification and recognition of the importance of the narrative.

My hypothesis is that what was pictorially portrayed was the *Battle of Gwen Ystrad* and that Koch was correct in linking it with the fight in 'Gwannanon' of 'The Gododdin' poetry. The topography of the area around North Berwick seems to fit well with the fragments of description within the poem. Those familiar with the beaches of this part of East Lothian would not find it difficult to locate a very distinctive 'white strath' close to the Law. That would be the *Broad Sands* already mentioned as the site of a very early pilgrims' ferry (see Map 3). There is still a *Ferry Gate* (attached to several sections of land and property) on the western edge of the town. It seems to be a possibility that in the decades after the Bear was placed in his tomb on the Law and more than five hundred years before record of the medieval sea-route over to Fife, the Broad Sands was known by the Britons as Gwen Ystrad. Given the antiquity of the much illustrated Law hill this white/holy strath may have an even earlier history of pilgrimage.

The wide beach is roughly triangular in shape with the mouth of the *Eil Burn* at its apex. I wonder whether this 'eil' may have originated in the Gaelic *'eileirg'* which was a triangular trap, natural or artificial used by huntsmen to ambush deer. Could it have been the name the Gaelic speakers, who would have been in Lothian in the 10th century, gave this water as a reference to a human slaughter on the beach once called Gwen Ystrad? The burn is situated between North Berwick and the village of Dirleton. The inland border of the beach is open and flat for about a mile before the ground rises gradually easterly towards the southern side of the Law and westerly, over a gently rising ridge of land (vicinity of Ferrygate Strip moving easterly to the hamlet of Kingston) which leads to the valley of the Peffer. A part of this area was the 'Mainis of Northberuik' and was called *'Dungrane'* in a land charter dated 15th June, 1596 (NAS catalogue GD110/177 (already referred to). There were two main meanings for the Scots word 'grane'. One was a branch, offshoot of a river, stream or valley and the other more likely meaning in this case, given the prefix of 'dun' (fortified hill) was a prong of a fork or Salmon spear (CSD 1987). This sloping land then had a name that perhaps commemorated such a battle remembered in ancient poetry as the *'Hill of Prongs/Spears/Fork Carriers'*. Interestingly the latter term was used by Gildas as a derogatory term for the Saxons (Moffat 1999, p202).

If my hypothesis is correct then the Gododdin force may have ridden to the 'Holy Strath' from Edinburgh along the sands of the Lothian coastline. At low tide there would be few if any obstacles for horses and a distance of around twenty miles could have been covered in a morning. Their destination was *'Catraeth.'* You may remember dear Traveller, my reference to the little ravine that was the physical boundary that divided the old royal burgh of North Berwick from 'Rodes', the site of the forgotten citadel? The Glen or Fairy Burn, a confluence of waters that run off the Law and the Heugh, flows over the floor of this gash through the cliffs and into the Milsey Bay (Mill Sea). The ruins of three grain mills can still be seen on its banks. These are the medieval *Mills of Kintreath*, one of which I have already noted was recorded as being the 'Wall Tower Mill'. Etymologically 'kin' (Gaelic) means *'head; principal'* whilst *'treath'* may, I will hazard, originate through the Welsh *'tref'* meaning *'homestead'* to the old Celtic *'trebo'* meaning *'dwelling'* or *'village'* giving a translation through the language eras of Scotland of: the *'mills of the main settlement/stead'* (Watson,1926p356). This would appear to be a direct reference to the citadel of Guinnion that is bounded by the glen on its west side. It seems possible from this that *Kintreath* was derived from *Catreath*. Given the place-name derivation perhaps there were mills there many centuries before the medieval priory had claim to them.

Further knowledge about Guinnion may be abstracted from the names associated with this place and its surroundings: *'Kintreath'; 'Canty'; 'cantref'* and arguably *Catreath*. A 'cantref' was the 'largest division of land in a lordship or dominion' (Watson 1926, p357). In medieval Wales a cantref was an administrative unit which was divided up into several 'commotes' with a court at which the main landowners *('uchelwyr')* and the king or his representative would gather and pass judgement ('Welsh Law' Wikipedia). According to the Welsh Laws concerned with land a cantref was a hundred trefs which amounts to 25,600 acres (one tref being 256 acres) which is roughly a seventh of the East Lothian territory (174,080 acres according to the Statistical Account of 1868). I would argue that such a portion of land would have encompassed the coastal Iudeu or Conspicuous Cape and its boundary lands along the Peffer valley with the forgotten citadel of Guinnion and the close-by fields as the 'main settlement' (Note 12)

It may also be of significance that the bay immediately east of the fortress of Guinnion was called *'Canty'*. Using Watson's (1926,p364) elucidation on the origins of the place-name *'Cantray'* as possibly etymologically derived from *'canto-treb'* meaning 'white stead' this sandy bay may be have been part of the white stronghold of Guinnion. From stone observations there had to have been an eastern disembarkation point to explain vignettes that show figures heading for the fortress along the coast edge from that direction. With several other pictorials a suspicion lurks that at some point there was a very large built harbour at Canty Bay.

Aside from all this there are arguably other significant topographical features of the Conspicuous Cape that were alluded to in the poetry which may bring us closer to being clear about the destination of the Gododdin. These are more difficult to locate because the passage of time has brought big changes to the landscape of East Lothian. The landowners of the county were at the forefront of the innovations of the agricultural revolution in the 18th and 19th centuries. Of particular relevance to this investigation was the drainage of the lands bordering

194

the Conspicuous Cape. In the time of the Gododdin a significant part of the valley of the Peffers would have been marshland. The place-names of the area provide the evidence of this for example *Fenton – 'farm by swamp'* (Williamson 1942); *Myreside- 'by a peat bog'* (CSD 1987) As already detailed, throughout what is now Scotland with a warmer and wetter climate there would have been copious amounts of bog-land and rivers would have been fuller and more numerous. Fords would have been important places and the one referred to in the 'Y Gododdin' *('Rough the ford before the warrier' (A version verse 17'); 'hard-pressed before the ford' (B version verse 9); 'firm in guarding the ford(' B version, verse 13)* (Translation by Thomas O.Clancy in 'The Triumph Tree' T.O.Clancy (ed)pp46-77 1998) seems to have been of great strategic importance as much strife was described around it. I have already cited sources which make clear that there was in all likelihood a substantial body of water surrounding the Conspicuous Cape in the 6th century (Chapter 3). An allusion to this feature may lie within another version of the 'dingle dousy' rhyme already conjectured as having some reference to raids on Iudeu (Note 13)

"Deuk's dub afore the door-

There fell I!

A' the lave cried 'Waly! Waly!'

But I cried 'Feigh, fye!"

(Chambers (1870, p21))

From the 18th century *'deuk's dub'* had the meaning *'duck pond'* and is still known as such in Fife, Kincardineshire and Dumfriesshire (CSD 1987) but given the the allusion to battle within the rhyme I wonder whether this term was part of a play on words. I would suggest that 'deuk' may have been linked to 'dux' the Latin for 'leader' and the name the Romans gave for a commander. The title was associated with Arthur as 'Dux Bellorum', leader of battles (Moffat 1999, p206). *'Dub'* as most Scots know it today is the word for *'puddle'* a small muddy pool of rainwater and is traced to the 16th century Lowlands meaning stagnant or muddy water. Whether the meaning was *'Dux's Water'* or *'Deuk's/duck's/dub'/pool* the rhyme could be a memory trace of the long gone natural barrier to entering Iudeu (*'afore the door'*) that has travelled through time by way of the oral tradition (Map3). Arguably it is a fragment of perhaps many stories that must have been told about an important battle fought long ago by Arthur and the Gywr y Gogledd/Gododdin that involved a particular stretch of water forever to be linked to the hero and that over a thousand years later lies unrecognised in a little rhyme sung to a child (Note 14)

The Peffer, a significant body of water in ancient times and a ford across it that seems to have been guarded, lay roughly two miles from the citadel. Where the ford was along the Peffer may be related to the presence of a *West Fortoun* now *West Fortune* and a *Fortoun Ester* now *East Fortune* in the valley of the Peffer (see Map 3). Were they 'fort-towns', settlements a mile apart with a purpose, to guard the fording place across the Peffer? I would conjecture now and suggest these place-names relate to inundation by the waters of the Forth as there was, close by, a *Fortoun Bank*. Certainly to the west may have been largely under water or difficult boggy ground suggested in the name 'Fenton'. 'Bloody lands' is a field name, near the mouth of the western Peffer, on a farm just a mile from West Fortune, called 'Prora' (Martine 1890/1999, p22) suggesting an oral/memory trace of past conflict(s) there. So does *'Stantilane'* meaning 'stand till one' which was the name of a farm at one time (Martine 1890). It can be found on old map and contemporary maps near Ballincrieff Castle which lies before the access point to the Iudeun Cape between the Garletons already described (see Map 3).

It may be that Adair's (1736) and Herman Moll's (1745) maps identified the ancient landward area of the Gododdin battle in placing a 'fford' and a 'Fuird' respectively in the vicinity of the lands called *Congalton* on the north side of the Peffer. Congalton is an interesting name with regard to the proximity of a fording place as according to Watson (1926 pp137, 487) *'cong'* means *'a narrow'* and was always used in connection with water. 'Alt' meant a 'height' and in Irish Gaelic it related to *'a narrow strait where a lake or river narrows itself'*. It is possible to argue that over many centuries etymology, stone narrative and poetry have collaborated in preserving a memory of the exploits of Arthur and those who came after him. With regard to the latter it may be that the encircling and possibly tidal Peffers constituted the 'echwydd' Urien was associated with. From my observations 'Catreath', a holy strath, a ford and an unpredictable waterway were in close proximity to each other on the coastal plain of East Lothian.

That the defeat of the Gododdin from Edinburgh took place here on the Conspicuous Cape may be revealed in what could be a poetical reference to the painted hill. In each version of the poem 'The Gododdin' warriors were at one point portrayed as:

"on each side of the Aled"

(The Gododdin Version A verse 82 and Version B verse 2 Translation by Joseph P. Clancy in 'The Triumph Tree' T. O.Clancy(ed) (1998, pp47-78))

'Aled' is a Welsh first name and means 'child'. Remembering the frequent portrayal of a baby bear at the summit of the Law and of a sea baby and warrior king on opposite sides of the same sculptures, I am suggesting this line from what is thought to be the oldest poem from Northern Britain, was a poetical allusion to the sacred hill. The hill may have become in some sense the embodiedment of the dead hero.

Some twenty or more years along the timeline from the founding of Lindisfarne, the coastal plain was arguably the site of another event this time recorded by Nennius in his 'Historia Brittonum'.   This was *Atbret Iudeu* or the *Ransom of Iudeu*. Two 12th century, not quite identical copies of the chapters from the Historia, described that in 655 or thereabouts, when the Anglo-Saxons/Northumbrians held sway over parts of Lothian, Penda, the king of Mercia in an alliance with thirty British kings went *'on the expedition as far as the urbs that is called Iudeu'* (Fraser 2009, p23).   Oswy, king of the Northumbrians was at Iudeu. To avoid an attack, he gave up or gave back to Penda, all the riches that were with him there in the city. Penda then distributed these to the British kings. After this in the same year, there was a battle called *Maes Gai* ('Field of Gaius' ie 'Caesar') near a river called *Winwead* which was won by Oswy in which most of the British commanders were killed.

The differences between the copies of the 'Historia' chapters are still the focus of historical debate with regard to the translation and usage of the Latin in which they were written. The debate has been about whether Oswy gave the ransom directly into the hands (*manu*) of Penda or whether he went to Penda who was on the plain of *Manau*, the land between the Carron and Avon Rivers, to give it to the Mercian. Fraser (2008) posited the theory that the scribe's use of words was to do with knowing that there was a connection between Manau and the fortress at Iudeu.   As Stone Archivist I am happy to corroborate such a connection inscribed as it was on the stone maps of the Uotadini. The link between the fortress/palace of Iudeu and Manau was inextricably woven into the ancient historical fabric of the lands of the Kyles, the Wall (Antonine), the beaches and the coastal hinterlands of the Forth and the Tay. A narrative of battles won against the Saxons and the Picts and others and the achievement of peace and stability across the lands over which Arthur was overlord (or Emperor) for a generation after Bouden (Badon). Bouden Hill and Camlaan (today Camelon) both lie on the plain of Manau (present day West Lothian and South Stirlingshire). Iudeu was consistently mapped into the military lines of attack and defence and it is from the plain of Manau that the Bear, dying, was taken to Iudeu, a city that had been connected with him since childhood and that had honoured him as its great saviour.

Fraser (2008) also argued that the correct interpretation of the word *'atbret'* is the Welsh meaning *'gave back'* and from this he suggests that Oswy had taken tribute from the Britons and this confrontation at Iudeu was about the return of this. It may very well have been the case but given the knowledge of the wealth of Iudeu itself and its cultural and religious significance to the Britons, then other possibilities come into view. For example, the native British who may have accepted the need to pay tribute and live in peace with the new overlordship of Northumbria were not prepared to accept his occupation of their sacred memorial palace. Whether it was down to greed or reverence the British princes may have demanded the commerative art treasures. Oswy faced with the possibility of war, promised to hand over Iudeun treasures in order to placate the Britons temporarily at least. He may have been in trouble with Celtic Church too as although perhaps not sure it wanted a popular sacred secular site may have, at the same time, had a public identity that was linked to the Christian hero. The decision to do battle somewhere else may have been due to all parties not wishing to destroy the site. Certainly according to the comment from Lambert de St Omer the palace may have been still intact centuries after this time. Seeking out a possible Maes Gai near a River Winwead may not be such a challenge if the Caesar that is being referred to is Arthur. You may recall Dear Traveller, that he was represented as a Caesar on the Emperor's map a choice of name for this stone prompted by seeing the laurel crown upon the Bear's head. It could be argued that searching for a field and a river associated with Arthur would necessarily include looking at the sites of his battles.

I would suggest that what is known about another conflict some three hundred years later may reveal the real location of Maes Gai. This was the *Battle of Brunanburh (937)* recorded in poetic form in the Anglo-Saxon Chronicles and described as between King Athelstan with his brother the Aetheling Edmund against a coalition led by Constantin king of the Scots, 'shipmen' (Vikings) and 'Northmen' (Cumbrians/Britons of Strathclyde)'. It was documented that this coalition was resoundly beaten *'in strife **around** Brunanburh'* (Winchester Manuscript (Anglo-Saxon Chronicles (Swanton 1996, pp106-110, my emphasis)). Brunanburh sometimes called *Brunandun* the whereabouts of which is apparently unknown today, was described as the *'meeting place of peoples'* (Winchester Manuscript, pp106-110). Arguably this would have been an apt description of Iudeu the scene pictorially of many visitations peaceful or otherwise.

There are even more names from different sources which were elucidated by Woolf (2007, pp168-173) such as *Wendun* (in northern annals) and from the 'Annales Cumbriae' *'bellum Brune'*. The 'brun' versions of the place-name fit well with the sacred bear hill. Williamson (1942, p85) noted in her analysis of non-Celtic names in the Scottish Borders, that in 'Brun' there 'may have been a personal name in a metathesized form' which would have been *Bruna* with a genitive ending in 'n' in southern Britain and *Brune* in Scotland which was later given a genitive ending of 'n'. Some explanation then for the spelling variations! Symeon of Durham apart from providing two 'brun' names for the location of this battle: *Brunnanwerc* and *Brunnanbyrig* also called it *Weodune*. From Williamson's interpretation of this latter name two meanings come into view, both have relevance to Guinnion and the painted hill. She suggested that Weodune may mean *'heathen temple'* derived from the Old English or alternatively it signified *'meadow-ford'* from taking *'weon'* to be the Old Norse *'vin'* for *'meadow'*. Cogent with regard to the battle three hundred years before, Williamson made a connection between the origins and meaning of *Weodune* and Bede's version of *'Winwead'* as *'Winwoed'*. On the basis of this finding the encircling Peffer may have been 'the river of the heathen temple' or the 'meadow river'. Respectively, both interpretations would fit with the stone evidence and the topographical characteristics of the Conspicuous Cape. It seems possible to argue from this that the arranged conflict at Maes Gai between Oswy and the Brittonnic/Mercian forces took place in the valley of the Peffers, site of one of the 12 Arthurian battles. It would be interesting to speculate with regard to the what was the situation within old Iudeu at time of the battle of Brunanburh given the bishop of Durham was still referring to it as a Pagan place in the 10th century.

The poetic account of the battle tells of a huge slaughter and retreat in a boat small enough to *'push afloat......over the fallow flood'*, suggesting that the survivors fell back towards a small river. Could this water have been the Peffer that encircled Iudeu? The Winchester scribe recorded that there was a subsequent transfer of the defeated into larger boats which departed on *'Ding's Mere'*. The 'deep water' alluded to I suggest was the Forth. *'Ding'* being related to *'din'*, is an earlier form of *'dun'* meaning *'fort*. The ancient stronghold of Guinnion may be the fort referred to. The nearby farm of New Mains (at Fenton north of Peffer boundary between Dirleton and North Berwick) that was, according to Martine (1890/90) 'anciently' called *'Dingleton'*. This may have been a faint trace of this era in the timeline of Iudeu's story as is the place-name *Duns Falde* in the same area. Already referred to earlier the meaning of the latter relates to an ancient fortification (ie meaning *'hill fort fold'* (Watson 1926).

You will have noticed dear Traveller that the date of the Brunanburh conflict may have made it exactly 400 years after the death of Arthur. Did such a momentous anniversary have some role in why the battle took place? Nearing the end of a long reign could Constantin have decided on a confrontation with the Saxon king with a view to snatching back Iudeu from the English? Had he seen the retrieval of the Conspicuous Cape as his memorial? He had on side the Britons of Strathclyde whose ancestors had a shared narrative and kindred links with the people on the Conspicuous Cape. Did the 'powerful eastern stone' and it's tomb of the iconic Arthur who had fought to keep the Saxons out of Lothian make the mustering of men easier?

There is a myth linked with the Anglo-Saxon king and the village of Athelstaneford in which the army of the Scots were victorious at the Cogtail Burn. Given the village's name, it seems unlikely that this commemoration would be given to the loser. Martine (1890,p21) a conscientious recorder of places, people and events in the parishes of 'Haddingtonshire' knew of this name and albeit unwittingly, I think identified its pre-Saxon lineage in a bracketed aside in which he gave the other name for the village as 'vulgarly called *Elshenford'*. Earlier in this chapter you will recall that *'Elphin'* meaning *'white rock'* or *'rock peak'* may have applied to the North Berwick Law. I suggest that this *'Elphin's ford'* would have been close to the western end of the significant stretch of water (Map3), stone detailed, where the two Peffers met and was matched to the east by Herman Moll's *'Fuird'* and Adair's *'fford'* near

Congalton. In addition I have suggested that there may have been a connection between the 'Elphin' of the poems *'The Verses of the Graves'* and *'The Brithwyr'* and the painted hill.

Woolf's analysis (2007, p177-181) of the recording of a raid by Constantin's successor Mael Coluim around 950 may be of some relevance with regard to the hill and the surrounding lands. More mythology seems to surround this event which either points to the old king pushing Mael Coluim into carrying out the raid or that he requested his kingship back for a week to do it himself. The raid was recorded in a 14th century copy of the *'Chronicle of the Kings of Alba'*. Of particular note for my investigation was the name the Scots called it:

" the raid of (the) Albidosi that is nainndisi"

(Woolf 2007, p177)

Expert study of the word 'albidosi' has come up with the meaning *'English Scotland'* which would presumably place the action in Lothian/East Lothian. It is tempting to see the raid as some sort of revenge for the defeat at Brunanburh. Hudson's interpretation of the word (1998, cited in Woolf 2007,p178) which he takes from the Latin as *'albi dorsorum'* was that 'albidosi' meant *'white ridges'* which he deduced referred to cattle. Without making such a connection this interpretation seems close to the stone portrayal of the Lothian-Forth coastline with its whitened signification. It would seem that different analytical/documentary pathways may have reached the same destination. What of 'nainndisi'? It may be too difficult to decipher due to scribal errors but what if Hudson's approach to the first word applied to this one too? My guess is that it may be the sort of word that reaches back millennia to the belief systems of the early peoples who settled on the estuary lands of the Forth and simultaneously carries an inheritance of language change that came about in Scotland over the many centuries. The pictorial cuts through the latter to some extent making some stone inspired theorising possible. For example, *'nainn- disi'* might be closer to a meaning, with *'nainn'* perhaps sourced to the ancient Celtic word *'nemetos'* meaning *'sacred; noble'*. *'Nemeton'* was a sacred place or *'local habitations of the gods'* (Watson 1926, p244). There are many place-names in Scotland in a range of spelling that can be sourced to this word explored by Watson (1926) in his chapter on early church terms.

Over the course of writing this book I have noted the presence of sculptured animals that were not native to Britain, in particular the crocodile and the baboon. I should mention that I have spied the head and neck of a camel on the Emperor's Map in the region of Angus and indeed a much larger version in stone can be viewed in that county today. Such pictorials have led me to consider the foundation legend of the Scots documented by Walter Bower in his 'Scotichronicon'. Bower, born in Haddington was an abbot of the Augustinian monastery on Inchcolm Island in the Firth of Forth. He wrote this huge historical work in the 1440's (Der Watt, 1998). It was the continuation of a chronicle by an earlier cleric John of Fordun. The legend goes that 'Scota' the daughter of an Egyptian pharaoh called 'Chencres' was driven out of Egypt with her husband Gaythelos Gal a prince of Greek origin. After a long journey Scota and her followers reached Scotland. Bower wrote that they stayed a while with the people there but then moved on to Ireland. According to the Egyptologist Lorraine Evans (2000) an Egyptian princess Meritaten the eldest daughter of the pharaoh Akhenaten (1353-1337) and Nefertiti left Egypt with her husband, possibly a prince of Tyre and undertook a journey which eventually brought her party to the shores of Britain. It was Evan's view that Bower's description of the route that the royal party took fitted well with what is now known from archaeological and genetic research. Several vignettes on the Emperor's Map including what looks to be a crewed ship off the East Neuk of Fife seem to hint at Egyptian sea voyagers. Whatever the details of that encounter/visit/sojourn it is clear from stone observations that the culture and religion of the ancient Egyptians left its mark on the lands of Atlantic, Central and Eastern Scotland. The people between the Walls apparently remembered and were proud to take ownership of that heritage.

In particular with regard to the painted hill there is the baboon head that I have sometimes observed configured into the shape of the North Berwick Law. To the ancient Egyptians the baboon represented the god Thoth, the god of wisdom, art and civlisation. The people of Ancient Egypt believed there were many gods (polytheism) and animals were seen as playing a major role in their worship of them. Some of these deities were linked to creation myths in which the Eygptians sought to explain how the world began. They came to be grouped together into what were called *enneads* (*Note 15*). The most important divine group called the *Great Ennead* was worshipped at a place in Lower Egypt about ten kilometres north-east of Cairo that the Egyptians called *Iuna* or *Yuna* (respectively 'Heliopolis' Wikipedia and McLeish, K (1996) which means *'place of the pillars'*. It was later to be called *Heliopolis* by the Greeks. Is this a coincidence or were the Uotadini on the sea plain of Lothian whose name could mean *'praise' 'support' 'pillar'* anciently linked to this sacred place ? I am reminded of the 2nd century geographer Pausanius who wrote of the *Genuini*, a people who were vassals to the Romans (Dunbavin (1998) referred to in Chapter 1) who lived north of Hadrian's Wall. Were the Brigantians raiding the lands of the Conspicuous Cape which as I have already argued, must have held great wealth as a place of kings and high priests?

Of particular relevance to this archive was the goddess Isis who emerged from the Great Ennead in the first millennium BC to become the chief goddess of ancient Egypt and a major cultic figure to the Romans. As goddess of goddesses she was the protector of kings and had the ability to prevent putrefaction and bring the dead back to life which according to myth, she did for her husband the god *Osiris*. The cult of Isis rivalled that of Christianity early in the first millennium and there are narrative similarities with regard to the existence of an afterlife and the *'joy of Isis'* when the 'Divine Tribunal' made her son *Horus* king (Pinch, 2002). Is it possible that 'nainndisi' was a trace of the Great Ennaed and the mother goddess Isis? That the Romans apparently associated the goddess with mystery religions and magic may point to and/or explain perhaps a Scots/ Latin origin for *'nainnd-isi'*. The 'Great Ennead' has a fair resemblance to the island called 'Grandena' in the Ravenna's Cosmography.

The Great Ennead of Iuna (Heliopolis) included Isis' husband Osiris. As the ruler of the underworld (ie.The Dead) and given the high status burials on the slope of the Law, perhaps he was the 'isi' referred to in the *'Chronicle of the Kings of Alba'*. All of Egypt's kings became Osiris in death. A further thread linking this deity to the chronicle record lies with the city of *Abydos* in the early kingdom (3200-3000 BC) of *This* or *Thinis* in Upper Egypt which on its outskirts had a royal necropolis. Many Egyptian kings were buried there. This place, the land of the dead, was the main cultic centre of Osiris (Nicholls et al 2008). A further possible link with the referral in the 'Chronicle of Kings' may lie with this ancient Egyptian city. *Abydos* was the Greek name that replaced the original Egyptian *Abdju* which means *'the hill of the symbol or reliquary'* ('Abydos' Wikipedia) and according to stone observation exactly describes North Berwick Law. Could 'Albidosi' be a Scottish trace of that ancient naming?

Isis' and Osiris' son Horus may also have had a place within the belief system of those who lived on the Conspicuous Cape. Horus like many Egyptian gods had various manifestations and functions. One of these in particular is of note concerning the narratives associated with the painted hill as he was known as *'Horus the child'* or *'Her pa khered'* (alexanderancientart.com). It is intrigueing don't you think, dear Traveller to ponder upon the parallels and connections between an Egyptian creation myth, P- Celtic oral/poetic tradition (ie 'Aled'/'child' in the 'The Gododdin') and a dead North British hero once a miraculous child, entombed in a northern 'pyramid'?

There were other enneads centred in Iuna whose members do appear on stone here beside the Wanton Wall. The Small Ennead of Heliopolis consisted of Thoth, Horus, Anubis and Maat Thoth's wife. The last two were associated with death ritual and belief. Anubis the jackal-headed god who was linked to mummification was sometimes called *'He who is upon his mountain'* which was a reference to his role as the protector of the tombs of pharaohs. This reminds me of the stone work that places a hound's head into the outline of the North Berwick Law and earlier in this archive I have referred to a dog with pups on the top of North Berwick Law (Mother Hound Agnes, Mae's narrative chapter 2). Amongst the pantheon of gods there was also a dog god from Abydos called 'Wepwawet' or 'opener of the ways' (Rice 1999). He was believed to inhabit graveyards marshalling the dead towards the goddess Maat who, as the embodiment of truth and justice, was responsible for measuring whether their souls were in an appropriate condition to reach the afterlife. Very early on I found a stone with what turned out to be a unique scene (so far in my observations) worked upon it. At the bottom of the little hill a woman was standing outside her house looking up towards a dog bounding towards the summit. I wondered what it signified. It was a puzzle and since it was the only one I have come across I had almost forgotten about it. In the mix of migrations and the concomitant changes in language and culture could this vignette be a remnant of an ancient North African contact millennium before the arrival of the Celts?

The crocodile sacred and revered in some parts of Ancient Egypt (Wenke 2009) has been stone identified in Fife and Argyll. One further sighting of this creature was as an outline of a headland or coastline just east of

Guinnion which would have been approximately the territory in which the ruined Tantallon Castle now stands. This once great fortress is thought to have been built on an older structure that may have been called *'Dentaloune'* (Bain 1958) which means most likely *'toothy rascal'* (CSD 1987). This quite affectionate name for a crocodile seems to chime well with the gentle stone portrayals of animals. The written record and the pictorial seem to be confirming in parallel another trace of the gods of Egypt in the Scottish landscape. Old Welsh poetry refers to such a creature as the crocodile in the context of describing the approach of a military force over water and the words suggest a ship with a resemblance (painted?) to this fearsome animal

"There passed an animal with wide jaws,

On it there were a hundred heads

And a battle was contested

Under the roof of his tongue;

And another battle there is

In his occiput"

(From the 'Battle of Godeu' in 'Arthur and the Britons in Wales and Scotland' Skene/Bryce (1988, p134))

These words seem to be describing hand-to-hand fighting on a ship. Don't you think it is interesting to speculate whether the inspiration for these words was sourced to a stone pictorial and a memory of a time when a wild creature of Africa had some sort of a presence near the Wanton Wall?

Another possible connection with the baboon-like profile outlined into the shape of the North Berwick Law may lie in the medieval name of *'Punton'* for the site of the old citadel. Three thousand years ago the Ancient Egyptians imported quantities of gold, myrrh, ebony and wild animals from a land called *'Punt'* including baboons which they kept as pets. Genetic research of the hair from mummified baboons seems to indicate that Punt was in modern day Eritrea and Ethiopia. The Eygptians sometimes referred to Punt as *'Ta netjer'* meaning *'land of the God'*. Some sources suggested that they thought of Punt as the land of their aboriginal ancestors ('Land of Punt' Wikipedia). More linkages to Scotland's 'oldest inhabitants' and the 'heathen temple', the burial place of kings and the appearance of non-native wild creatures more commonly found in Africa may be uncovered with further observations.

One final mysterious link with Ancient Egypt has been the observation on stone of the distinctive *nemes* headdress only worn by Egyptian kings (Wenke 2009, p304). The folded cloth has been sculpted as upon the head of the Bear on a goodly number of narrative stones. Aside from these I have found one pyramidal shaped stone obviously representing the Law upon which there are what looks to be the coloured stripes that are usually associated with the nemes scarf.

Moving forward over two thousand years to the times of early monastical documentation perhaps I have been unfair to the religious men of those times in suggesting they were silent in their annals and tracts as to the fate of such a major site of pilgrimage as Iudeu. As you will have gathered from the many versions of 'Brunaburh' in just such records it seems clear that monks did write about Iudeu. It is just that over the centuries due to the changes in language other names came to be associated with the place. There may be an instance when the Iuduen identity was remembered as there was recorded in the Anglo-Saxon Chronicle ('D' text) in 952 AD a Northumbrian bishop called Wulfstan who had been imprisoned on the orders of the Saxon king Eadred in a place called *Iudanburh* (Woolf 2007,p189)

Perhaps another hint of the citadel's existence may lie hidden in Bede's *'An Ecclesiastical History of the English People'* (*'Historia ecclesiastica gentis Anglorum'*) written around 731. For example he described the healing powers of a wooden cross that in 634 King Oswald had placed in the ground before a battle and identified the site as 'in the English tongue *Hefenfeith' or the Heavenly Field'* which he described as 'near the wall in the north' (Bede, Chap2 Christian Classics Ethereal Library). Arguably this may have been a referral to the Peffer Valley beside the sacred hill, the place I think that was called *'Heaven's Haven'* (Clancy 1998) in the 'Gododdin'. Bede in his account of the building of a church by Oswald on the site of the cross locates it in the lands of the Bernician people. As already detailed these 'gap people' are thought to have been well settled in the Christian Gododdin lands of East Lothian by the end of the 6th century. Yet Bede wrote that this church was much needed as

"..it appears that there was **no symbol** of the Christian faith, no church, no altar erected throughout all the nation of the Bernicians."

(In 'An Ecclesiastical History of the English People' Chapter II. (Christian Classics Ethereal Library (my emphasis)))

That Bede was known to nurse an antipathy towards the North Britons seems borne out in this statement as stone evidence arguably provides a very different picture of the East Lothian part of what was Bernicia. Such a culturally iconic place and a hugely important pilgrimage site must have been difficult to avoid making allusion to. Fraser (2009, pp106-107) suspected that there was some sort of earlier ecclesiastical centre that was rival to Lindisfarne and hazarded that it might have been an Ionan monastery at Portmahomack in Easter Ross. Stones in vast quantities point to the East Lothian pyramid, 'hill of the symbol' as an earlier contender for the souls of the people.

With regard to the time after Brunaburh I suspect that due to its earlier significance, Iudeu may still have figured prominently in some portion of the religious and secular history of Scotland. I suggest that these stone pictures may have a contribution to make in historical research. I have found a possible example of this that concerned the boundary of Lothian. According to Woolf (2007 pp 234-240) there is uncertainty with respect to what was the 'Lothian' referred to in the annals. Keeping this in mind there may be something written that flagged up the existence of Iudeu. In Rollason's (2003, pp275-276) analysis of how Lothian became part of Scotland in the reign of the Anglo-Saxon king Edgar (957-975) one of his sources seemed cogent to this. According to Rollason's reading of an 11th/12th century text called the *First Coming of the Saxons* Edgar gave 'Lothian' to the Scottish king Kenneth as a way of securing his north-eastern border. Kenneth II was presented to Edgar by the two earls in charge of Northumbria. He did homage to the Saxon king and was duly given 'Lothian'. Of the two earls one being Oslac earl of York, it is Earl Eadwulf's (with the added moniker of 'Evil Child' (Note 16)) domain that is of the most interest concerning Iudeu. He was described as ruling:

"Over the Northumbrians from the Tees to **Myreford**"

(Rollason (2003, p275), my emphasis.)

Is it possible that 'Myreford' relates to the same ford on the Peffer that had been at the centre of the conflicts around Iudeu/Brunaburh? The old maps have *Mayrtoun* close to Drem and Prora(Adair 1682); *Myreton* and close by *Myrtoun* (Adair 1736) all in the vicinity of Herman Moll's late 17th or early 18th century map with *'Fuird'* on the Peffer Burn. If this

Myreford was on old Iudeu's watery boundary then in the 10th century the Earl of Bamburgh (Eadwulf) held sway over the southern part of today's East Lothian. What Kenneth may have received then was this portion of present day Lothian south of the bog land of the Peffer. If the ancient boundaries of the Emperor's Map signified 'Lothian' then this territory's southern boundary may have been the Lothian Tyne a few miles south of North Berwick. In other words the 'Lothian' referred to consisted of the Conspicuous Cape and surrounding lands.

Could it be that the stories attached to this coastal territory were at the root of a 150 years of Scottish kings invading 'Lothian' and the eastern border lands after the union of the Scots and the Picts in 844 AD under Kenneth MacAlpin? (Watson 1926 p133) Perhaps the Saxon king was ridding himself of a particular bone of contention in any relations with the Scots. Was the prize for the Scots Iudeu, Punt, Agned, Grandena, Aled, Brunaburh, Catreath, Arthur?

The Bear who had sculpted ties of blood with the western kyles and islands of Atlantic Scotland, the peoples between the old Roman walls, and those from the forests and mountains beyond seemed to embody all that united Northern Britain. A mix of people, belief systems and histories were documented in stone as integral to Arthur's story. From miraculous sea-baby to emperor he appeared to have been well remembered by the people of the North for many centuries after his death.

Auld Mur

Dear Arthur has been gone now over forty winters and I have come home. I have a place at Owen's hearth, my grandchild's man. Old and tired as I am I still manage a stint of guard duty at the foot of Agned. Long gone are the settled times. Here only I remember first hand peace between all the Northern Kindred. I shall not live to see it again but perhaps those who come after the children who listen to my stories may.

****

Chapter notes

Note 1
For example there seems to be one sort in which shells are used as the medium for representing the Bear's last resting place.

Note 2
Originally the meaning of the ankh was 'life' and it later took on a further sense, that of immortality. There is uncertainty as to what the symbol actually is.

Note 3
Perhaps the *Pow Burn* which empties into the Forth at *Airth*.

Note 4
Incidentally, there are two present day Elphinstones within the bounds of the ancient Emperor's Map. One in East Lothian near Gladsmuir and the other a little north of Airth and the Pow Burn, on the south side of the Forth. I wonder whether their locations may be significant as territorial markers for the stone depicted white ridges of land ruled over by the chiefs of the Uotadini.

Note 5
On the subject of cloaked figures it is of interest to note that in the 14th century the Cistercian nuns at the Priory of North Berwick wore black habits rather than the usual white of the order (Sutherland 1999). Could this have been because the Druids in their flowing white robes were still a potent memory in this part of Scotland? Indeed one could speculate whether there were still people (religious or otherwise) in such garb caring for the sacred site in the medieval period.

Note 6
Stone observations suggest there were specific sites that were part of Arthur's story at Iudeu, such as the earth cliff (small amphitheatre or 'round table'), and the lower part of the Law. The latter may have been the represented by a holy well which is situated in the Lodge grounds and was known as St Andrews Well in medieval times.

Note 7
I read the copy of this charter made in 1842 by William Fraser held in the National Archives of Scotland GD158/271

Note 8

'The White Cockade' by James Grant was set in the North Berwick/Auldhame part of East Lothian just before the rebellion. The relevance to this archive is early in the narrative when two Jacobites come ashore near North Berwick and proceed to walk eastwards towards Auldhame. Grant refers to a 'Temple House' placing it near the coastal road on the outskirts of the town. In other words he seems to have known of such a place in the vicinity of the citadel site.

Note 9

I have observed a pillar on one stone. Perhaps this suggests an alternative/additional meaning attached to the Uotadini concerned with their city.

Note 10

Other *Kilmorys* in Argyll and Bute: Kilmory a village on the *Knapdale coast* with a *Kilmory Bay* and a *Kilmory Burn* situated opposite the group of islands of which *Eilean Mor* is the largest. Kilmory is a village on the south-western coast of the island of *Arran* with an *Eilean Mairi* off-shore. *Kilmory Castle* lies on the southern outskirts of the town of *Lochgilphead* (OSL 55, 68, 62). In addition there is a Kilmory on the island of *Rum* and on the *Ardnamurchan Peninsula*.

I would hazard that there may be other traces of that time in the places associated with an early saint called Cormac (Irish) or Cormag (Scottish). There is a *Cormac's Cave* on *Eilean Mor* the largest of the *Mc Cormaig Islands* in the Sound of Jura that lies about two miles off another Kilmory on the *Knapdale coast*. There on elevated ground looking over to the Paps of Jura is a chapel and a cross. Cormac is thought to have founded a monastery at *Keills* on the *Tayvallich Peninsula*. All these sites fall within the landscape that witnessed the dramatic flight of the baby Arthur with the last most likely being the embarkation point for the travellers from Dunadd. I wonder whether all these locations were part of an ancient pilgrimage pathway that perhaps was an example of a merging of narratives between those of the Northern Christian Church with its cult of the Virgin Mary, and that of the stone sculptures powerfully illustrated with the identifiers of much earlier religions and beliefs.

Note 11

Vrÿston in 'Scotia Regnum' (1635) by W J Blaeu; *Vrymston* in 'Scotiae pars australis' (1636) by H Hondius and *Vrimston* in 'The north part of England and the south part of Scotland Quarter-Master's Map' (1644) by T Jenner and W Holler. John Adair (1683) has the place called 'Magdalans' (meaning possibly - good enclosure?).

Note 12
I have carried out a rough measurement of the lands on the seacliffs east of the Glen ravine and on the southern side of the Tantallon Road that were from stone pictures, the possible bounds of the citadel and these amounted to 51 acres.

Note 13
According to Chambers (1870) *'dingle dousies'* were about placating young children by making a fiery ring from a lighted stick that was vigorously waved in front of a young child creating a distracting circle of fire while reciting a particular rhyme. The meanings of the words 'dingle' and 'dousie' suggest a play on words that would link the rhymes to long forgotten conflict - *'douse'* from 'dousy' related to *'doose'* meaning *'heavy blow'* etc or to *'doozie'* a *'lighted flame'*. Another possible meaning then is *'clobbered fort'* (CSD 1987). With regard to this rhyme is it possible that it is a long forgotten reference to a battle near 'dingsmere' or earlier again 'Deuk's dub' and the much fought over watery boundary of Iudeu?

Note 14
'Dux' is still in use in Scotland usually with regard to academic achievement at school. The dux is the top student overall in the final year of high school.

Note 15
This is a Greek term meaning a group of nine. Greek was used by Greek and Roman writers to describe all things Egyptian.

Note 16
It seems quite a coincidence that the Earl of Bamburgh had such a nickname given my theory that the Aled (Child) was a reference in 'The Gododdin' to the North Berwick Law. It seems possible that Eadwulf may have earned this name with regard to his governance of the Conspicuous Cape.

Last Words

Stone-gained knowledge has led me to finding out that Arthur Bear of the North was interred in a tomb that was a mystery or wonder to the world right here in this seaside town with the hill at its back. Observations of the miniatures that depict this wonder communicate the art and skill that was invested in providing a resting place fit for such a miraculous being who had survived the Cauldron when so tiny. I think that the great Maen or Stone of Iudeu that was envisioned in several totemic guises that represented millennia of belief for countless generations of peoples who came to live on the coastal plain of Lothian was a place of worship and pilgrimage both Pagan and Christian. Called the 'powerful eastern stone' in an 11th century Gaelic poem, it may be that this power continued long after the Gododdin were no more. That this longevity was due to Arthur's presence in the sacred hill seems likely. After a thousand years there still remained vestiges of the clifftop citadel, its towers, bridges and meal mills in the place-names on early paper maps. Over many of these years it appears that Iudeu in whatever name form, was sometimes the focus for conflict yet left untouched and perhaps for a while treated as a protected zone. The knowledge that this place existed may shed light on some of these events. Much of the history of the people of what is now Scotland before and after The Bear would seem for whatever reason, to have been lost to them. Yet I suspect that if the stone narratives were taken seriously more would be known of this country's rich heritage. I hope so

Over millennia the artists and craftsmen who created the story stones of North Berwick and the surrounding coast had much to document including the arrival of new peoples and the battles that sometimes must have ensued. The identity and beliefs of a people were displayed in their bird and animal totemic identifiers in the landscape and on the participants in the many bloody actions. There were special events such as marriages, the celebrations and honours bestowed after victory, the arrival of ships at a sea citadel, a bird catching contest and the recordings of burials as well as a very important funeral. Detailed familiarity with the coastal lands and sands of the eastern estuaries of the Forth and Tay was transcribed onto stone enabling even a 21st century observer to recognise and attempt an interpretation of the stone maps found.

One map in particular provides a layered narrative that contextualises the events and times of the Gwyr y Gogledd and the story of Arthur and in the process portrays something of the Roman action and influence on the North centuries before. The Emperor's Map holds the images of the enemies of the Romano-Britons, the Saxons and some of the peoples north of the Antonine Wall. Also with regard to the latter, the stone map seems to indicate that very ancient ties with the peoples north of the Forth and Tay were remembered and built upon through marriage by the Romano-British coalition of Arthur's time.

The lineage of the Sea Baby seems pivotal to the story of Southern Scotland remembered in stone. The Bear's life may have been spent in east and central Scotland but the map makes clear that his origins were with the very earliest settlers, the Bear People, perhaps the Atacotti or 'ancient inhabitants' or the other Neolithic peoples of the North who hunted and gathered across pre-Scotland and had a homeland in Cowal and Bute that stretched to the banks of Loch Lomond. Alt Clut or Dumbarton Rock features strongly in the story of these people. There, is set a narrative which links Arthur to the Romans and a people with a wolf totem in the form of a marriage approved and witnessed by a range of northern community representatives. Arthur's mother was a queen or princess of the Horse Folk of Kintyre, a people who were of Brittonnic and Irish descent. In one tiny stone map it is made clear that Arthur's origins flagged up a narrative shared amongst the Northern peoples.

There is a distinctive subset of crafted work which focuses on a violent and tragic set of events that were portrayed as having taken place on the Kintyre peninsula and at Dunadd around the time Arthur was born. This narrative does point the finger of blame at a particular figure and I have conjectured who this may have been. Often on the same work the arrival of the dying Arthur at Iudeu and his last resting place on the Maen has been documented. I have argued that the vast quantity of worked pieces that record the location of the Bear's tomb suggests that a cult developed around the Christian hero that would have made the Conspicuous Cape a major place of pilgrimage for many centuries. I have postulated that perhaps this commemoration of Arthur with its Pagan associations may have been very acceptable to a population on the cusp of religious change and helpful to the early Celtic Christian Church. Eventually however church leaders may have come to see the Arthurian narrative as a threat and so any related 'paperwork' could well have been disposed of. However, from the number of crafted works that commemorated the story of the Sea Baby, the emperor and the secular saint I have argued that it was very widely known and remembered into the future in the place-names, stories, rhymes and poetry of the people of Scotland.

Stone portrayals of the sea citadel as well as the Druid presence in the colourful and shaded niche of minute painted hills led to the uncovering of Puntoun and Ponti[fc]raig. They take the story of the Conspicuous Cape of East Lothian to a time long before the Romans when this quiet part of the world was at the epicentre of cultural and religious life of Scotland's oldest peoples and visitors/migrants included the Egyptians. The use of a multitude of wonderfull skills and techniques that appear to have had the objective of telling a story artfully will if studied open a window out into a vista of complexity with regard to the identity and culture of 'dark age' Scotland.

It has been a long journey of words for one now completely enamoured by the pictorial. My objective was to put some of the unnoticed records of the old peoples of Scotland 'out there'. It was an experience in which I was always aware of how little I know of history or etymology or art or many other forms of knowledge that the stone narratives sent me off to explore. Inevitably there will be evidence of this and I would like apologise now for the errors I have made in this book.

More travelling awaits me in the little heap on my desk.

Appendix 1: The Emperor's Map

Approximate dimensions: length 5.0 cm; breadth 4.0 cm; height 1.5 cm.

There are 6 separate surfaces, all worked.

A tiny limestone plaque which can be viewed from all perspectives and another scene/story depiction comes into view. This suggests to me that an effort has been made to encapsulate as much of the life and times of Arthur as possible. The scenes individually are exquisite and many are explicable to modern eyes. Those that are not, is due only to unfamiliarity with all the events depicted. To the owner of this treasure, it must have been like having a romantic novel, a thriller and a tragic plot for a play all merged into one small piece of art lying in the palm of his hand.

On the largest surface there is a stylised map that seems to encompass the whole of the Central Lowlands of Scotland and tip into the Highlands. It appears to lay out the defences and areas of control and threat and battle within this territory. This is achieved using a variety of methods:

The use of colour, for example the same colour that is used to depict the face of Arthur is used I think to make it easier to identify where he had control or fought throughout the territory.

The working carved surface upon carved surface (ie one scene can distinguished using no magnification and another even smaller carved scene is found, using magnification, carved upon this for example:the sails of the ship carrying the wounded Arthur has a minute battle scenario worked upon it's sails. A x6 magnification brought these stories to light.

As with the majority of the sculpted work the use of animal 'totems' such as bears, horses, birds and cats assists in working out who were the protagonists. For example, there is a tiny scene of men rushing towards each other near to what I take to be Dunipace and close by there is the head of a cat. It is possible to conjecture from this that the Picts or Pechs were involved in this battle scene.

Of particular note with regard to what is known about Arthur's campaigns and what the other maps that I have found have revealed, this map provides something more in that Fife and Angus were represented. There is some detail concerning Arthur's activities in Fife and into the Tay estuary. Another interesting feature of this map is that it appears to provide some inkling as to the existence of sub-kings or chiefs. My reason for this conclusion is finding several king-like figures (ie men with distinctive hair and seated frequently in chairs).

Fights/events represented by bear heads etc: south bank of Carron; vicinity of the River Bonny or Dunipace; Castle Rock Edinburgh; Carlton Hill Edinburgh; Tay Estuary ; Mouth of the River Leven, Fife; Guinnion (east North Berwick); Glencourse (and invaders at mouth of the Esk at Musselburgh); Old Battle (west of North Berwick); Aberlady Bay; stony banks of Carron south of Stenhousemuir; vicinity of St Andrews or Cupar with attack coming from the west ,bear looks ensconced on the coastal St Andrews area ie seated figure; the Larbert/Torwood almost to Airth area (large male(hatted) and female figure possibly with offspring; south of Forth River, possibly Pow burn around Airth area; North Berwick Law; Bouden Hill Linthithgow area small bear and head of an older man faint outline of a hill; Camelon area, several warrior figures and a woman's head, dark hair; prostrate bear slightly east of Stenhousemuir;tiny boat with tiny bear coming from north west on Carron before Dunipace area; 'north' of the Carron and on the edge of the stylised map side there is a mysterious shining hollow/pool in which there is a young man's face and several small male figures outside it and linked to it is a goddess figure head of young woman with an elongated body/legs.

There is one other distinctive feature of the map side which was a puzzle for a long time. It is a deep and long indent, whitened with some sort of infill, which seems to start in the vicinity of Musselburgh and almost reaches to the coastline of West Lothian, pushing through a coloured part of the map in which there are faint traces of the recorded military maneovres that took place in the Lothian hinterlands. Of course, at Musselburgh there is the River Esk, a navigable river which is the confluence of two rivers the North and South Esks. It is the former, I think, which is part of the map indent. The North Esk reaches the Pentlands, flowing through Roslin Glen and reaching Greenlaw where the Glencourse Burn empties into it. At this point the NorthEsk veers off westwards along the edge of the Pentlands but the valley of the Glencorse is a route through the hills to Balerno and thence, almost in a straight line to Torphicen and the Bouden Hill, Nennius' 'Badon Hill'. At the end of the indent there is a faint figure, a bear, a hill and the face of an old man (needs good magnification and perserverance!) There are minute traces of what I take to be gold paint still evident on the corner of the shortest and slanted sides. That there are traces elsewhere suggests that this carved narrative was very richly decorated.

Appendix 2: The Glass Map

Approximate dimensions: 4.5 mm x 5.5 mm x 1.5 mm.

This worked stone is a very different piece from the Emperor's Map. It is dark coloured with some signs of dye used in certain parts. There is some inlaid quartz in evidence. The purpose of using this apart from denoting the sea (these quartz areas turn blue using the digital camera) seems to be to highlight stories or vignettes. I have concluded this from examining the large number of little pits that have lost their glassy covers and have small scenes crafted in their bases. Generally the piece is in a poor condition particularly on one face where it is very difficult to discern the meanings and structure of the work.

The other face is a good deal clearer. Here there are some remnants of quartz, enough to suggest that it represents the upper reaches of the River Forth. To the east there are more pits but there are also featured a sprinkling of recognisable figures of people. It is darker than the surrounding stone and is irregularly segmented. Look closer and there are minute scenes being played out beneath th/e dark surface. The lines between each segment are a cream colour. Look very closely and some tiny figures can be seen on these dividing lines. The familiar distinctively shaped beaches of Lothian are discernible in a lighter shade to that of the segmented land. There are seventeen separate segments which as a whole outline the shape of a seated bear put together jigsaw fashion. I think that what they represent is how the land was carved through with rivers and burns. Perhaps this division by water provides a possible insight into how this part of present day Scotland at least, was perceived by the people who lived there. Apart from a Celtic reverence for water, it was water that was the main means of transport. The movement of people and goods was done by boat. It was safer and quicker than a land route when wild animals, rough ground and possibly the odd bandit would have had to be faced.

Another distinctive feature is positioned parallel to the 'back' of the bear. This is a series of lines, of which four have been more deeply carved. My interpretation of this is that it is the Antonine Wall and the three rivers that flow west to east on each of it's sides. The most northerly of these waters being the Carron, then the Avon and Almond Rivers. Further lines appear to be part of the numerous boats being sailed or rowed upon them. They are full of passengers, tiny figures distinguishable along the length of vessels. Some of these passengers may be soldiers. One small rowing boat has what appears to be a Christian religious figure (brown clothing). There is much more to be interpreted from this piece. More technology than I have needs to be used to decipher it. Perhaps an expert in the legends and myths of ancient Britain may enjoy recording the huge number of vignettes presented upon the most unlikely of surfaces.

Appendix 3: Sketch Maps

Map 1
Scotland with the old Roman walls

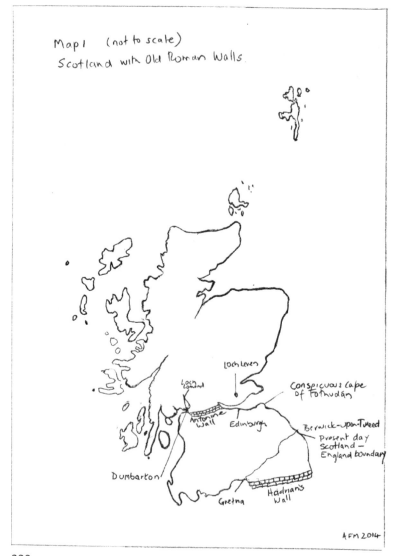

Map 2
North Berwick today (not to scale)

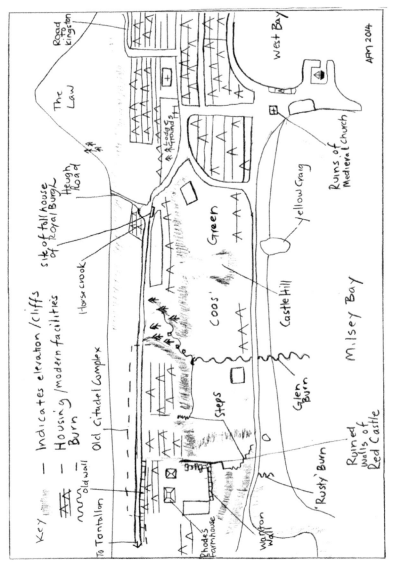

Map 3
The Conspicuous Cape of Fothudán

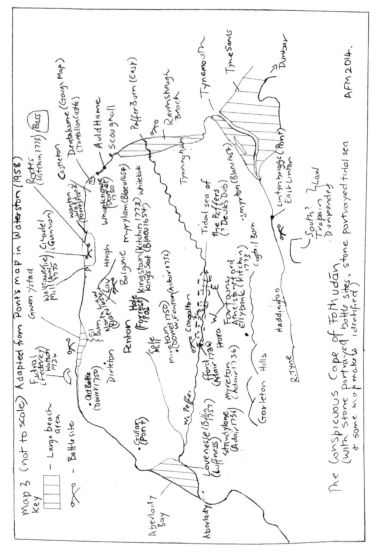

Map 4
Stone-portrayed Guinnon

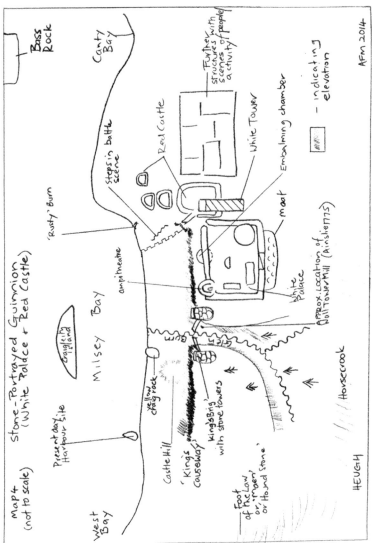

Map 5
Location of the twelve Arthurian battles (not to scale)

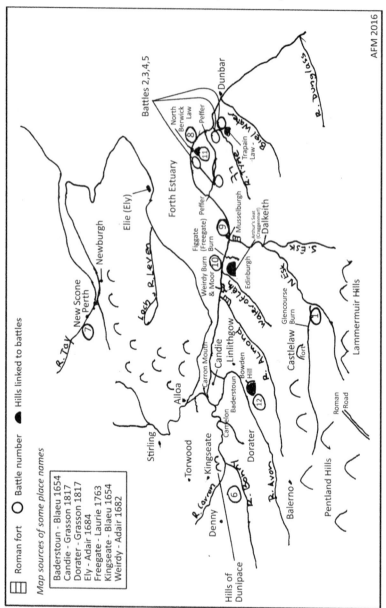

AFM 2016

Map sources of some place names

Baderstoun - Blaeu 1654
Candie - Grasson 1817
Dorater - Grasson 1817
Ely - Adair 1684
Freegate - Laurie 1763
Kingseate - Blaeu 1654
Weirdy - Adair 1682

Map 6
Journey of the Sea Baby

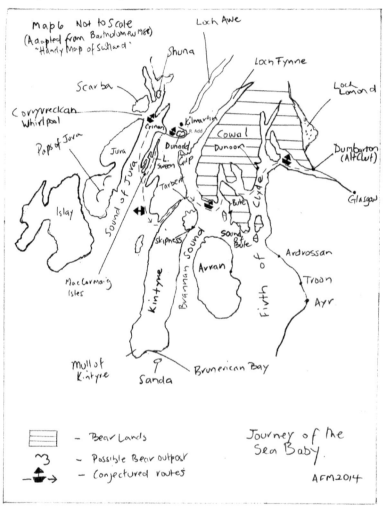

Map 6 Not to Scale
(Adopted from Bartholomew 1988)
"Handy Map of Suhard"

Loch Awe

Shuna

Loch Fynne

Scarba

Loch Lomond

Corryvreckan Whirlpool

Crinan · Kilmartin
R Add

Cowal

Paps of Jura

Jura

Dunadd

Dunoon

Dumbarton (Alt Clut)

L. Sween

Crip

Sound of Jura

Tarbert

Glasgow

Islay

Bute

Clyde

MacCormaig Isles

Skipness

Brannan Sound

Sound of Bute

Ardrossan

Arran

Firth of Clyde

Troon

Kintyre

Ayr

Mull of Kintyre

Sanda

Brunerican Bay

▭ – Bear Lands

〜 – Possible Bear outpost

⛵→ – Conjectured routes

Journey of the Sea Baby.

AFM 2014

Map 7

The lands north of the Gannet's Bath (inspired by the Emperor's Map)

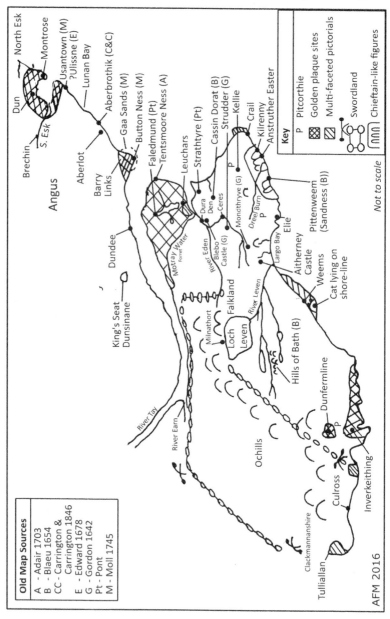

Map 8
Location of the Battle of Mons Graupius

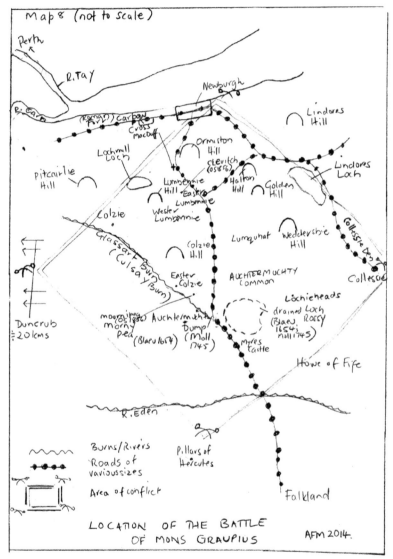

References and Bibliography

Ackroyd, P. (2002), The origins of the English imagination, Chatto and Windus, London.

Anderson, A.O. (1908), Scottish Annals from English Chroniclers AD500-1286, David Nut, London.

Anderson, J. (1981), Sir Walter Scott and History, The Edina Press, Edinburgh.

Baird, W. (1898), The Annals of Duddingston and Portobello, Andrew Elliot Edinburgh (Republished 1993 by West Port Books), Edinburgh.

Baldwin, J. R. (1985/ (minor revision1989)), Exploring Scotland's Heritage. Lothian and Borders, The Royal Commission on the Ancient and Historical Monuments of Scotland Her Majesty's Stationary Office, Edinburgh.

Bannerman, J. (1993), 'MacDuffs of Fife' in Medieval Scotland. Crown, Lordship and Community Editors Grant, A. and Stringer, K. J. Edinburgh University Press, Edinburgh.

Barrow, G. W. S. (1992), Scotland and its Neighbours in the Middle Ages, The Hambledon Press, London.

Barrow, G.W.S (1959), Traverlen, Duddingston and Arthur's Seat, The Old Edinburgh Club, Vol30, pp1-9.

Bates, C. R. and Oakley, D. J. (2004), 'Bathymetric sidescan investigation of sedimentary features in the Tay Estuary, Scotland', International Journal of Remote Sensing, Vol 20, No. 22, pp. 5089-5104.

Beckensall, S. (2005), The Prehistoric Rock Art of Kilmartin, Kilmartin House Trust, Kilmartin, Argyll.

Berger, J. (1972), Ways of Seeing, Penguin Books, Harmondsworth.

Broun, D (2000), 'The church of St Andrews and its foundation legend in the early 12th century: recovering the full text of Version A of the foundation legend', pp108-114 in Kings, Clerics and Chronicles in Scotland, 500-1297. Edited by Taylor, S. Four Courts Press, Dublin.

Buchan, D. (1984,) (editor), A collection of Scottish Folk Literature, Routledge Kagan Paul London.

Budge, E. A. Wallis (1925), The Mummy. A Handbook of Egyptian Funerary Archaeology, 2nd edition reprint (1989), Dover Publications Inc., New York.

De Bono, E. (1967), The use of lateral thinking, Penguin Books, Harmondsworth.

Carr, D. (1981), 'Knowledge in Practice' American Philosophical Quarterly,Vol 18, no.1 Chapter 6, pp53-61

Calise, J.M.P. (2002), Pictish Sourcebook : Documents of medieval legend and dark age history, Greenwood Press, London.

Chambers Popular Rhymes of Scotland, (1870), W and R Chambers, Ltd Edinburgh.

Chambers Concise 20th Century Dictionary (1985) Edited by Davidson, G. W., Seaton, M. A., Simpson, J. W. and R Chambers Ltd., Edinburgh

Clancy, T. O. (1998), The Triumph Tree. Scotland's earliest poetry 550-1350, Canongate Classics,Edinburgh.

Clancy, T. O. (2000), 'Scotland, the 'Nennian' recension of the Historia Brittonum and the Lebor Bretnach', pp 87-107, in Kings, Clerics and Chronicles in Scotland, 500-1297, edited by Taylor,S., Four Courts Press, Dublin.

Clancy, T. O. (2004), 'Philosopher King: Nechtan mac Der Ilei' Scottish Historical Review, Vol LXXXIII, no216 October pp125-149.

Clancy, T. O. (2007), 'The poetry of the court: Praise' in The Edinburgh History of Scottish Literature Volume 1 From Columba to the Union (until 1707), Brown, I. (General Editor), Edinburgh University Press, Edinburgh pp63-71.

Clancy, T. O. (2007), 'A fragmentary literature: Narrative and Lyric from the early Middle Ages', in The Edinburgh History of Scottish Literature Volume 1 From Columba to the Union (until 1707), pp123-131, Edinburgh University Press, Edinburgh.

Clarkson, T. (2010), The Men of the North. The Britons of Southern Scotland, John Donald, Edinburgh.

Collins Latin Dictionary (1997), 1st edition, Harper Collins Publishers, Glasgow.

The Concise Scots Dictionary (1987), 3rd edition Robinson, M. (editor-in-chief), Aberdeen University Press, Aberdeen.

Cowie, T. (1999), 'The Romans' in A Reason for Inveresk compiled by Burnet, J. E. pp15-18 Courtyard Press, Inveresk.

Crawford, B.E. (1997), 'Are the dark ages still dark?' pp1-4 in The worm, the germ and the thorn pp1-4, Pinkfoot Press, Balgavies, Angus.

Crumley, J. (1991), Discovering the Pentland Hills, John Donald Publishers Ltd, Edinburgh.

Cowley, D. C. (2008), 'Crop marked aerial survey and the plough-levelled archaeology of East Lothian' Transactions of the East Lothian Antiquarian and Field Naturalists Society, Vol XXV11,pp1-19.

Drummond, P. (1991), Scottish Hill Names. Their origin and meaning. Scottish Mountaineering Trust.

Dunbavin, P. (1998), Picts and Ancient Britons. An Exploration of Pictish Origins, Third Millennium Publishing, Nottingham.

Duncan, A. A. M. (2000), 'Sources and uses of the Chronicle of Melrose, 1165-1297', in Kings, Clerics and chronicles in Scotland, 500-1297 Edited by Taylor, S (ed) pp146-185,Four Courts Press, Dublin.

Duncan, J. (1997), Perth and Kinross. The big country, John Donald Publishers, Edinburgh.

Ellis, P. B. (1994, 2002), A Brief History of the Druids, Robinson Running Press, London.

Ferrier Rev, W. M. (1980), The North Berwick Story, Royal Burgh of North Berwick Community Council, Atholl Lodge North Berwick, East Lothian.

Foster, S.M.(1997), 'The Picts. Quite the darkest of the peoples of Dark Age Britain?' in The Worm, the germ and the thorn, pp5-17, The Pinkfoot Press. Balgavies, Angus.

Fraser, James. E. (2008) 'Bede, the Firth of Forth, and the Location of Urbs Iudeu' The Scottish Historical Review,Vol LXXXVII, 1, no223, April 2008, pp1-25.

Fraser, James .E. (2009), From Caledonia to Pictland. Scotland to 795, Edinburgh University Press Ltd, Edinburgh.

Friar, S. and Ferguson, J. (1993), Basic Heraldry, The Herbert Press, London.

Giles, J. A. (1808-1884)(2000online) translation of The History of the Britons by Nennius Gutenburg text Cambridge Ontario Inparenthesis Publications Medieval Latin Series

Gillies, W. (2007) 'The Lion's Tongues: Languages in Scotland to 1314' in The Edinburgh History of Scottish Literature Volume 1 From Columba until the Union (until 1707) (General Editor Brown, I.) Edinburgh University Press Edinburgh pp52-62.

Gray, Forbes. W. (1938) 'The Falls of Dunbar: a notable Scots family' in Transactions of the East Lothian Antiquarian and Field Naturalists' Society Vol3, pp120-141

Gray, Forbes. F. (1948), 'The Bass Rock in History', Transactions of East Lothian Antiquarian and Field Naturalists Society, Vols IV-V, pp51-68.

Groome, F H. (1885), The Gazzetteer of Scotland ,Vol 1, p152.

Henniker, H. (1996), 101 Bike Routes in Scotland, Mainstream Publishing Company (Edinburgh) Ltd, Edinburgh.

Hicks, C. (2012), Girl in a Green Gown. The history and mystery of the Arnolfini Portrait, Vintage Books, London.

Hill, H. (1791-1799), 'North Berwick' in Statistical Account of Scotland, John Sinclair (editor), p524, Wakefield EP Publishing, (1973-1983).

Hudson B T (2002) 'The Scottish Gaze' in History literature and music in Scotland 700-1560', Mc Donald, R. A. (Editor) pp29-59, Toronto University Press Incorporated, Toronto.

Hudson. B. (2007), 'One Kingdom from many Peoples: History until 1314' in The Edinburgh History of Scottish Literature Volume1 From Columba to the Union (until 1707), (General Editor Brown, I) pp33-43, Edinburgh University Press, Edinburgh.

Johnston, T. (1999), Our Scots noble families, Argyll Publishing, Glendaruel, Argyll.

Jones, D. (1995), Boats, The British Museum Press, London.

Kirke, T. (1679), 'A modern account of Scotland by an English gentleman' in Early travellers in Scotland, Hume Brown (Editor (1891)), P David Douglas, Edinburgh.

Laing, A (1872), 'Newburgh and Neighbourhood' in The Kingdom of Fife in Days gone by, Ballingdale, W., Edmonston and Douglas, Edinburgh, Antiquarian reprint, Lang Syne Publishers Ltd, Newtongrange, Midlothian.

Lamont-Brown, R. (2002), Fife in history and legend, John Donald Publishers, Edinburgh.

Lethbridge, T. C. (1954), The Painted Men, Andrew Melrose Ltd, London.

Markus, G. (2007), 'Saving verse: early medieval religious poetry' in The Edinburgh History of Scottish Literature Volume 1 From Columba until the Union (until 1707), pp91-102, Edinburgh University Press, Edinburgh.

Marsden. J (1997), Alba of the Ravens. In search of the Celtic Kingdome of the Scots, Constable and Company Ltd, London.

Martin Martin (1660-1719), 'Jura and Islay from a description of the Western Islands of Scotland' in Cradle of the Scots: an Argyll Anthology, Osborne,B.D.; Armstrong,R.; Renton,R. (Editors 2000), pp184-191, Birlinn, Edinburgh.

Martine, J (1890 republished 1999), Reminiscences and notices of the parishes of the county of Haddington, East Lothian Council Library Service, Macdonald Lindsay Pindar PLC.

McCrie. Rev., T. (1848, 1912), The Bass Rock. Civil and Ecclesiastical History, W. P Kennedy, Edinburgh.

McDiarmid, M.P. (1983), 'The Gododdin and other heroic poems of Scotland' in Scotland and the Lowland Tongue, McClure, J.D. (Editor), Aberdeen University Press, Aberdeen.

MacAlpine, N. (1929), A Pronouncing Gaelic-English Dictionary, Alexander McLaren and Sons, Glasgow.

McDonald, R. A (2002) ''Soldiers most unfortunate': Gaelic and Scoto-Norse opponents of the Canmore Dynasty, c1100-1230)' in History, Literature and Music in Scotland, 700-1560, McDonald, R. A., (Editor), pp93-119, Toronto University Press Incorporated, Toronto.

McHardy, S. (1997), 'The wee dark fowk o' Scotland:the role of oral transmission in Pictish Studies' in The worm the germ and the thorn, Pinkfoot Press, Balgavies, Angus.

McNeish, C. (1999), Scotland's 100 Best Walks, Lomond Books, Edinburgh.

MacLennan, M. (1925), A Pronouncing and Etymological Dictionary of the Gaelic Language, John Grant, Edinburgh.

MacQuarrie, A. (1993), 'The Kings of Strathclyde c400-1018' in Grant, A. and Stringer, K. J. Medieval Scotland, Crown and Lordship and Community, pp1-19 Edinburgh University Press, Edinburgh.

Moll R J (2002), 'Offquhat nacioun art thow?' National identity in Blind Harry's 'Wallace' in History literature and music in Scotland, editor MacDonald, R. A. pp120-143,Toronto University Press Incorporated, Toronto.

Montrose History Society (2004), Ebb and Flow. Aspects of the History of Montrose Basin, Pinkfoot Press, Balgavies, Angus.

Montrose Basin Heritage Society (2008), Flowing Past More Historical Highlights from Montrose Basin, Printmatters, Brechin, Angus.

Moffat, A. (1999), Arthur and the Lost Kingdoms, Phoenix, London.

Moffat, A (2005), Before Scotland The history of Scotland before history, Thames and Hudson, London.

Morris, J. (1973), The Age of Arthur. A history of the British Isles from 350-650, Phoenix, London.

Morrison,J. Oram,R. Oliver,F. (2008), ' Ancient Eldbotle unearthed and archaeological and historical evidence for a long-lost early medieval East Lothian village', Transactions of the East Lothian Antiquarian and Field Naturalists' Society, 28, pp21-45.

Nicolaisen, W.F.H. (1997), 'On Pictish rivers and their confluences' in The worm, the germ and the thorn, pp113-118, Pinkfoot Press, Balgavies, Angus.

Nicolaisen, W. F. H. (2001), Scottish Place-Names, John Donald, Edinburgh.

Osbourne, B.D., Armstrong,R., Renton,R. (eds) (2000), Cradle of the Scots, An Argyll Anthology, Birlinn, Edinburgh.

Padel, O. J. (2008), 'Some South-Western sites with Arthurian Associations' in The Arthur of the Welsh. The Arthurian Legend in Medieval Welsh Literature, (2nd edition), Editors Bromwich, R., Jarman, A.O.H., Roberts, Brynley. F., pp229-248, University of Wales Press, Cardiff.

Paterson, J. (1858), History of the Regality of Musselburgh with numerous extracts from the town records,, James Gordon, Musselburgh.

Robertson D M (2008), Goodnight my servants all. The sourcebook of East Lothian Witchcraft Grimsay Press, Glasgow.

Reid, J.J. (1885), 'Early notices of the Bass Rock and its Owners', Proceedings of the Society of Antiquities, Dec14th, pp54-60.

Rennie, A. (2008),The Harbours of Elie Bay. Elie and Earlsferry History Society, printed Aberdeen.

Robinson, C. and Maolalaigh, R. (2007), 'The Several Languages of a Single Kingdom: The languages of Scotland, 1314-1707' in The Edinburgh History of Scottish Literature Vol I . From Columba until the Union (until 1707), Brown, I (General Editor), pp153-163, Edinburgh University Press, Edinburgh.

Rollason, D. (2003), Northumbria, 500-1100 Creation and destruction of a Kingdom, Cambridge University Press, Cambridge.

RCAMCS (1933), The Royal Commission on Ancient Monuments and Constructions of Scotland 11th Report with inventory of monuments and constructions in the counties of Fife, Kinross and Clarkmannan, HMSO, Edinburgh, HMSO.

Royan, Nicola with Broun, D. (2007), 'Versions of Scottish Nationhood c850-1707 in The Edinburgh history of Scottish literature vol1 From Columba to the Union (1707) pp168-183. Period editors Thomas Owen Clancy and Murray Pittock, General editor Ian Brown, Co-editor Susan Manning, pp168-183, Edinburgh University Press Ltd, George Square, Edinburgh.

Rowland, J. (2007), 'Aneirin, the Gododdin' in The Edinburgh History of Scottish Literature Volume 1 From Columba to the Union (until 1707), (General Editor Brown, I.), pp72-76, Edinburgh University Press, Edinburgh.

Rush, C (1994), A Twelve Month and a Day, Canongate Press Ltd, Edinburgh.

Sharpe, R (2000), 'The thriving of Dalriada' in Kings, Clerics and Chronicles in Scotland 500-1297, pp47-61, edited by Taylor, S., Four Courts Press, Dublin.

Simpson, W. Douglas (1958), 'Tantallon Castle' in Transactions of the East Lothian Antiquarian Field Naturalists Society, Vol 7, pp18-26.

Sims-Williams, P. (2008), 'The Early Welsh Arthurian Poems' in The Arthur of the Welsh. The Arthurian Legend in Medieval Welsh Literature, (2nd edition), editors

Bromwich, R., Jarman, A. O. H., Roberts, Brynley. F., pp33-71, University of Wales Press, Cardiff.

Skene, W. (1868), (ed. Bryce, D. (1988)), Arthur and the Britons in Wales and Scotland, Llanerch Enterprises, Dyfed.

Sommerville M (1873, edited by D MacMillan (2001)), Queen of Science. Personal recollections of Mary Sommerville, Canongate Classics, Edinburgh.

Sutherland, E. (1999), Five Euphemias. Women in Medieval Scotland 1200-1420, Constable, London.

Swanton, M. (1996), (editor), The Anglo-Saxon Chronicle, J. M. Dent, London.

Sydeserff, D (1996), 'East Lothian field names: some researches into past and present names' in Transactions of the East Lothian Antiquarian and Field Naturalists' Society vol.23, pp49-85.

Stephen, W. (1938), The story of Inverkeithing and Rosyth, The Moray Press, Edinburgh.

Taylor, S. (2000), 'The coming of the Augustinians to St Andrew and version B of the St Andrews foundation legend' in Kings, Clerics and Chronicles in Scotland 500-1297, pp115-123, edited by Taylor, S., Four Courts Press, Dublin.

Thomson, R. L. (2008), 'Owain: Chwedl Iarlles y Fyynnon' in The Arthur of the Welsh. The Arthurian Legend in Medieval Welsh Literature, (2nd edition), editors Bromwich, Rachel, Jarman, A.O.H., Roberts, Brynley. F., pp159-169, University of Wales Press, Cardiff.

Watson, W.J. (1926), (2011 introduction by Simon Taylor), The Celtic Place Names of Scotland, Birlinn, Edinburgh.

Watson, W.J. (2002), Scottish Place Name Papers, Steve Savage Publishers, London/Edinburgh.

Way, G. of Plean and Squire, R. (1994), Scottish Clan and Family Encyclopaedia, Harper Collins, Glasgow.

Welsh, M. and Isherwood, C. (2003), Walks in Argyll and Bute, Clan Walk Guides, Clan Books, Doune, Perthshire.

Wenke, R.J. (2009), The Ancient Egyptian State. The origins of Egyptian Culture (c 8000-2000BC), Cambridge University Press, New York.

White, D.B. (1990), Exploring old Duddingston and Portobello, Mainstream Publishing, Edinburgh.

Whitehead, Rev. W. Y. (1948), 'David Calderwood. Historian of the Kirk', in Transactions of the East Lothian Antiquarian and Field Naturalists'Society, Vol 4, pp69-74.

234

Whyte, I. and K. (1988), Discovering East Lothian, John Donald Publishers, Edinburgh.

Whyte, D. (2000), Scottish Surnames, Birlinn, Edinburgh.

Woolf, A. (2007), From Pictland to Alba 789-1070 The New Edinburgh History of Scotland, Vol. 2, Edinburgh University Press Ltd, Edinburgh.

Yeoman, L. (2005), Reportage Scotland, Luath Press Limited, Edinburgh.

Archival works held by the National Archive of Scotland Edinburgh (NAS)

National Archive reference numbers as follows:

GD1/453/5 no15;

GD1/453/5 no17;

GD6/4;

GD6/13;

GD110/20;

GD110/177;

GD110/211;

GD110/218;

GD110/177.

Online References

Alexander Ancient Art, 'Confusing number of Deities in Ancient Egypt', http://www.alexanderancientart.com/info/numberofgods.html, retrieved 15/02/2013.

Am Faclair Beag (An English-Scottish Gaelic Dictionary incorporating Dwelly), http://www.faclair.com

Ayto, J. (1990,2005) , World Origins (2006), http://www.credoreference.com/entry/acbwordorig/gannet.

BBC Science and Nature-Horizon TV and Radio Follow-up (2005) Neanderthal pp. 1-4, http://www.bbc.co.uk/sn/tvradio/programmes/horizon/neanderthal_prog_sum mary.html, Retrieved 20/06/2011

Bede's Ecclesiastical History of England-Christian, Classics Ethereal Library, http://ccel.org/bede/history.v.ii.xx.html, retrieved 26/01/2013, www.behindthename.com

Breeze, A., 'The Names of Rheged', James Williams Memorial Lecture 2011 (DGNHAS), Summary by H Gough-Cooper, retrieved 03/12/2011

Campbell (1964), Kilmory Oib (archaeological note), http://www.canmore.rcahms.gov.uk/on/site/39194, retrieved 16/05/2013

Cassell's Peoples, Nations and Cultures 'Attacotti' (2005), retrieved from http://www.credoreference.com/entry/orionpnc/attacotti

Chalmers, G. (1887), Caledonia or a historical and topographical account of North Britain from the most ancient to the present times with a dictionary of places chorographical and philological, Alexander Gardiner (publishers), Paisley, Library of the University of California, Los Angeles.http://www.archive.org/stream/caledoniaorhisto01chal/caledoniaorhist o01chal_djvu.txt

Christison,D (1904), Kilmory Oib (archaeological note), http://www.canmore.rcahms.gov.uk/on/site/39194 retrieved 16/05/2013

Collins English Dictionary 2000, retrieved from 2Fwww.credoreference.com/entry/hcengdict/osco_umbrian

Dictionary of the Scots language, www.dsl.ac.uk

Dodson, A, (2004), 'Eygpt, Ancient Hieroglyphics and Origins of the Alphabet', Encyclopaedia of African History (2005), retrieved from 2Fwww.credoreference.com/entry/routafricanhistory/Egypt_ancient_hieroglyphi cs_and _origins_of_alphabet.

Franciscus, R., cited in
http://www.bbc.co.uk/sn/tvradio/programmes/horizon/neanderthal_prog_sum
mary.shtml retrieved 20/06/2011.

www.fiffhs.org/maps/stats/falklandstats.htm, Retrieved 08/01/13

Fisher, I. (2001), Kilmory Oib (archaeological note),
http://www.canmore.rcahms.gov.uk/on/site/39194 retrieved 16/05/2013

Grant, M. (1986), Guide to the Ancient World, H.G. Wilson
http://connect.nls.uk2060/2Fwww.credoreference.com/early/gttaw/asia

Green, T. (2009), Lambert St Omer's 'Floridus' from www.arthuriana.co.uk/notes
and queries/N&Q2_ArthFolk.pdf.

Highland Council, Ambaile Highland History and Culture Eilean Mor,
http://www.ambaile.org.uk/en/item, retrieved 15/05/2013

Historic Scotland, Society and Culture. The Symbols, http://www.pictish
stones.org.uk/pictishstoneshome/aboutthepicts/society/sy, retrieved
30/12/2010

Hunter-Mann, K. (2001), 'The Last of the Romans: The life and times of
Ambrosius Aurelianus' The Heroic Age Winter Issue 4 pp1-14
http://www.mun.ca/heroicage/issues/4/Hunter-Mann.html

Johnston, James B. (1892), Place Names of Scotland. David Douglas. Edinburgh
University of Toronto Libraries. Robart's Collection
http://archive.org(details)/placenamesofscot00johnuoft, retrieved 07/05/2012

Johnstone, James Brown (1892), Place-names of Scotland D Douglas Edinburgh
on openlibrary.org Carlifornia Digital Libraries collectioncdl:Americana

Johnston, F.I. (5/11/62), Trapain Law. Field Sheet of the National Monuments
Record NT580747, www.rcahms.gov.uk

Lamont, J. (1649-1671), The Diary of John Lamont of Newton, books.google.co.uk

MacFarlane, W (1906), Geographical collections relating to Scotland made by
Walter McFarlane, OpenLibrary
http://www.archive.prg/stream/geographicalco102macfgoog(geographico102ma
cfgoog.

McLeish K.M (1996), Bloomsbury Dictionary of Myth,
http://www.credoreference.com

Mc Killop, J. (2005), 'Hags' from Myths and Legends of the Celts pp1-2 'Taliesin'
from Myths and Legends of the Celts pp1-2,
http://www.credoreference.com/entry/penquinmlc/hags

National Library of Scotland, 'Timothy Pont', http://maps.nls.uk/pont

Neanderthal DNA. (2003), In Encyclopaedia of the Human Genome, http://www.credoreference.com/entry/wileyhg/neanderthal_dna.

Nichols, D. Convey, R.A. Kamyar Abdi (2008), 'Rise of Civilisation and Urbanism' Encyclopaedia of Archaeology Elsevier Science and Technology, 2Fwww.credoreference.com/entry/starch/civilisation_and_urbanism_rise_of, retrieved 13/2/13

Nimmo, W. (1770), History of Stirlingshire, 3rd edition, revised by Gillespie, R. (1880), Vol II, Chapter 32, www.electricscotland.com/history/stirlingshire/chap32.htm.

Ora et Labora: All Saints of Britain and Ireland pp1-12, posted by Culpa, Felix http://ishmaelite.blogspot.com/2010/06/allsaints-of-Britain-and-ireland.html, retrieved 12/08/2010

The Penguin English Dictionary, 2Fwww.credoreference/penguineng/oscan, retreived 25/02/2013

Pinch, G. (2002) 'Isis' (Egyptian Deity), http://www.credoreference.com/topic/isis_egyptian_deity

Pococke R., Tours in Scotland Vol 1, Edinburgh University Press by T&A Constable for the Scottish History Society (1887), https://www.openlibrary.org

Rice (1999), 'Who's who in Ancient Egypt (2003), Routledge Http//credoreference.com/entry/routwwac/thegods_of_Egypt

Skene, Felix J H (Translator) (1872), The Historians of Scotland Vol IV., John Fordun's Chronicle of the Scottish Nation Edmonston and Douglas Edinburgh, Editor Skene William F Skene, Library of the University of California Collection cdl; Americana archive.orgEbook and Texts Archive California Digital Library.

Welsh Academy Encyclopaedia of Wales (2008), 'Taliesin' p1, http://www.credoreference.com/entry/waencywales/taliesin_fl_late_6th_centu ry_poet

Whyte, B and Whyte, B. (1974), Tobar an Dualchais/Kist of Riches, ID 36963, www.tobarandualchais.co.uk

Wikipedia, 'Montrose, Angus' pp.1-15, http://en.wikipedia.org/wiki/Montrose.Angus 4/06/2012

Wikipedia, 'Land of Punt', pp.1-4, http://en.wikipedia.org/wiki/Land_of_Punt, retrieved 02/10/2013

Wikipedia, 'Welsh law', pp.1-12, http://en.wikipedia.org/wiki/Welsh_law, retrieved 12/09/2012.

Wikipedia, 'Heliopolis', http://en.wikipedia.org/wikiHeliopolis_(ancient), retrieved 13/03/2013

Wikipedia, 'Sanda', http://en.wikipedia.org/wiki/Sanda_Island, retrieved 23/03/2013

Wikipedia, 'Bear', http://en.wikipedia.org/wiki/Bear, retrieved 16/12/2012

Wikipedia, 'Abydos, Egypt' Retrieved http://en.Wikipedia.org/wiki/Abydos_Egypt, retrieved 18/02/2013

Williamson, May. G. (1942), The Non-Celtic Place-Names of the Scottish Border Counties Unpublished PhD thesis University of Edinburgh, www.spns.org.uk

Woodland Trust Dura Den Wood pp.1-2, http://www.woodlandtrust.org.uk/en/our-woods/Pages/about-this-wood.aspx?wood=4895, retrieved 07/05/2012.

Wooliscroft, D. J. (University of Manchester), Signalling and the Design of the Gask Ridge System , pp.1-26, http://www.theromangaskproject.org.uk/Pages/Introduction/Gask signalling.html, retrieved 20/03/12

Maps accessed from the online map site of the National Library of Scotland.

Abbreviations:

NLS – National Library of Scotland

OSE – Ordnance Survey Explorer map

OSL – Ordnance Survey Landranger map.

All maps below accessed from the National Library of Scotland Maps online site http://maps.nls.uk

Adair, J. (1682) Map of Midlothian (manuscript).

Adair, J. (1684) The East Part of Fife Surveyed and designed by John Adair (manuscript)

Adair, J. (1703) Frith and River of Tay with all rocks, sands and shoals etc and surveyed by John Adair Edinburgh

Adair, J. (1736) A Map of East Lothian. Cooper Edinburgh

Ainslie, J. (1775) The Counties of Fife and Kinross with Rivers Forth and Tay Cooper London

Bartholamew (1912) Survey Atlas of Scotland. The Edinburgh Geographical Institute Edinburgh

Bellin, J. D. (1757) Carte du Golphe d'Edinburgh. Paris

Blaeu, J and C (1654) . Lothian and Linthquo. Amsterdam.

Blaeu, J (1654) Fifae Vicecomitatus. The Sherifdome of Fyfe. Amsterdam.

Blaeu, J. (1654) Fifae pars Occidentalis (West part of) Amsterdam.

Blaeu, J. (1654) Fifae pars Orientalis (East part of) Amsterdam.

Blaeu, (1654) TBA Insulae Albion et Hibernia cum minorbus adjacenti. Accessed 07/04/10.

Blaeu J. (1654) Atlas of Scotland contributor of a description of the Lothians David Buchanan or William Forbes of Innerwick and translator Ian C. Cunningham. P37.

Carrington, F A and Carrington G W (1846) A Map of Scotland divided into counties shewing the principil roads, railways, rivers, canals S.Lewis London

Collins, G. (1693?) Edinburgh Firth. F.Collins? London?

Dorret, J. (1750) A General Map of Scotland and Islands thereto belonging. London.

Dorret, J. (1751) A Correct Map of Scotland divided into shires from the most authentic surveys. Kilmarnock.

Elphinstone, J. (1745) A New and Correct Map of North Britain.

Forrest (1802) Map of Haddingtonshire Edinburgh.

Gordon, J. (1642) Fyfeshire MDCXLII Manuscript map

Grasson, J. (1817) To the Noblemen and Gentlemen of the County of Stirling (map of Stirlingshire). Stirling.

Hondius, H. (1632) Scotiae pars australis Amsterdam.

Kitchin, T. (1773) A New and Complete Map of Scotland and Islands thereto belonging London

Marr, J. (1666) A Chart of the Mouth of the Firth of Tay (Manuscript)

Mercator, G. (1595) Scotie Regnum (south sheet) Duisberg.

Meuro, J. (1780) A New and Accurate Map of Scotland divided into shires from the most authentic surveys. Kilmarnock.

Moll, H. (1708) North Part of Great Britain. Rhodes, Nicholson and Bell.

Moll, H. (1745) The Shire of Linlithgow or West Lothian, the Shire of Edinburgh or Midlothian and the Shire of Haddington or East Lothian. Bowles and Bowles. London.

Moll, H. (1745) The Shires of Fife and Kinross. Bowles and Bowles London.

Moll, H. (1745) The Shire of Angus or Forfar. Bowles and Bowles London.

Pont,T. Map 15 Argyll North of the Crinan Canal

Pont, T. Map 17 Loch Lomond

Pont, T. Map 29 Middle Strathmore (Manuscript map)

Pont, T Map 32 The East Central Lowlands (Stirling, Falkirk, Kilsyth)

Pont, T Map 26 Lower Angus and Perthshire east of the Tay (Manuscript map)

Pont, T. Serenissimo Potentissimo Iacobo I Magnae Franciae et Hibermiae Regi printed in Waterston, R. (1958) 'Timothy Pont Map of the Tyne Valley' Transactions of the East Lothian Antiquarian and Field Naturalists Society Vol7 pp44-45

Pont, T (Gordon) Map 54 North-West Fife.

Pont, T and Hondius, H. (1630) A New description of the Shyres of Lothian and Linlithquo/ T Pont; Jadocus Hondius cae lavit sumptibus Andre Hart. Amsterdam.

Speed, J. (1610) Kingdome of Scotland. Sudbury J and Humbell

Thomson, J. and Johnston, W. (1832) Atlas of Scotland J. Thomson Co. Edinburgh

Other Historical Maps

The Gough Map of Great Britain (circa 1370's) Linguistic Geographies (2011) King's College London. www.goughmap.org/map

Donaldson, G. (1966) 'Map of the Siege of Leith 1560' Old Edinburgh Club Vol32

Lawrie, J. (1763) Duddingston Parish and Neighbourhood as in 1763 in Baird, W. 'The Annals of Duddingston and Portobello Andrew Elliot Edinburgh republished 1993 by West Port Books Edinburgh.

Contemporary Maps

Ordnance Survey (2001) Explorer 351 Dunbar and North Berwick. Southampton.

Ordnance Survey (2008) Landranger Map 53 EditionB2 Blairgowrie and Forest of Alyth. Southampton.

Ordnance Survey (2007) Landranger Map 54 Edition B2 Dundee and Montrose. Forfar and Arbroath. Southampton.

Ordnance Survey Landranger (2001) Map 55 Edition C1 Lochgilphead and Loch Awe . Southampton

Ordnance Survey Landranger (2007) Map 56 Edition C2 Loch Lomond and Inverary. Southampton

Ordnance Survey Landranger (2000) Map 59 Edition C3 Saint Andrews.Kirkcaldy and Glenrothes. Southampton

Ordnance Survey (2003) Landranger Map 62 Edition C North Kintyre and Tarbert. Southampton.

Ordnance Survey (2007) Landranger Map 65 Edition D2 Falkirk and Linlithgow Southampton.

Ordnance Survey (1999) Landranger Map 66 Edition C Edinburgh Penicuik and North Berwick. Southampton

Ordnance Survey (2007) Landranger Map 68 Edition B2 South Kintyre and Campbeltown. Southampton

RCAHMS (2008) The Antonine Wall. World Heritage Site. Scotprint Edinburgh

Index

A

Abdju, 203
Aberlady, 45, 49, 51, 189, 216
Abydos, 203
Achnabreck, 163
Aedan mac Gabran, 105, 128, 140
Aedilfrith, 140
Agned, 82, 115, 208
aide-memoires, 168
Airth, 67, 77, 209
Albidosi, 201, 204
Aled, 197, 204, 208, 211
Alt Clut, 49, 67, 72, 73, 100, 101,
    155, 156, 157, 160, 161
Altar of the Blessed Virgin Mary,
    187
Anubis, 204
Arfynydd, 142, 145
Argoed, 142, 143, 145
Arthur of the Cauldron, 108, 112
Atacotti, 158, 159, 161, 213
Atbret Iudeu, 197
Athelstaneford, 45, 200
Athernis, 138
Auchtermuchty, 120, 123
Auldhame, 51, 210

B

baboon, 36, 60, 118, 126, 129, 180,
    185, 202, 205
badger, 58
Badon, 57, 85, 86, 88, 108, 174, 198
Bagh Dail nan Cean, 98
Balgone, 50
Bass Rock, 11, 32, 33, 34, 38, 46,
    186
battle stones, 46
battles of Arthur, 62

Bear People, 72, 105, 125, 156,
    158, 159, 185
Bear territory, 96, 105
bear with a cross, 70
Bede, 49, 51, 52, 141, 199, 206, 207
Belhaven Bay, 55, 64
Benarty Hill, 136
Bernician people, 14
black bull, 119
black horse, 106, 109, 125
Blaeu Atlas, 47, 50, 138, 139
Blebo, 147
boar, 47, 97
boat, 97, 118, 164
boatful of warriors, 65
Bouden Hill, 85, 86, 87, 216
Brechin, 108, 127, 149
Bregion, 57, 82
brown, 36, 37, 61, 93, 96, 97, 125,
    157, 167, 178, 219
Brude, 26
Brunalban, 158
Brunanburh, 199
Brunerican Bay, 95
Brunnanbyrig, 199
Brunnanwerc, 199
bulrush, 171
busy hair, 77, 78

C

Cailleach, 98, 113
Caledones, 67
Cambrune, 80
Camelon, 89, 178, 198, 216
Carlton Hill, 78, 80, 81, 82, 216
Carpow, 121, 123
Carron River, 16, 66, 177
Castle Rock, 59, 78, 80, 81, 82
Castlesteads, 88
Cat Coit Celidon, 57, 67
Catreath, 140, 191, 194, 196, 208

Cats, 67, 72, 82, 123, 124, 125, 149
Cellawr Brewyn, 141
chair sculptures, 137
chieftain lists, 26
chieftain with a feline appearance, 129
Christian religious figure, 68, 219
citadel carvings, 22
City of the Legion, 57, 71, 74, 76
Claw Walls, 152
Clevitch, 122
colour, 2, 5, 10, 59, 60, 61, 79, 81, 82, 95, 96, 103, 106, 112, 137, 147, 162, 163, 167, 176, 190, 215, 218
Columba, 111, 182
column of heads, 26
Colzie, 122, 123
Comgall, 106, 109
Comgellaig, 136
Congalton, 196, 201
conspicuous cape, 49
Corryvreckan, 98
Cowal, 96, 107, 109
Craggenmarf, 79, 125
Crail, 130, 147
Croceflatt, 28
crocodile, 103, 126, 130, 134, 180, 202, 204
crow, 137

D

deer, 58, 67, 68, 89, 118, 119, 129, 137, 139, 156, 193
Denny, 66, 67, 89
Dentaloune, 205
Dingleton, 200
dog, 21, 36, 42, 53, 60, 84, 204
Domongart, 105, 109
Dreel Burn, 143
Drem, 50, 207
Druids, 6, 7, 178, 183
Duddingston, 79, 80, 187
Duglas, 57, 64

Dunadd, 97, 99, 106, 107, 183, 187
Dunaverty Castle, 95
Dunbar, 29, 117
Dunfermline, 134, 136
Dungrane, 193
Dunipace, 66, 67, 84
Dunning, 122
Dura Den, 147

E

Eadwulf, 207
Earlsferry, 29
East Fortune, 51, 196
echwydd, 146, 147, 196
Eden River, 139
Elshenford, 200
Endrick Water, 16
Epidii, 96
Epona, 99
Esk Mouth, 76, 84

F

Falkland, 120, 131, 132, 146
feathered headdress, 70
Fergus mac Erc, 158
Fidra, 48
Forthridge Muirs, 134, 135
fox, 95
Freegate Burn, 81
funeral, 100, 175, 182

G

Gabran, 105, 127
Galbraith, 166
Gana, 34, 40, 47, 186
gannet, 22, 38
Garleton Hills, 45
Gask Ridge, 120
Genuini, 11, 203
Gergenn, 129
Giudi, 48

Glassart Burn, 122
Glencorse, 63, 83, 216
Gododdin, 34, 38, 84, 86, 104, 117,
    137, 140, 167, 172, 186, 191,
    192, 193, 194, 196, 197, 204,
    206, 211, 212
Golden Hill, 121, 123
golden plaque, 82
Grandena, 186, 203, 208
grave-mapping, 52
Great Ennead, 202, 203
Great Inveresk, 75
guidhe, 55
Guinnion, 26, 35, 49, 69, 110
guledig, 88
Gwanannon, 34
Gwyr Y Gogledd, 37

H

handling coals, 34
hare, 23, 48
headgear, 58, 72, 129, 130
Her pa khered, 204
Herbertshire, 177
hills and boats, 100
Historia Brittonum, 24, 56
Hole, 38
Holyrood Park, 80, 82
Horus, 203, 204
hound racing, 36

I

Inveresk, 1, 10, 63, 75, 76, 79, 153
Inverkeithing, 135
Isis, 203, 204
Iudanburh, 206
Iudeu, 48, 49, 51, 55, 83, 183, 189,
    190, 197, 199, 206, 207, 208
Iuna, 202

J

Jura, 97

K

Kellie, 139, 143, 148
kenspeckle, 125
Kettle, 132, 145
Kilmartin, 138, 162, 163, 164
Kilmory, 187, 210
Kilmory Oib, 187
Kingston, 23, 193
Kintreath, 193

L

Larbert, 67, 216
Largo Bay, 131
Leuchars, 129, 151, 171
Lindisfarne, 189
Linlithgow, 85
long-beaked bird, 102
Lumbennie, 122

M

Maat, 204
Mac Arthur, 166
Maes Gai, 197
Manau, 9, 64, 197
marital discord, 66
marriage scene, 129
Matheson, 27, 166
Mathriue, 138
Medcaut, 189
Mehyn, 143
military line, 67, 85, 198
Milsey Bay, 25
miniature work, 4, 5, 7, 8, 165, 178
Mons Graupius, 1, 68, 121, 149,
    227
Monthryve, 138
Montrave, 138, 144

Montrose, 106, 109, 125, 126
Morcant, 140, 144
mosaic, 7
Motray Water, 120, 138, 142, 148
Musselburgh, 74, 153, 216
Myreford, 207

N

nainndisi, 201
Nennius, 57, 83, 115, 147, 184, 197
North Berwick, 18, 25, 26, 27, 28,
    29, 30, 31, 36, 48, 49, 50, 54, 84
North Berwick Law, 46, 47, 49, 192,
    200

O

Ochills, 120, 122, 145, 148
Offeris, 177
old capped and bearded man, 69
Ormiston Hill, 123
Osiris, 203
Owain, 132, 143

P

Peffer, 45, 46, 50, 51, 65, 66, 188,
    189, 193, 194, 196, 199, 200,
    206, 207
Perth, 67, 84, 89, 149
Picts, 14, 76, 78, 79, 81, 82, 84, 123,
    129, 134, 135, 149
Pictstonhill, 68
pinemartin, 58
Pitcorthie, 133, 147
pony tail, 70, 76, 86
Portobello, 79, 80, 81, 82
ptarmigan, 155
Punt, 28, 205
Puntoun, 27, 28
Putikin Burn, 130

R

Ravensheugh Sands, 65
regnal list, 26
Rheged, 132, 140, 141, 142, 143,
    144, 146, 147
Rhun, 133, 147
Roman presence, 72, 74
Rome Bay, 147
Rosyth, 135
row of babies, 31
row of king-like figures, 131
rushes, 129, 152, 171

S

Salt Springs of Wardie, 79
sand lands, 61, 65, 78, 128
Saxons, 12, 62, 69, 84, 86, 140, 143,
    144, 193, 197
scriptural number, 188
sea bird, 23, 91, 155
sheep, 56, 72
signage, 60, 77, 124, 190
sleeping bears, 188
stone maps, 57, 60, 62, 85, 116,
    142
story pathway, 72
swan, 94, 130, 132

T

Ta netjer, 205
Tantallon Castle, 29, 30, 205
Thomas the Rhymer, 76, 90
Thoth, 202
thoughts and dreams, 178
tiny bears, 60, 120
Tollzies, 137
totems, 84, 112, 130, 165, 215
translation scene, 160
Trapain Law, 10, 46, 65
Trat Treviot, 80
Traverlen, 79

Tyninghame, 50

U

Uchterutherstruther, 139, 154
Uotadini, 9, 10, 11
Urien, 132, 191
use of metal, 7

V

veneration of water, 101
vignette, 58, 61, 68, 70, 72, 74, 76,
    82, 90, 94, 99, 106, 114, 117,
    118, 120, 127, 130, 134, 160,
    161, 178, 204

W

Wall Tower, 30, 36, 84, 193

Weirdy Burn, 78
Wemyss, 134
Weodune, 199
Wepwawet, 204
Winwead, 197, 198, 199
Woad Isle, 153
wolf, 58, 73, 157, 213
Woolies croft, 39
wren, 7

Y

youthful bear, 60
Yuna, 202

Z

zoomorphic representation, 7

Printed in Great Britain
by Amazon